EXCEEDING GRATITUDE *for the* CREATOR'S PLAN

JAMES P. GILLS, M.D.

CREATION HOUSE
A STRANG COMPANY

EXCEEDING GRATITUDE FOR THE CREATOR'S PLAN by James P. Gills, M.D.
Published by Creation House
A Strang Company
600 Rinehart Road
Lake Mary, Florida 32746
www.creationhouse.com

Unless otherwise noted, all Scripture quotations are from the Holy Bible, New King James Version. Copyright © 1979, 1980, 1982 by Thomas Nelson, Inc., publishers. Used by permission.

Scripture quotations marked NIV are from the Holy Bible, New International Version of the Bible. Copyright © 1973, 1978, 1984, International Bible Society. Used by permission.

Scripture quotations marked KJV are from the King James Version of the Bible. Copyright © 1979, 1980, 1982, by Thomas Nelson, Inc., publishers. Used by permission.

Scripture quotations marked The Message are from THE MESSAGE: THE BIBLE IN CONTEMPORARY ENGLISH, copyright © 1993, 1994, 1995, 1996, 2000, 2001, 2002. Used by permission of NavPress Publishing Group.

Scripture quotations marked NAS are from the New American Standard Version of the Bible. Copyright © 1960, 1962, 1963, 1968, 1971, 1972, 1973, 1975, 1977 by the Lockman Foundation. Used by permission. (www.Lockman.org)

Scripture quotations marked AMP are from the Amplified Bible. Old Testament copyright © 1965, 1987 by the Zondervan Corporation. The Amplified New Testament copyright © 1954, 1958, 1987 by the Lockman Foundation. Used by permission.

Scripture quotations marked NCV are from The Holy Bible, New Century Version. Copyright © 1987, 1988, 1991 by Word Publishing, Dallas, Texas 75039. Used by permission.

Greek definitions are derived from *Strong's Exhaustive Concordance of the Bible*, ed. James Strong, Nashville, TN: Thomas Nelson Publishers, 1997.

Cover design by Terry Clifton

Author's note about the cover: The artist's image of the DNA helix shows the Creator's template for life—its beauty and complexity.

Library of Congress Control Number: 2006936882
International Standard Book Number: 978-1-59979-155-5—Paperback;
978-1-59979-162-3—Hardback

First Edition

07 08 09 10 11 – 9 8 7 6 5 4 3 2 1
Printed in the United States of America

EXCEEDING GRATITUDE
for the
CREATOR'S PLAN

This book is dedicated to Dr. Jim Rowsey. Dr. Rowsey has shown continued appreciation for his Master through tremendous trials. Jim, thank you for being a 1 Thessalonians 5:16–18 kind of man. "Be joyful always; pray continually; give thanks in all circumstances, for this is God's will for you in Christ Jesus." You have given all of us a gorgeous example of how to undergo trials that have made you a greater man and a stronger man in Christ. May we challenge each other to live this life of joy and romance and mystery in abandoning ourselves to the grace of God so that we may be enthralled with Him both now and forever! Thank you for giving us a living example of that grace of God and the joy of the Lord as the believer's strength.

ACKNOWLEDGMENTS

I would like to acknowledge my indebtedness to my patients who have shown me so many truths. I have seen daily that my greatest sin of omission is my lack of appreciation and my greatest sin of commission is worrying about things that are not realities. I am also thankful for people such as John Piper, Augustine, Jonathan Edwards, Oswald Chambers, and Gary Carter, who have shown me the real Word of God living within individuals. My thanks go to such men as Michael Behe, Tom Woodward, and Steve Meyer, who are spearheading the Intelligent Design movement. Their appreciation of the complexity, beauty, intricacy, and wonder of the Creator and His creation is making an impact on our generation.

Contents

BY ELLEN VAUGHN

There are certain people in this life who overflow with enthusiasm, expertise, curiosity, compassion, and concern for others. These people are thriving, generous, and full of energy. One sometimes wonders what they eat for breakfast.

In Dr. Jim Gills' case, though I'm sure he eats his Wheaties, there is a far deeper reason for his spiritual and physical vigor. His exuberance clearly flows from a profound, abiding relationship with God. He overflows with gratitude for God's great gifts. God's grace spills into every arena of Dr. Gills' life, which are many. He is a world-renowned eye surgeon, founder of St. Luke's Cataract and Laser Institute, prolific author, mentor, philanthropist, athlete, husband, and father, to name just a few.

The great thing is, when you read this book, you'll find that Dr. Gills' rollicking enthusiasm is contagious. You will come away with a mixture of awe, wonder, and practical ideas about how to worship and cultivate a relationship with God the Creator in the midst of your day-to-day life.

This book explores the overwhelming natural wonders of God's creation as starting points for learning more about the supernatural wonders of His amazing grace. Nature proclaims the glory of God, whether in the mind-bending enormity of star systems beyond our own, or the exquisite construction of the human eye. The world is full of incredible, intricate beauties, from the elegance of astrophysics to the life-giving properties of human blood.

And if we read the "book of nature" like a good detective novel, the evidence surely points to the One behind it all. Design points to a Designer. As Romans 1 puts it, "Since the creation of the world

His invisible attributes [His eternal power and divine nature] are clearly seen, being understood by the things that are made."

Many of us would agree with this common-grace conclusion about creation, and it is good. But there is more that is even better—special grace. By this we mean that God has not only disclosed Himself through the wonders of nature, but with irrepressible love He came to live among us in the Person of Jesus Christ, as revealed through Scripture.

Without faith in Christ, the natural world is a wondrous thing, of course. But *with* faith in Him, we perceive everything on a different level. We see what has been there all along, but hidden. Nature becomes a great concert of praise. The heavens declare the glories of God. The stones cry out with hosannas.

As we discover more about the Creator's plan and more about His grace, life can become a tremendous adventure. And, as Dr. Gills says, the organic response to these wonders is a tide of sheer, overwhelming, radical gratitude.

Obviously, and happily, this kind of gratitude is not a discipline. It's not another dry "to do" to add to our morning list or a box to be checked off at the end of the day. It is a gift of God, so woven with His grace that it's hard to separate the two. Because we've received grace, we give thanks to God for His good gifts. In those times when life is tough, when we face difficulties and brokenness, we can still give thanks. We are not grateful for the terrible situations themselves, but for the fact that *God is God* and *He is with us.*

When we praise God in the midst of pain, thanking Him for His power, strength, love, grace, and other qualities, the Holy Spirit keeps on giving. He can fill us with God's power in the midst of our weaknesses. He can give joy and real comfort regardless of our circumstances.

This is an ambitious book. It weaves together enormous themes: the wonders of science, the greater mysteries of God's grace, the power of supernatural gratitude, and the challenges that you and I face every single day. I pray that God will use it in your life to His own glory, and that you might enjoy a fresh infusion of enthusiasm, energy, and joy—whether or not you eat your Wheaties!

—ELLEN VAUGHN
AUTHOR, *RADICAL GRATITUDE*

BY TOM WOODWARD, PH.D.

The closing chapter of Hebrews exhorts us to "continually offer the sacrifice of praise to God," and then it describes this flow of praise as "the fruit of our lips, giving thanks to His name" (Heb. 13:15).

So, what does praise have to do with man's exploration of the cosmos? To put it differently, how is our view of God impacted by the growing tsunami of scientific evidence flooding in from astronomy, physics, chemistry, and biology, all of which point to a master intellect? As we uncover new layers of complexity in these worlds—the cosmos and the baffling micro-cosmos that we call "the cell"—should this not drive us to our knees?

You have in your hands a remarkable book, brilliantly executed with a bold and penetrating thesis: the twin universes of "natural science" and "Christian faith" are really one and the same universe. There are, to be sure, different methodologies for scholars to use in "getting to the data." Yet, there is no divorce and no separation in content. These realms are masterfully integrated into one glorious, colossal tapestry.

Answering the naysayers

This is an important truth, and one that is radical, timely, and practical. It is even viewed in some quarters as a dangerous idea! Some would attack this truth and try to drown out all glimpses of brilliant design in nature by pointing to "evil in the cosmos." Yet, leaving aside the doctrine of the fall of mankind, how would an atheist have any solid standard for calling anything objectively "evil"?

Other naysayers who take potshots at the intelligent design of nature say, "They have no connection whatsoever. Science is based on facts, while religion and Christianity is a leap of faith." Richard Dawkins, a biologist and feisty evangelist for atheism at Oxford, has gone so far as to call the Christian religion a "virus of the mind."[1]

Dawkins' myth of the antagonism of Christian faith and scientific fact faces ever more stringent challenges as the months pass, and as scientists unravel the intricacies and "computer-like complexity" of the innards of our bodies' molecular machinery. Many in the Dawkins crowd are now reduced to evolutionary storytelling. This is fine in a class on the literature of mythology, but is it science?

In this book, Dr. James Gills accomplishes two wonderful feats: First, he explodes into smithereens the Darwin myth (or shall we now call it the Dawkins myth?) about random or law-like motion of particles leading to the wondrous complexity of life and of the universe. For this, the good doctor deserves our highest kudos. But second, he follows the sage advice of the Book of Hebrews and shows how naturally, how beautifully, how powerfully this scientific vista should lead us into new worlds or worship of our truly awe-inspiring God and Maker.

It is a rare privilege, and a deep honor, to have known Dr. Gills for the eighteen years since I began teaching at Trinity College and began lecturing at universities on the debate over origins. He has been more than a rare friend. He inspired me, taught me, encouraged me, teamed up with me, mentored me, and propelled me in a myriad of ways toward greater Christlikeness. (Yes, Dr. Gills, I *did think about my pancreas today,* and I praised its brilliant Designer!)

Through this book, you too will meet Dr. Gills, but best of all, you'll meet both his mind and his heart. His mind and heart are graciously captivated by Christ, and they are enthralled by God's mastery of the dance of atoms and the swirling majesty of galaxies. You'll meet an ophthalmologist who has applied the "eye-opening" skills to the eyes of our own hearts and minds. Here we learn in a new way what it is to weave together Christ-centered faith and scientific fact and to explode with joyful exultation in a way we have never before experienced. You'll learn about a new world of worship and a new flow of fruit from our lips that the Book of Hebrews sketched out for us. Best of all, you'll never be the same.

—Tom Woodward, Ph.D.

FOREWORD

BY TOMMY NELSON

The most basic, blatant, inescapable, and irrefutable signature of God is the creation. "The heavens declare the glory of God…Their line has gone out through all the earth, And their words to the end of the world" (Ps. 19:1, 4). "Since the creation of the world His invisible attributes are clearly seen, being understood by the things that are made…so that they are without excuse" (Rom. 1:20).

But as majestic a statement as creation is, man has learned to navigate around it. Ancient polytheism made idols to account for the phenomena of nature. Pantheism simply made God the creation. Darwinism and naturalism have made the creation a closed system of natural causes. Modern man and modern science have built an entire intellectual system upon unverified and illogical speculations. It is interesting that in the judgment of God, revealed in the Book of Revelation, humankind is judged for a refusal to worship the God of creation. He is told to "Fear God and give glory to Him, for the hour of His judgment has come; and worship Him who made heaven and earth, the sea and springs of water" (Rev. 14:7).

Dr. Jim Gills has made a career studying Darwin's self-professed evolutionary enigma—the human eye. He is more than equipped to examine and extol that which scientists of the intelligent design movement have proclaimed as demonstrating irreducible complexity—the creation. Dr. Gills combines a scientist's insight, a saint's worship, and a common man's vocabulary to bring the divine mind within arm's reach. His is a read that should produce insight, amazement, worship, and a confident faith in God's chief apologetic.

In a day where virtually all possible ideas and alternatives to God have been ventured and have failed, man is faced with two possibilities: either all is nothing and there is no ultimate meaning to life, or man has stumbled over square one—the self-evident, infinite, personal Creator of all, from whose image man is cast. It is still the creation that cries out to man in every facet of nature. A creation not reserved for the Einsteins, Newtons, and Max Plancks, but equally accessible to the simple, honest eyes of common men.

—TOMMY NELSON

During a banquet sponsored by Fellowship of Christian Athletes in Tampa Bay, Florida, I was privileged to listen to some captivating remarks presented by Tommy Nelson. A former athlete, Tommy has been pastor of the six-thousand-member Denton Bible Church in Denton, Texas since 1977. His passion for Christ has been recognized by many; he has been featured on *Focus on the Family*, in Josh McDowell's teaching videos, and in other national broadcasts.

The evening of the banquet, Tommy outlined for us the dramatic change in the worldview of our American culture since the time our nation was founded. Our founding fathers embraced the belief in a God who created nature. He is outside of nature and is infinite and sovereign. Yet, He is personal, having given mankind His Word (the Bible) and His only Son, Jesus Christ, to die for the atonement of mankind's sin. God can convert man and answer prayer. And He will return to judge the world. This cultural worldview of those who founded our nation, accepted nature as God's creation and understood history in that light. Outside of the history of mankind, in divine contrast to human finiteness, stood the absolutes of God and the Bible.

However, over the next two centuries, there was a comprehensive shift from that biblical worldview, which resulted in a philosophical "tsunami" in the twentieth century. This "perfect storm" transformed the religious and philosophical paradigms for all succeeding generations. Tommy asserted that this catastrophic shift in worldview is the most monolithic change in the history of western civilization. He cited a number of seismic pressures leading up to this cataclysmic shift in belief systems.

Philosophers of the seventeenth and eighteenth centuries began to approach their view of life and reality (epistemology) without the Bible; they tried to expound the meaning of "truth" without acknowledging God as the source of absolute truth. For example, two main groups of early modern philosophy (as categorized by Kant) were the rationalists and the empiricists. The rationalists (including Descartes, Spinoza, and Leibniz) believed that all knowledge can be gained by the power of our reason alone. Empiricists (including John Locke, George Berkeley, and David Hume) rejected that idea, believing that all knowledge has to come through the senses, from experience rather than through the reasoning mind. Though this distinction is somewhat oversimplified, it helps us to understand the slow process of the detachment of philosophy from theology in seventeenth- and eighteenth-century Europe.

David Hume (1711–1776), a renowned eighteenth-century empiricist, was influential in spreading the belief that all human knowledge comes to us through our senses. He did not believe we could know anything that we had not first felt or "sensed." He referred to these perceptions as "impressions" and "ideas." Impressions come from what we hear, see, feel, love, hate, desire, or will. Ideas, which are the less lively perceptions, are reflections on any of the sensations or movements relating to impressions. To Hume, it is impossible for us to think of anything which we have not felt by our external or internal senses. Hume's assumptions of reality and truth made it impossible to know if God, a soul, or a self exists without receiving proof of that existence through sensual knowledge.[1]

With this shift in philosophical paradigm, nineteenth-century philosophers like Friedrich Nietzsche (1844–1900) moved even farther away from the assertion of absolute truth of the Bible into a philosophical position known as *nihilism*. Nihilism argues that the world, and especially human existence, is without objective meaning, purpose, comprehensible truth, or essential value. "Nihilists generally believe all of the following: God does not exist, traditional morality is false, and secular ethics are impossible; therefore, life has no meaning, and no action is preferable to any other."[2] Further, you cannot even really know if you exist. This position reduces mankind to the level of an animal that must simply fend for itself to survive.

During this time Charles Darwin (1809–1882) argued his theory of evolution, Einstein (1879–1955) introduced his theory of relativity (concluding that nothing is absolute), and Sigmund Freud (1856–1939) and a host of others pressed their godless philosophical and scientific views on a society in transition of worldview based in the definition of "truth."

Soren Kierkegaard (1813–1855), the "father of existentialism," asserted that "truth is subjectivity and subjectivity is truth." This means that human beings can be understood only from the inside, in terms of their lived and experienced reality and dilemmas, not from the outside in terms of a biological, psychological, or other scientific theory of human nature. There is no place for the existence of a sovereign, Creator-God that stands outside creation in this philosophical approach to life.[3]

There is the "Christian" form of existentialism, which states that a person can choose to create meaning in life by taking a leap of faith to believe that God exists and that God is good. However, this personal choice does not make God an objective reality who created mankind and gave him absolute moral law. Rather, it simply makes God a subjective interpretation for the person who chooses to make Him a part of their meaning in life. Existentialism tends to view human beings as subjects in an indifferent, objective, often ambiguous, and absurd universe in which meaning is not provided by the natural order, but rather can be created, however provisionally and unstably, by human beings' actions and interpretations.[4]

Eventually, these godless, humanistic philosophies found their way into our seminaries and influenced the theology of pastors and spiritual leaders of the twentieth century. The approach to Scripture, called "higher criticism," denied the Bible as a supernatural book; it is rather a compilation of men and an imperfect story of the history of ancient peoples. Students who embrace higher criticism deny the divine Trinity of God, scoff at the Son of God coming to Earth through a virgin birth, and do not accept the possibility of miracles. As a result, many churches have been reduced to accepting a social gospel—salvation is man bringing about social change. The onset of this liberal theology of the 1920s concluded that there is no need for salvation, for man is not lost.

The influence of philosophies like nihilism, existentialism, relativity, evolution, and higher criticism created a powerful paradigm shift in the worldview of millions of people. No longer was our culture accountable to a higher moral law, as taught in Scripture and woven into the fabric of our American Constitution. There was no longer broad acceptance of moral right and wrong, of the reality of evil, or of mankind's desperate need for reconciliation to God.

Instead, the relativistic model of man postulated by Sigmund Freud makes us merely icebergs controlled beneath the surface by the subconscious which makes us do what we have to do. This theory was generally adopted as the philosophy of the day. Nature is all that is left; man is a determined animal; there is no God, no Christ, and no divine revelation of God and His purpose for mankind in the Bible.

Thankfully, this atheistic "tsunami" was countered by a vibrant movement, called fundamentalism, within the church in the early twentieth century. Fundamentalists, those who held to the truth of the Bible, of Christ as the Savior of mankind, and of salvation through rebirth, in Tommy Nelson's words, "began to circle the wagons." These evangelicals organized large Bible conferences at Nyack, Niagara, Mt. Hermon, and in other places. A. W. Tozer and other fundamental theologians wrote and spoke eloquently, expounding the doctrines contained in the infallible Word of God. Many new denominations were formed and non-denominational seminaries sprang up to accommodate those who believed in the integrity of the Bible. During this time, many faith missions were also established, in which missionaries would raise their own support to win the lost, because the established church had ceased to believe in the Fall of man and his need for salvation.

During the following decades, many parachurch groups were founded, including Intervarsity, Campus Crusade for Christ, Navigators, Youth for Christ, and Fellowship of Christian Athletes. These organizations and others filled the gap left by evangelical churches that took the posture of "huddling together," protecting their gospel from the world's bombardment of godless philosophies. So overwhelming were the atheistic philosophies of the day that fundamentalists felt intimidated and separated themselves from the world and did not fulfill the Great Commission to "go into all the world and preach the gospel to every creature" (Mark 16:15).

Some historians credit World War II veterans, who fought in deadly battles in Europe and survived, with helping to establish effective parachurch ministries that changed the cowering mentality of the evangelical churches during that time. When American Christianity was deeply wounded and chose to withdraw from the world, these Christian men and women declared that Christians must be willing, like Martin Luther, Calvin, Zwingli, and other saints of old, to die for what we believe. They believed in salvation by faith in Christ and in life everlasting. They believed that the purpose of the church was not predominantly to bring about social change, but to bring renewal through teaching men and women the truth of Scripture regarding the born-again experience of salvation through Christ alone.

Tommy concluded his remarks by referring to his own testimony. The power of the truth of the gospel, spoken to him through a fellow athlete, changed his life, brought peace to his soul, and revealed the destiny and purpose of God for his life. As a Christian athlete, he was forced to give up football because of injury. Tommy then began a career as a teacher. One day a coach invited him to speak to athletes about his faith in God. Hesitantly, he accepted the invitation, and many young people received Christ as a result. For Tommy Nelson, as they say, the rest is history.

Godless philosophies do not offer the answers that the human soul craves regarding questions of significance, meaning, and purpose for life. They do not answer the logical questions of why we came into such exquisite existence, how we were designed, and what sustains life itself in our universe. Only as we choose to humble ourselves before our awesome Creator and seek to be reconciled to Him can we discover answers to the deepest questions of the human heart: "Who made me?" "Why am I here?" "What is my purpose?" and "After this life, what?"

Thankfully, today the biblical tenets of the Christian worldview are intact and spreading around the globe as millions of people turn from their false religions to embrace the love of the Savior, Jesus Christ. A cursory study of religious movements today, as published even by mainstream media, show a sharp rise in Christianity in many nations of the world. This book is, more than anything else, an apologetic for the reality and power of the Christian worldview to change lives and transform defeated people into positive, successful, joyful, and loving souls who discover their personal destiny—the reason for which they were born. That is only possible when people discover and learn to appreciate fully the "Creator's plan."

The Christian Worldview

To clarify the basic beliefs held by Christians, John Piper formulated "six stages of Christianity,"[3] which I have adapted here for your understanding of the foundational truths of the Christian worldview:

1. **Predestination**—The creation and all of life was planned and detailed by God in explicit, intricate, and massive detail—it is beyond any human comprehension or understanding. No man can do it or could do it; it is the work of God, preplanned and glorious. In creation we see and appreciate and worship the mind of the Creator who planned every detail before he brought it to pass.

2. **Creation**—All of life and creation was created by God, by Jesus. John 1:3 says concerning Jesus, "Through him all things were made; without him nothing was made that has been made" (NIV). The creation was planned and accomplished in such a way that the peoples of the world look alike. We have one common, intelligent piece of information that is in all of us—DNA. The plants and species have never changed. They have had microadaptation but never macro. It was designed with an irreducible complexity and an intelligent design, then carried out and created as planned by the Lord. There are a hundred conditions that are necessary to have life on Earth, from the atmosphere to the angle of the tilt of the Earth, and many other precise details such as the distance of our planet from the sun; the thickness of the Earth's crust; the amount of water, oxygen, and carbon dioxide in the atmosphere; our place in the Milky Way Galaxy; the kind of star that our sun is compared to others that would be harmful to life—all of these conditions and many other amazing details show that we live on a privileged planet and it is designed for us to recognize that privilege and study God's creation from it.

3. **The Incarnation**—Christ, who is God the Son, came
to Earth and took upon himself perfect humanity
so that he was fully God and fully man, two natures
joined together in one Person forever. This concept is
one that has changed the entire world and given purpose to it. It was man that sinned, but only God could
pay an infinite penalty. The solution is the God-man,
God the Son, the second Person of the blessed Trinity,
Jesus. Through Him, ultimately, God communicates
His will and knowledge of truth. In Colossians 1:9,
Paul prays for "God to fill you with the knowledge of
his will through all spiritual wisdom and understanding" (NIV). In essence, He said, "My desire is that you
come to know the will of God and His wisdom and
have a godly understanding." That is why Christ came
and sacrificed His life as the Savior—to give us the
"power to become the sons of God" (John 1:12, KJV).
Through relationship with Him, we gain the knowledge of God and enjoy intimacy with Him.

4. **Imputation**—Imputation can be described simply as
God imputing our sin to Jesus on the cross and God
imputing Jesus' righteousness to us as believers. So
it was not just Christ's life, but His death and resurrection, that brought us salvation. His death pays
for our sins! This imputation is most important. He
took our place of judgment; we receive His standing
as righteous. Paul would often plead with men to be
reconciled to God and the understanding of imputation was the foundation of his plea: "Be reconciled to
God. God made him who had no sin to be sin for us,
so that in him we might become the righteousness of
God" (2 Cor. 5:20–21, NIV). When Christ's perfect

righteousness is put into our account we are declared justified or declared righteousness. Now God views us as He does His Son—and "If God is for us, who can be against us?" (Rom. 8:31, NIV).

5. **Righteousness**—Righteousness (sanctification) is living in right relationship with our Creator because of Christ. Walking uprightly before the Lord and living to please Him is the essence of a sanctified, righteous life—the basis for the Christian walk. It is not possible for the proud person. Righteousness comes with surrender to the lordship of Christ and humility of realizing we can't do anything without Him. As we embrace Christ with a passion, our role is to love Him with all our heart, soul, and mind and our brothers as ourselves (see Mark 12:30–31). The power to live to please God flows out of a life that receives His love and joy and responds with love and joy in Him and in all that He wants us to do.

6. **Consummation**—The sixth stage of the panorama of the true knowledge of God is *consummation*. This is the reality of being joined in heart and affection in an all-consuming joy with our Lord. Our consummation in God will be ultimately fulfilled when we, as believers, see Jesus face to face in heaven. However, this "consummation principle" has already begun to be reality now in our union and communion with the risen Savior, our heavenly Bridegroom. He is no longer one of the many things that we pay attention to; He is the *One* we pay attention to.

Jamie Buckingham talked about the fact that at his life's end he became joyfully aware that it was just "Jamie and Jesus." He had finished his responsibilities at his church; he had no more books to write or author's deadlines to meet; no more magazines to publish; he accepted no more of the many speaking engagements he had enjoyed—it was just Jamie and Jesus. His personal life was better. Everything was better. For even though he was about to die, his life had become focused solely on his relationship with Jesus. I know several people who have retired and gotten rid of everything besides Jesus. They read Scripture four to six hours a day and have no distractions—life is just Jesus and them. They have reached consummation now, along with many people who really seek after their Lord. The great consummation that we long for in eternity will be rewarded to us in proportion to the degree of closeness and intimacy with our Lord that we have pursued in this life. "You will be repaid at the resurrection of the righteous" (Luke 14:14, NIV). I pray that you are consumed with His glory, the wonderful Person of Jesus, and His majesty, and that you humbly realize that you can do nothing of a gracious nature without Him.

We humbly present these six stages of Christianity so that they can be a road map as we walk along the path that leads to the celestial city. This overview makes sense of Christianity and our life with Jesus. It gives us the *big picture* in which to fit our lives. May we all, as Christian pilgrims, keep these six landmarks before us as signposts along the way. May we anticipate with joy crossing that river into the celestial city in order to enjoy the ultimate consummation—being totally consumed with the Creator and Redeemer of all. May we discover, as C. S. Lewis says, that heaven is all we ever dreamed of throughout our life but never found here below. May God bless you!

—JIM GILLS

I am convinced that the cause of many of life's failures is that we, as human beings, lack *exceeding gratitude* for our Creator. As a result of taking His divine gift of life for granted, we live in discontent and misery, complaining about what we don't have and failing to express genuine appreciation for what we do have.

I am also convinced that by simply stopping to appreciate the world around us, as well as the marvelous "world" of life within us—our human body—our perspective of life can be transformed. This new perspective will reveal to us the Creator's redemptive plan and fill our hearts with exceeding gratitude for our Creator-Redeemer. That divine relationship will transform us into joyful, ennobled, Christian steward-servants.

No appreciation without knowledge

David Jeremiah, well-known pastor and author, declares that without *knowledge* it is impossible to experience appreciation. You cannot hold in high esteem something (or someone) about which you know nothing. It is impossible to value that of which you are not aware. For example, if you are not aware of the marvels of creation, you cannot properly appreciate them, value them, or be grateful for them. If you know nothing about the love of God, you will not be grateful to Him for His love, grace, and mercy. Knowledge is requisite to appreciation. In short, you cannot properly appreciate the Giver of life or the gift of life when lacking knowledge of either.

As a young medical student more than four decades ago, I explored the wonders of DNA and the astonishing secrets of life that have been unlocked by molecular biology scientists. Observing the fantastic function of microscopic particles whose only mission was to establish and maintain life, my perspective of life was radically changed. I found myself becoming filled with appreciation to the Creator of life for His unfathomable gift of life.

Today, the scientific evidence discovered about our world is leading more and more people to the acknowledgment of a Creator. Out of that springs understanding of God and His amazing love for mankind, which inevitably leads the seeking heart to a revelation of His Son, Jesus Christ. As you learn to receive the redemption found in Christ alone, you will discover your personal destiny—the reason for which you were born. As a result of the deep gratitude born in your heart for your Creator-Redeemer, you will know the joy and freedom of living an anointed life—releasing the "dance" of your DNA.

No knowledge without grace

Guillermo Gonzalez and Jay Richards, authors of *The Privileged Planet: The Search for Purpose in the Universe*, discuss the fascinating fact that, not only does complex human life exist on our planet, but we have the *intelligence* and ability to understand our planet and the universe in which we exist in great depth of detail. This superfluous intellectual ability is not part of the Darwinian theory of evolution, which states that intelligence is evolved only to the level needed for survival. We don't have to know how the universe functions to live here—to survive.[1]

Our capacity for knowledge, without which we cannot appreciate life or the Giver of life, must be understood as a special gift from our Creator. His grace—divine favor—bestowed upon mankind gave us intelligence with which to pursue knowledge. Each individual must choose the source of knowledge on which he or she will rely for meaning in life. Your choice of worldview, philosophy, religion, or non-religion will ultimately determine your level of appreciation for life as well as your destiny.

In David Jeremiah's book, *Captured by Grace*, he asserts that *grace* is a stained-glass, impersonal word until *it happens to you*. He challenges us to "compare our Lord to the gods of all the world's religions and find that grace is the difference maker":

> [Grace] is the x-factor that radically sets Him apart. Our God is "the God of all grace" (1 Pet. 5:10). He is kind, benevolent, and longsuffering. We need not beg Him, bribe Him, or appease Him. He actually longs to bless us every single moment, every single day. He comes down to us rather than demanding that we climb the impossible ladder to infinity to reach Him. Grace is God taking the initiative."[2]

Dr. Richard Swenson, in his DVD presentation, *More Than Meets the Eye*, declares that in God's greatness, His grace is one of His perfections that is life-changing when it touches humanity.[3] It is that divine grace or favor coming to your heart that births thankfulness and gratitude for your Creator. In her book, *Radical Gratitude*, Ellen Vaughn, writes: "Cultivating a thankful heart is not about autonomy, self-sufficiency, and self-congratulation, but dependence and thanks to Another. We perceive each day's experiences as gifts given, or opportunities allowed, by a Giver's sovereign purpose."[4] Entering into a relationship of dependence on your Creator-Redeemer opens to you an eternal perspective of life filled with hope, joy, and love—all a part of God's divine favor.

What is your worldview? Where are you on the appreciation scale? Do you live in self-centered misery or have you discovered the secret to personal destiny and deep satisfaction in life? Instead of suffering the effects of selfish unhappiness, you can learn to cultivate a lifestyle of radical gratitude by gaining knowledge of the wonders of life. This new perspective can be transforming as you learn to truly appreciate the divine gift of life you have been given.

The purpose of this book can be summed up in four key words:

- *Appreciation,* simply defined, means "to grasp the worth and value of something or someone; to esteem and properly revere them."[5] God is Creator of the laws of nature; therefore, all of nature reveals God to us. Appreciation for the Creator's "intelligent design" deepens as we gain knowledge of the unfathomable generosity of our Creator-God, revealed in His creation.

- *Adoration* is the spontaneous heart response to a revelation of our loving God and Savior, who desires intimate relationship with His highest creation—mankind. Adoration for our God fills us with praise and thanksgiving for His gift of life and brings us to repentance for our great sin of omission—our lack of appreciation in taking His gift of life for granted.

- *Anointing* is the divine charisma of God Himself and it characterizes the beauty of a life lived in intimate relationship with God. As we learn to appreciate our Creator-Redeemer and ask Him to anoint our hearts, lives, and even our DNA, we can rest in the joy and peace of Christ's redemption.

- *Antiquated* most accurately describes Darwin's theory of evolution in the light of twentieth- and twenty-first-century scientific discoveries revealing strong evidence of "intelligent design" in creation. Current scientific knowledge is causing many to abandon the antiquated theory of evolution, resulting in an openness of heart and mind to the potential of intimate relationship with their Creator.

Biblical analogies reveal eternal truths.

The Bible is filled with pictures of earthly life that help us to understand heavenly truths. It seems that the Creator delights in "showing off" His creation, using its natural imagery to teach supernatural realities. For example, Psalm 23, the beloved psalm of comfort, begins: "The Lord is my shepherd." Though our Lord is not a shepherd in the natural sense, this comforting analogy helps us grasp the supernatural protection, provision, and providential care that Christ, our "good shepherd" (John 10:11), bestows upon the sheep of His pasture (see Ps. 100:3).

One of the most prolific analogies in Scripture teaches eternal truths through the imagery of trees, vineyards, flowers, and other wonders of the plant kingdom. For example, in the Old Testament, the righteous are portrayed as beautiful trees:

> Blessed is the man Who walks not in the counsel of the ungodly, Nor stands in the path of sinners, Nor sits in the seat of the scornful; But his delight is in the law of the Lord... He shall be like a tree Planted by the rivers of water, That brings forth its fruit in its season, Whose leaf also shall not wither; And whatever he does shall prosper.
>
> —Psalm 1:1–3

In the New Testament, Jesus refers to Himself as the vine and to His followers as branches:

> I am the true vine, and My Father is the vinedresser... I am the vine, you are the branches. He who abides in Me, and I in him, bears much fruit; for without Me you can do nothing.
>
> —John 15:1, 5

The natural connectedness (and dependency) of the branch to the vine gives us a vivid picture of the intimate, abiding relationship with Christ that is necessary to live useful and fruitful lives. These descriptive, biblical analogies strengthen our grasp of abstract, eternal realities.

Similarly, this devotional is designed to deepen your appreciation of the Creator through gaining knowledge of the marvels of creation—from the awesome galaxies of the universe to the microscopic wonder of your DNA. As you discover the facts of infinite design present in every molecule of creation, you will realize how truly special you are in the eyes of your Creator. His incredible love and desire for relationship ordained your existence before time began. The grace of God—His divine favor—can be seen throughout His creation, but is never more exquisitely revealed than in the creation of mankind.

The "flowers" designed for each devotional message depict a central biblical truth about our Creator. The center of the flower is labeled to reflect the core of the eternal truth discussed, with related truths forming the "petals" surrounding it. Of course, some truths that form a "petal" of one flower are powerful enough to be the center of another flower, forming its own "petals" of related truths. For example, *grace* is a powerful truth forming a "petal" around *Christ*. Yet, *grace* itself is a central truth, forming other divine attributes around it as well. Of course, no divine truth stands alone; each is blended into an exquisite bouquet of eternal realities, ultimately revealing the wonder of the Creator's divine design for life.

If you want to live a joy-filled life, you will need to develop a profound appreciation for your Creator, who designed you before time began. Knowledge of that unfathomable design will birth appreciation within you. As you develop an attitude of exceeding gratitude for the Creator-Redeemer and His awesome gift of life, you will learn to live in satisfying, intimate relationship with Him.

From a faulty to a faultless worldview

In an earlier century, Charles Darwin tried to separate science from God. Scientists today have compiled irrefutable evidence of intelligent design—from the unfathomable immensity of the galaxies to the microscopic DNA—that explodes the myths of Darwin's theory of evolution. I believe that as you learn to appreciate the One who created "science" through His incomprehensible, irreducibly complex, intelligent design, your heart will become filled with exceeding gratitude for your Creator.

The biblical truths of this devotional can lead you into a deeper *appreciation* of the Creator, enable you to express sincere *adoration* to God, and teach you to live a satisfying, *anointed* life. Jesus promised: "I have come that they may have life, and that they may have it more abundantly" (John 10:10). May you become like a tree, "planted by the rivers of water" (Ps. 1:3). May you bask in the exquisite comfort of the "good shepherd" (John 10:11). And may your life blossom with the radiance of joy and peace that emanate from a heart filled with "exceeding gratitude for the Creator's plan" for the life He has given you to enjoy.

Know that the LORD, He is God; It is He who has made us,

and not we ourselves; We are His people and the sheep of His

pasture. Enter into His gates with thanksgiving, And into His

courts with praise. Be thankful to Him, and bless His name.

—PSALM 100:3–4

TRACING THE HAND OF THE CREATOR

The Darwinian theory of evolution that has driven scientific thought for over a century declares that all of life is the product of purely undirected natural forces: time, chance, and natural selection. *Natural selection*, in simple terms, means that all of life evolved from one simple cell produced in the primordial oceans of the Earth. However, Charles Darwin cited a potential flaw in his theory of origins:

> Natural selection acts only by taking advantage of slight, successive variations. She can never take a great and sudden leap, but must advance by short and sure, though slow steps. If it could be demonstrated that any complex organ existed, which could not possibly have been formed by numerous, successive slight modifications, my theory would absolutely break down."[1]

Scientists today are viewing far distant galaxies now visible through powerful telescope lenses. And they are using equally powerful microscopes to penetrate the tiny, molecular world of the human cell. Their twentieth- and twenty-first-century scientific studies have discovered precisely what Darwin feared—complex structures that could not have developed through "numerous, successive slight modifications." These "irreducibly complex" wonders, such as the DNA buried in the nucleus of our cells, which serves as a blueprint for tiny, molecular machines, have indeed caused Darwin's theory of evolution, to use his words, to "absolutely break down." As year by year new layers of complexity are revealed within living cells and in the intricate crafting of the cosmos, it has become more and more difficult to resist the conclusion of "intelligent design" revealed in every functioning aspect of creation.

THE TRANSFORMING POWER OF APPRECIATION

My life story can be summarized in four words: "I'm not appreciative enough." In living life, I have not always experienced the humble reality of a heart filled with exceeding gratitude for the Giver of life and the gift of life itself. I have a tendency to take all of the good things of life for granted. I have not appreciated my parents, my neighbor, or my Lord enough. Too often, I have embraced the mind-set of many Americans, even Christians, who simply strive to get more, do more, and continually want (covet) even more.

In this mind-set of frantic discontent, we fail to experience or express appreciation for all that we have been given. Our ingratitude causes us to lose the powerful impact on our lives that true appreciation can bring. One reason for our lack of appreciation may be that we don't understand the marvelous gift of life we have been given.

More than four decades ago, I was a medical student at Duke University. Sir John Eccles had recently been awarded the Nobel Prize in medicine for his work on the cell and its electrophysiological transmembrane potential. Eccles had exposed the cell as an active and intricate entity possessing dynamic relationships between a number of cell systems. As a young medical student, I developed a tiny instrument, called a *nanopipette*, which could measure these electrical potentials across a single cell membrane, as proposed by Eccles. I found that the electrical field the cell generates, as measured by this instrument, can be at times larger than the electrical field found near power lines.[2] As I gazed at the phenomenal activity of life produced by the hundreds of functioning entities within one microscopic living cell, and its ability to integrate perfectly with more than sixty trillion other cells of the human body, my ingrained philosophy of evolution was jolted.

It was becoming more and more illogical to reconcile the odds of "formation by chance" to such a complex organism when the obvious criterion of "design" was necessary to its flawless form and function. During the decades since then, scientists in the world of molecular biology have continued to explore the phenomenal design of the cell, with similar conclusions.

For example, Michael Behe, author of *Darwin's Black Box*, has concluded that the *irreducible complexity* of the microscopic, functioning "motors" within each cell preclude the possibility of their evolution. His original definition of "irreducible complexity" is "a single system composed of several well-matched, interacting parts that contribute to the basic function of the system, wherein the removal of any one of the parts causes the system to effectively cease functioning."[3] In other words, these microscopic entities, comprised of several functioning parts, could not begin to function without all of their parts being present simultaneously. Thus, for one of the parts to have to *evolve* slowly over time would make the existence of the system impossible.

Eternal benefits

As my knowledge of the design of human life grew through scientific discovery, it transformed my entire perspective of life. I knew a growing sense of deep appreciation for the astounding gift of life as I observed it under the microscope, which caused me to begin a pilgrimage toward a deep, intimate relationship with the Designer—the Creator of all of life. In my personal journey to faith in God, the Creator-Redeemer, I have come to believe that a lack of appreciation for our eternal Creator, is one of humankind's greatest sins.

We often refer to two types of sin: sins of *commission*—what we *do*—and sins of *omission*—what we *fail to do*. Perhaps the greatest sin of *omission* is our failure to properly appreciate the gift of life. Lack of appreciation, like all other sin, may be a result of genuine ignorance. Lack of knowledge, for example, of the wonders of creation, will inevitably result in a lack of appreciation for them. Yet, sin always brings with it terrible consequences. Illnesses in our physical body, negative syndromes in our mind, broken family relationships, and most importantly, lack of a relationship with God Himself are potential consequences of a lack of gratitude for the gift of life.

And the presence in our lives of the sin of commission—*worry*—can also be a result of failing to appreciate God. To worry is to not view life in relation to God's sovereignty, design, and faithfulness. Worry emanates from a life that is distracted and diverted into a self-centered perspective that is self-destructive, unproductive, and joyless.

Knowledge of the creation reveals to us the nature of our Creator. As we behold the Creator's infinite hand in our universe, we begin to understand that He is outside of "time" or any other finite, limiting force. He is eternal. And if He designed life with a divine purpose, it must be to unlock the secrets of eternity to our hearts. Jesus asked the Father to give eternal life to as many as He had given to the Son (John 17:2). He continued: "And this is eternal life, that they may know You, the only true God, and Jesus Christ whom You have sent" (v. 3). Learning to appreciate the Creator can be a beginning point to unlocking for us the eternal benefits of knowing God, receiving His Son, Jesus Christ, and thereby entering into eternal life.

Yet, it has been my observation that even people of faith, born-again believers in Christ who love their Creator-Redeemer, often lack appreciation for His creation. They fail to comprehend the wondrous beauty all around them and often abuse the gift of physical health He has given them. Their lack of knowledge of the handiwork of their Creator keeps them from full appreciation of the eternal benefits of life they have been given. Again, I have observed unbelievers who have not surrendered to Christ as Savior, who nevertheless enjoy a deep appreciation for the wonders of creation. Their scientific knowledge of the mysterious workings of life and the beauty of the laws of physics, for example, give them a wondrous perspective of life that evokes deep appreciation for the gift of life. It often sets them on a journey, as it did me, to surrender to the love of their Creator-Redeemer.

When these two realities—appreciation for creation and surrender to the Creator-Redeemer—unite in a person's heart, there is an explosion of hope, love, joy, purpose, and destiny. Only believers who learn to appreciate their Creator can truly enjoy the eternal benefits of the abundant life, which Jesus promised: "I have come that they may have life, and that they may have it more abundantly" (John 10:10). That deep appreciation in a believer's heart evokes adoration and worship of God. And that divine relationship in turn manifests the power of God's anointing in a life of worship, fulfilling our eternal destiny. It is that anointed life, restored to relationship with the Creator-Redeemer, that brings the deepest satisfaction to the human heart. We never tire of reflecting on the wisdom of John Piper's maxim: "God is most glorified in us when we are most satisfied in Him."[4]

Understanding appreciation

What does it mean to truly appreciate? To be grateful? Webster's dictionary defines the terms for us:

> To *appreciate* is to grasp the nature, worth, quality, or significance of; to value or admire highly; to judge with heightened perception or understanding: be fully aware of; and to recognize with gratitude."[5]

Similarly, the noun *appreciation* is defined as:

> A judgment, an evaluation, especially a favorable critical estimate; a sensitive awareness, especially in recognition of aesthetic values, and an expression of admiration, approval, or gratitude.[6]

To be *grateful* means, first of all, "to be appreciative of benefits received."[7] In order to be grateful and to fully appreciate anything in life we must acquire an increased awareness of its worth and a heightened perception of its significance. Appreciation involves placing such high value on something that it evokes our deep admiration. It also implies recognition of aesthetic values, which gain our unabashed approval and our expression of generous gratitude. It follows that to truly appreciate the *gift* of life, we must learn to appreciate the *Giver* of life.

Lack of appreciation will inevitably cause us to take all of life for granted—not only ours, but also the precious lives of those around us. I believe this sin of omission is one of the greatest failures of mankind. When we truly appreciate our Creator, we will not take for granted the awesome gift of life He has given to us. For me, the personal discoveries of the gift of life, as seen through the microscope, caused an explosion of appreciation within my heart and mind for the Creator. Out of sheer gratitude for the unimaginable complexities of every cell, which form over two hundred different kinds of tissues in our body, my heart reached out to thank the One who made it all possible. In my humble acknowledgment of a

Creator, I desired to know Him. And as I sought to know Him, I discovered Him, not only as my Creator, but as my Redeemer as well.

Radical gratitude

True appreciation for God evokes the most profound expressions of gratitude, admiration, and worship of which the human spirit is capable. Ironically, it is in those humble expressions of adoration to our Creator-Redeemer that we also find ultimate fulfillment and satisfaction in life.

Ellen Vaughn, in her book, *Radical Gratitude*, recounts how the transcending power of a grateful heart caused men and women, who faced hardship and tragedy, to win in the face of life's overwhelming challenges. She cites the powerful views of gratitude that philosophers in the classical Western tradition have held:

> The Roman sage Cicero called gratitude not only the greatest of virtues but the parent of all others...Plato and Socrates wrote that citizens have a duty of obedience to the state based on gratitude for its benefits. Shakespeare wrote, 'O Lord that lends me life, lend me a heart replete with thankfulness!' Immanuel Kant said that ingratitude was the 'essence of vileness.'[8]

The power of gratitude to impact our lives, according to the philosophers, lies in understanding that "gratitude is not only the greatest of virtues, it is parent of all others."[9] Conversely, all kinds of evil—the "essence of vileness"—gains entrance to our lives through the terrible vacuum in our hearts created by our lack of appreciation for our Creator. Every eternal virtue in life triumphs over evil when we learn to allow our hearts to be filled with gratitude—radically. The apostle Paul confirmed the impact that expressing gratitude has on our lives:

> Rejoice in the Lord always. I will say it again: Rejoice!...Do not be anxious about anything, but in everything, by prayer and petition, with thanksgiving, present your requests to God. And the

peace of God, which transcends all understanding, will guard your hearts and your minds in Christ Jesus.

—PHILIPPIANS 4:4, 6–7, NIV

Personal relationship with God counteracts the destructive power of anxiety from our lives. The apostle Paul had his share of troubles, yet he declared confidently: "Who shall separate us from the love of Christ? Shall tribulation, or distress, or persecution, or famine, or nakedness, or peril, or sword?...Yet in all these things we are more than conquerors through Him who loved us" (Rom. 8:35, 37). David Jeremiah comments on Paul's attitude toward life expressed in these verses. He writes:

> Paul takes his stand at the very crosshairs of the devil's target and says, "I'm here...Nothing will deny me from being the conqueror that Christ has made me to be through the power and redemption of His love...Therefore I will laugh and sing with the joy of heaven through the worst of storms, and just try to stop me! I will live every moment in the abundance of gratitude that flows from the power of grace.[9]

As we learn to place high value on the Creator and on His creation, we discover the great value of our own life as well as of the lives of others. This sense of significance in itself is a powerful impetus for overcoming life's difficult challenges. Often our lack of appreciation can be heard in our whining complaints of, "If only I had this," or, "If only I could do that." These and similar statements reveal our selfish nature that lacks appreciation for God's divine gift of life to us. Instead of expressing gratitude daily for what we have, we focus on what we do not have. As a result, we are blinded to all of life's good things we could be enjoying.

There are internal obstacles to seeing the beauty of life clearly. Our degree of spiritual sight hinges on the honesty and sincerity with which we appreciate our Lord. Many people do not appreciate the Lord and His gifts because they are content with the attractions of superficial observations and desires, and they are selfish and proud. This question may be a beginning of a new vision of life: How can we remain indifferent to the marvelous design of our bodies and the Creator's eternal plans written within them?[10]

Of course, in acknowledging that we owe our life to the Creator of life, we are expressing dependence on Another, which is uncomfortable to our independent minds. However, if we admit the fact that we did not create ourselves, it follows that we cannot know for what purpose we exist without consulting with the Creator. If we choose to go blindly through life without acknowledging our dependence on our Maker, we are doomed to live in the misery of ingratitude. Ellen Vaughn explains:

> The biggest obstacle to gratitude is refusing to admit that apart from Christ, we can do nothing. We are dependent on Him. All our lives, we will have needs that we cannot fulfill by ourselves. Paradoxically, this way of dependence is not slavish. In it we find real, rollicking freedom.[11]

Eternal consequences

Worry, the opposite attitude to appreciation, is a grave consequence of our lack of appreciation. Worry is a prevalent disease in our culture today. When our thoughts are filled with worry and anxiety, we inhibit the creative and energetic ideas we could otherwise produce. If worry makes it difficult to eat or sleep, it becomes even more difficult to focus our minds on life's demands. We become indecisive, fearing that we will make wrong decisions, so we can't make any decisions.

Charles Mayo, cofounder of the Mayo Clinic, confirmed that worry affects the circulatory system, the heart, the glands and the nervous system, as well as other parts of the body. He used to say that he never knew of anyone who died of overwork, but he knew of people who died of worry.[12] So, it is possible to *worry ourselves to death*, but it is not possible to worry ourselves into a longer, healthier, happier life.

If we give ourselves to worry, it makes us irritable and more susceptible to panic attacks. Anxiety can cause us to become depressed, negative, critical, judgmental, domineering, and controlling. As a result, we isolate ourselves from people and become lonely. As a progressive disease, worry depletes us emotionally. It can sometimes cause hypertension and destroy our ability to fight against other diseases by decreasing our natural immunity. Scripture describe a society that is characterized by these negative perspectives of life:

> But know this, that in the last days perilous times will come:
> For men will be lovers of themselves, lovers of money, boasters, proud, blasphemers, disobedient to parents, unthankful, unholy, unloving, unforgiving, slanderers, without self-control, brutal, despisers of good, traitors, headstrong, haughty, lovers of pleasure rather than lovers of God.
>
> —2 TIMOTHY 3:1–4

Cultivating a personal relationship with God, our Creator-Redeemer delivers us from the negative consequences of a life lived without gratitude. My prayer is that I can help you avoid some of these consequences, which I have experienced in my own life when I have failed to appreciate God and others as I should.

Our loving Creator

The key to living a life filled with gratitude is to acknowledge our loving Creator. As Richard Swenson, physician, physicist, and scientific researcher, astutely observes:

> When we gain a picture of what this creative God has done within us, it helps us to understand that we are more than a random collection of organized atoms. Within the miracle of the human body, there is sanctity, hope, and glory. More important, this

same awareness also helps us to appreciate that such a Creator is rightly regarded with awe...When we see Him more clearly, we have more faith in His power and less anxiety about our circumstances.[13]

Cultivating an attitude of appreciation for the unfathomable beauty of design formed by the hand of our loving Creator can deepen into profound gratitude and awe for the Giver of life.

Divine destiny

I invite you to personally evaluate your level of appreciation for the gift of life, and the Giver of life, as you continue to read this devotional. To know the satisfaction of discovering your eternal destiny—the divine purpose for which you were born—demands such an evaluation. Take the challenge to consider your lack of gratitude, first for the Creator, and then for each aspect of the wondrous gift of life He has given you to enjoy. In such honest confrontation you need fear nothing except the lack of appreciation that keeps you bound to failure in areas of your life. I encourage you to receive the promise God made many years ago to His people, Israel, for the fulfilling of divine destiny:

> I have set before you life and death, blessing and cursing; therefore *choose life, that both you and your descendants may live.*
> —DEUTERONOMY 30:19, EMPHASIS ADDED

For since the creation of the world His invisible attributes are

clearly seen, being understood by the things that are made, even

His eternal power and Godhead.

—Romans 1:20

Tracing the Hand of the Creator

The level of precision of the universe is 10^{10} to the [27th], a number that is humanly impossible to describe. The minute details of every movement of the stars, every element of the planets, every formative attribute of the Earth are precisely what is needed to sustain life, to the unfathomable degree that the most brilliant scientist could never begin to reproduce (see Appendix A). The sheer magnitude of the universe that has been discovered to date is beyond our comprehension.[1]

The planet Venus is the size of the Earth. But it has very long days because it takes eight months to rotate one time. And it is the only planet that is retrograde—it rotates in the opposite direction of all the others in our galaxy. As a result, its atmospheric pressure is ninety times greater than the Earth's. The upper clouds of Venus drip sulfuric acid, and there are surface hurricane winds constantly, along with deafening thunder and lightning strikes, and a one thousand degree Fahrenheit surface temperature.[2]

Jupiter, the largest planet in our galaxy, could hold one thousand Earths. It rotates so fast that one day is only eight hours long. It has surface winds of one thousand miles per hour. While it cannot sustain any known form of life, it performs a very important role for our Earth. If Jupiter were not placed precisely where it is, comets would strike the Earth one thousand times more frequently than they do, threatening our very existence. Saturn is the beauty queen of the Milky Way's planets. Its gigantic rings are exquisite to behold. (See photo on page 221.) It contains seven hundred fifty times the volume of the Earth. Two of its moons perform an extraordinary feat. Every four years they shift in their orbits, looking as though they are about to crash into each other. But then, at the last "moment" they do a kind of "dance"—and switch orbits.[3]

DISCOVERING THE CREATOR

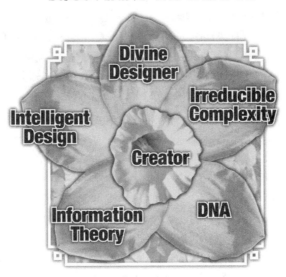

We are all familiar with the Darwinian theory of evolution that has driven scientific thought for over a century. Charles Darwin, in his book, *On the Origin of the Species*, declared that all of life is the product of purely undirected natural forces: time, chance, and natural selection. It was Darwin's attempt to explain the appearance of design without a Designer—a designer substitute. He concluded, "Natural selection acts only by taking advantage of slight, successive variations. She can never take a great and sudden leap, but must advance by short and sure, though slow steps"[4] Yet, Charles Darwin himself feared that his theory of origins could be successfully refuted if scientists could discover a complex organism, "which could not possibly have been formed by numerous, successive slight modifications."[5] Scientists of the twentieth and twenty-first centuries have done just that.

Dr. John Polkinghorne, who studied under the quantum physicist, Paul Dirac, made his name as a particle physicist in the 1960s and 1970s. In 1979 he quit his post of twenty-five years as professor of mathematical physics at Cambridge University to train as an Anglican priest. After serving as a parish priest in Bristol, England, and later as vicar in Kent, Polkinghorne returned to academia in 1986 to become dean of Trinity Hall, Cambridge. He then became president of Queens' College Cambridge from 1989 until he retired in 1996.

Polkinghorne has written fourteen books on science and religion. He believes that science and theology are not opposed to one another; rather, they provide a different perspective on the world. In 2002, Polkinghorne was awarded the Templeton Prize, recognized as the world's best-known religion prize and awarded each year to a living person "to encourage and honor those who advance spiritual matters."[6] In his book, *One World*, Polkinghorne discusses the wonder of creation, as paraphrased by Ravi Zacharias:

> When you reflect on creation and reflect on this world it is so fascinating, so intricate, and so marvelous and so tightly knit in its design. If you were to go into the early days of the formation of the universe the expansion and contraction rates have to be so precise, the margin of error must be so small, it would be the equivalent of taking aim on a square inch target at the other end of the universe twenty billion light years away and hitting it head on-bulls eye![7]

Irreducible complexity

The complexity of the universe as understood by physicists like Polkinghorne today was not apparent a century ago. In Darwin's day, it was believed that cells were very simple entities, like blobs of gel. But as science has progressed, it has discovered that cells are extraordinarily complex. The cell, which is the basic unit of every living thing, is a fascinating microscopic world of "irreducible complexity." That is, it could not possibly have been formed by numerous, successive slight modifications, as Darwin supposed. For example, molecular biologists now know that the amount of information in the DNA of even the single-celled bacterium, *E. coli*, can be as high as 4.5 million pairs of letters—greater than the information contained in our largest books.[8]

Michael Behe, biochemist at Lehigh University describes *irreducible complexity* using a standard household mousetrap as an illustration. It has five parts, all of which must be present at the same time for the trap to work. If you take away any of the parts, you don't have a functioning mousetrap. You can add the parts one by one, but until you get to the full five parts, you have no function. It is an all or nothing scenario. Scientists now know that the most fundamental single cell demonstrates this phenomenon of irreducible complexity.[9]

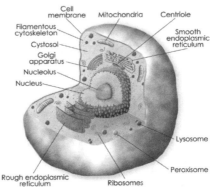

I invite you to place your eye on the lens of a powerful microscope and observe with me some of the functions of the life of one human cell. The cell itself is made up of many tiny specialized structures. The *membrane*, or skin, of the cell is a microscopic phenomenon, whose function is to exchange important materials needed for its health. *Mitochondria* are tiny, complex engines in each cell, which busily make the fuel, ATP (adenosine triphosphate). Food is oxidized within the cells. Carbon dioxide and other waste products are dispatched through the membrane of the cell to the lungs or kidneys to be expelled. Meanwhile, oxygen and other nutrients enter the cell. In short, life and health happen continually on the cellular level for more than sixty trillion cells in the human body.[10] Viewing these microscopic marvels evokes the awe of appreciation for the gift of life we take so much for granted. But that is not all.

While the membrane is the *skin* of the cell, and the mitochondrion is the *heart* of the cell, the DNA, packed away in the nucleus, is the *brain* of the cell. In 1953, James Watson and Francis Crick proposed the model of the double helix DNA molecule and were rewarded with a Nobel Prize for their work. The DNA is an amazingly delicate filigree, containing massive volumes of information used to form and maintain the health of its life entity. If the DNA from a single human cell was stretched out, it would extend over five feet in length. And it is only fifty trillionths of an inch wide.[11] Every living thing, whether in the plant or animal kingdom, contains this brainy DNA molecule. This amazing molecule is also complete with all assembly instructions necessary to develop and maintain its particular life form.

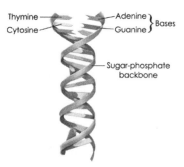

Lets look again through the lens of the microscope to observe *enzymes*, a class of proteins that help the cell digest other kinds of proteins. We watch as they are created in one compartment, called the *endoplasmic reticulum*. But we understand that they do their work in another compartment, the *lysosome*. To get from one compartment to the other, we see the enzymes being "stuffed" into a kind of bus, a *vesicle*. This bus then travels to the destination compartment and eventually merges with it, spilling its contents into the compartment. And the complex process continues.

The point is that virtually all of the proteins needed for this process must be there from the beginning or you simply don't get any function. There is no room for Darwin's theory of "short and sure, though slow steps." Observing these microscopic functions of the cell also makes it tough for Darwinists to argue that design is simply an illusion that has been produced by mutation and natural selection. As pointed out in the delightful video documentary, *Unlocking the Mystery of Life*, just one microscopic cell is teeming with complex wonders. You will observe "trucks" that carry supplies from one end of the cell to the other, "machines" that capture the energy from sunlight and turn it into usable energy, and other machines that clean the cell. There are as many molecular machines in the cells of the human body as there are functions that the body has to do. Hearing, seeing, smelling, tasting, feeling, blood-clotting, respiratory action, the immune responses, and so on all require a host of complex molecular machines functioning in complete harmony in every one of your sixty trillion cells—and all at the same time.[12]

We see that Darwinian theory fails in light of the perfect functioning of these complex cellular machines, because every part of the machine must be present *simultaneously* and function perfectly in order to exist. In short, none of their parts could have "evolved" in the progressive, small, variations that Darwin's theory of origins relied upon; they are irreducibly complex.

One spectacular, tiny molecular machine you will observe in the cell is called the *bacterial flagellum*. (See page 222 for illustration.) Scott Minnick, a scientist who has studied this machine for over twenty years, explains its functions for us. The parts of this machine are visible when a cell is magnified fifty thousand times. It has a propeller, drive shaft, motor, rotor, filament, u-joint, and so on and functions like an outboard motor on a motorboat. There are over forty different parts necessary for the bacterial flagellum to function. Some of the parts are running at one hundred thousand rpms and are hard wired into a sensory mechanism so that they are getting feedback from the environment. And even though they are spinning that fast, it takes only a quarter turn to stop and shift directions to start spinning one hundred thousand rpms in the other direction. Scientists call it the most efficient machine in the universe. All components of this irreducibly complex system must be present *simultaneously* for this molecular machine to perform.[13]

Scott Minnick concludes that even more complex than the machine itself is the set of *assembly instructions* that require a precise sequence of assembly of the parts of the flagellum motor. He describes this tiny motor as being built from the inside out. There is a counting of the number of components needed for the ring structure, and then the feedback says there is enough of that component. It is then time to add the rod, then a ring, and after that a u-joint, which must be a certain size and become bent to a certain angle. The "machines" that regulate the building of the motor must themselves be assembled by yet other machines within the cell, which also exhibit irreducible complexity.[14] Remember, all of these machines with their multiple "parts" are microscopic, and they occur in trillions of cells that form a living human body.

Intelligent design

Because of these scientifically based phenomena, many scientists are acknowledging the "genius" of an intelligent designer, who people of faith acknowledge as our loving Creator. As Dr. Stephen Meyer explains: "If we observe design, it is not wrong to infer a Designer. If we observe life, it is not wrong to infer a Life-giver. If we see DNA, it is not wrong to infer the precision of a Genius."[15]

As a young medical student, I came to feel the intellectual tension between polar opposites tugging me more in the direction of creation and away from popular theories of evolution. My honest conclusions from personal observation caused me to embrace the reality that codiscoverer of the DNA molecule, Francis Crick, declared: "The origin of life appears . . . to be almost a miracle, so many are the conditions that would have to be satisfied to get it going."[16]

Some argue that "common sense" should be allowed as we consider how our lives and this universe got here. For example, archaeologists will say that a clay pot is solid evidence that a civilization once lived there. No one believes that the ground, or wind, or chemicals randomly assembled to form that clay pot and accidentally painted a design on it. People made it. If a simple clay pot shows human design, what do we conclude about an object whose makeup is far more complex? Like the human eye, which can distinguish among seven million colors.

Are we to believe that though a clay pot did not arise from natural means, the human eye just came about from elements in the atmosphere? Some would say that science demands such a conclusion, because to believe in God is not scientific. How is that different from finding the clay pot and starting with the assumption that people didn't exist in that location, so scientists must now find out how the clay pot developed from the elements in the ground or air.[17] Logic tells us that behind a designed object there must be a designer.

The argument for intelligent design is based on what we do know of the known world. For example, *intelligent agents* are required before *information-rich* systems can be produced. We know that there is no *natural* cause that produces information—not natural selection, self-organizational processes, not pure chance, which Darwin suggested. Yet, we know a cause that is capable of producing information—that is *intelligence*. Meyer explains that during the nineteenth century, scientists dealt with two entities: *matter* and *energy*. But in the twenty-first century, we have to deal with a third entity: *information*. And information presumes intelligence.[18]

According to Meyer, when we find an information-rich system in the cell, in the DNA molecule specifically, we can infer that intelligence played a role in the establishing of that system, even if we weren't there to observe its coming into existence. When we observe an outboard motor and see how the parts interact, we know that someone with intelligence made that motor; it is the same for molecular biological machines of microscopic size that form the basis of cellular life. Many scientists have concluded that the vast information stored in the DNA molecule is the result of a *mind*, which can only be explained by a theory of beginnings that involves *intelligent design*. They conclude that a healthy science is science that seeks the truth and lets the evidence speak for itself. And these scientists believe the great promise of *intelligent design* to be a new "tool of explanation" that belongs in the tool kit of science.[19]

Scientists acknowledge that, though there are profound religious implications to such a theory, they must be accepted according to the facts science is empirically observing in creation. The incredible pattern of interrelated organisms of irreducible complexity is strong evidence for believing that such incredible design reveals the presence of a divine Designer.

If life truly is a gift of God and an expression of His grace and divine favor, then getting to know God must be the ultimate expression of human life. David Jeremiah describes grace as "the bridge over a chasm that seemed infinite—the canyon between our depravity and His holiness. That bridge is wide and sturdy and sure, beckoning us to cross over into a life too wonderful for us to imagine."[20]

Philosophical debate: the divine Designer

Dr. Armand Nicholi, a Harvard professor, has taught a course for twenty-five years that compares the philosophical arguments of two of the most brilliant men of the twentieth century; Sigmund Freud and C. S. Lewis. Though the two men never met, Dr. Nicholi presents the writings and letters of Lewis and Freud side by side, allowing them to "speak" for themselves on the profound topics of God, life, and love.[21]

Sigmund Freud, a devout atheist, and C. S. Lewis, an atheist-turned-believer, express polarizing views of the most fundamental issues of mankind, which determine meaning in life. For example, on the question of the existence of God, Freud asserts that we all possess intense, deep-seated "wishes" that form the basis for our concept of and belief in God. In our helplessness, we seek protection; in our loneliness, we seek companionship and comfort. Therefore, we "create" God in our image to meet our needs; He exists only in our minds as a fantasy of our wish fulfillment. Because we looked to our earthly father for protection in our childhood, most people exalt that idea and create a fantasy image of a divine Father to be our God. Freud advises us to grow up and give up the "fairy tales of religion."[22]

C. S. Lewis countered Freud's "wish fulfillment" argument with the assertion that the biblical worldview involves a great deal of despair and pain, which is certainly not to be *wished* for. To embrace the biblical worldview, one must first come to the realization that he is in deep trouble because he has transgressed the moral law and desperately needs forgiveness and reconciliation. The Christian worldview, according to Lewis, only begins to make sense "after you have realized that there is a real Moral Law, and a Power behind the law, and that you have broken that law and put yourself wrong with the Power." Lewis concluded that finding God "does not begin in comfort; it begins in dismay."[23]

Secondly, Lewis refutes the "wishful thinking" argument of Freud on the basis that living in relationship with God also involves pain. Scripture teaches that we must submit our will to the will of God. Lewis notes that the process of "rendering back one's will which we have so long claimed for our own, is, in itself, extraordinarily painful. To surrender a self-will inflamed and swollen with years of usurpation is a kind of death."[24]

Finally, Lewis reasons that wishing for something does not rule out the existence of the object wished for—it may itself be evidence *for* its existence. We usually possess desires for things that exist. Lewis asserts, "Creatures are not born with desires unless satisfaction for those desires exists." He then implies we all have a deep-seated desire, or wish for, a relationship with the Creator and for an existence beyond this life, though we often mistake it for something else.[25]

Lewis reasons: "If I find in myself a desire which no experience in this world can satisfy, the most probable explanation is that I was made for another world. If none of my earthly pleasures satisfy it, that does not prove that the universe is a fraud. Probably earthly pleasures were never meant to satisfy it, but only to arouse it, to suggest the real thing. If that is so, I must take care, on the one hand, never to despise, or be unthankful for, these earthly blessings, and on the other, never to mistake them for the something else of which they are only a kind of copy, or echo, or mirage. I must keep alive in myself the desire for my true country, which I shall not find till after death...I must make it the main object of life to press on to that other country and to help others to do the same."[26] Lewis' purpose in life was expressed in those statements.

Freud recognized a similar unfulfilled desire in himself as that which Lewis defines. In a paper published in 1899, Freud described a "longing" that haunted him all of his life. This longing he associated with a desire to walk in the woods with his father, as he did as a child. He writes: "I believe now that I was never free from a longing for the beautiful woods near our home, in which...I used to run off from my father, almost before I had learnt to walk."[27]

Lewis writes: "All your life an unattainable ecstasy has hovered just beyond the grasp of your consciousness. The day is coming when you will wake to find, beyond all hope, that you have attained it, or else, that it was within your reach and you have lost it forever."[28]

Thousands of years ago, King Solomon, declared to be the wisest man who ever lived, warned: "Remember now your Creator in the days of your youth" (Eccles. 12:1). There is no other way to appreciate the gift of life you have been given. And in no other sphere can you hope to understand the divine purpose for which you have been created. The Old Testament prophet declared: "Have you not known? Have you not heard? The everlasting God, the LORD, The Creator of the ends of the earth, Neither faints nor is weary. His understanding is unsearchable" (Isa. 40:28). Seeking to know this God is a lifetime adventure that will unlock the mysteries of the wonderful gift of life you have been given.

Scripture teaches that everything that has been created had its origin in the bosom of the Triune God—Father, Son, and Holy Ghost. Grasping this spiritual reality by faith will bring you into deeper worship and love for the One who formed you. And seeking to know His purpose for your life will not only bring fulfillment to you in your journey on Earth, it will also reap great rewards for your future. According to Scripture, that future is forever—eternity spent with God, your Creator, your Father, your Savior.

As you observe creation in its beauty and appreciate the intricate details that point to a divine Designer, you can discover many secrets about your Creator-God. And as you seek to know God as your Savior through Christ, the Son of God, the Holy Ghost will do His wonderful work of grace in your life. He will open your heart and mind to the truths of the Word of God. You will be able to express with the songwriter, Maltbie D. Babcock, the wonders of God's creation:

> This is my Father's world, and to my list'ning ears,
> All nature sings, and round me rings,
> The music of the spheres.
> This is my Father's world, I rest me in the thought
> Of rocks and trees, of skies and seas
> His hand the wonders wrought.
>
> This is my Father's world, The birds their carols raise,
> The morning light, the lily white,
> Declare their Maker's praise.
> This is my Father's world, He shines in all that's fair;
> In the rustling grass I hear Him pass,
> He speaks to me ev'rywhere.[29]

Let the heavens rejoice, and let the earth be glad; Let the sea

roar, and all its fullness; Let the field be joyful, and all that is in

it. Then all the trees of the woods will rejoice before the Lord.

—Psalm 96:11–12

Tracing the Hand of the Creator

Each bit of matter in the universe is influenced by only four forces. These forces are the gravitational force, the electromagnetic force, the weak nuclear force, and the strong nuclear force. Each of these forces works with different strengths on different particles over vastly different distances. Of the four, the strong nuclear force is the most powerful, and gravity is by far the weakest. Yet if even an infinitesimal change in the strength of one of these forces with respect to another were to occur, life as we know it would not be possible.[1]

In 1692, Sir Isaac Newton wrote in a letter: "So then Gravity may put the Planets into Motion, but without the divine Power it could never put them into such a circulating motion as they have about the sun; and therefore, for this, as well as other Reasons, I am compelled to ascribe the Frame of the System to an intelligent Agent...The Cause of Gravity is what I do not pretend to know."[2]

THE PHENOMENA OF NATURE

Have you marveled as you read of the scientific discoveries that are unlocking the mysteries of DNA and the intricate functioning of a living cell? No matter what form of life you view under the microscope—plants, insects, birds, animals, creatures of all kinds—the same amazing secrets of nature can be discovered there. For example, did you know that spider silk has a higher tensile strength than nylon, and can be stretched twice as much? The sticky material is fairly acidic, and thus old webs are not readily broken down by bacteria or fungi. This insect's body fabricates, without education, the material it needs for alluring food, and somehow the spider "knows" how to spin its intricate web.[3]

And were you aware that there are about twenty thousand different species of ants, or that they live almost anywhere on the planet in large colonies or groups? There are three types of ants in each species: the queen, the sterile female workers, and males. The male ants only serve one purpose—to mate with future queen ants; they do not live very long.[4] Therefore, the only ant we could observe working above ground is the female ant. When the Bible instructs us to "Go to the ant, thou sluggard; consider *her* ways," (Prov. 6:6, KJV, author's emphasis), it is amazingly accurate.

Have you paused to observe the fascinating little hummingbird hovering motionless in the air while delicately feeding on flower nectar? Their wings beat at times at an unbelievable seventy-eight beats per second. The North American Ruby-throated and Rufous travel two thousand miles or more during migration. Astonishing as it may seem, these little birds make their migratory journeys in total solitude, not in safe flocks like some other birds.[5]

Wonder and awe

Do you have a favorite "part" of nature, or a favorite place where you love to breathe deeply and meld your psyche with the view of God's nature you are reveling in? If you live in a temperate climate that generates four seasons, which is your favorite? Spring, with the trees and bushes bursting forth with new spring greenery, the soft breezes blowing fragrances of every kind, and birds filling the air with their song? Or summer, with the warmth of its sunshine and fields producing their crops, and vacations in the mountains or on the beaches? Is it the peaceful autumn, with the sudden hushing of activity, the magnificently colored leaves, luxurious harvested fields, and crisp cool mornings? Are you a person who loves the cold winters, fresh snows, frosty mornings, and ski slopes?

Who can describe the awe that looking into a darkened sky filled with tiny sparkling lights of billions of stars can evoke from our hearts? There are those who revel in watching a powerful thunderstorm with its lightning. Others cannot take their eyes off a tiny, brilliantly colored wild flower blooming under a rocky crag where no one else will even see it. You probably have a favorite nature sight or sound that fills your heart with happiness, if only for a moment.

The phenomena of nature's beauty seem infinite in number and are exquisite in beauty to the beholder.

Our privileged planet

Of course, it would be impossible to appreciate any of the natural phenomena of nature unless the laws of nature were functioning without the slightest deviation for even a second. For example, the law of gravity controls the balance of power in the entire macroscopic universe. Gravity is, in fact, the dominant force of the universe at distances greater than the size of molecules. Although Sir Isaac Newton clarified the law of gravity several hundred years ago, it remains a mysterious force.

One possible explanation for gravity is found in the observance of theoretical gravitons. It is postulated that gravitons are tiny energy quanta that function within gravitational fields in a way similar to that of photons carrying light. But if so, how exactly do these gravitons constitute an attraction between the Earth and the moon? We don't know.[6] As Isaac Newton acknowledged: "The Cause of Gravity is what I do not pretend to know."[7]

While scientists today are still searching for the answers to "the Cause of gravity," many of them have concluded from their observations that planet Earth as we know it is a *privileged planet* within our galaxy, as well as among the planets of thousands of other galaxies they have discovered. Let's consider for a moment the role of our tiny planet—Earth—in the grand scheme of the universe.

Why are there such perfect environmental conditions for sustaining life on Earth and for the growing of food to nourish so many different species of living creatures? What is the source of the unlimited oxygen needed to sustain life? What forms the climates conducive to all kinds of living plants and animals? What sustains all the necessary environmental elements needed for mankind, the highest form of life that has been found anywhere in the vast universe, to survive? And why do we have the level of intelligence even to ask these questions? How do these mysteries of life relate to purpose? Guillermo Gonzalez, a research astrobiologist in the NASA astrobiology program, concludes, "The most habitable places in the universe also offer the best opportunity for scientific discovery. I believe this implies purpose."[8]

Purpose

Gonzalez and Jay Richards, coauthors of the book, *The Privileged Planet: The Search for Purpose in the Universe*, reveal fascinating discoveries about our planet and the universe beyond. In 1990, during the space exploration of Voyager I, it approached the outer reaches of the solar system, and then turned back to face our sun. With its wide-angle cameras, it captured unprecedented views of our home star—the sun—and six of its orbiting planets. One of them appeared as a small pale dot, engulfed by a ray of sunlight. It was the Earth as seen from nearly four million miles away. This incredible perspective of our planet creates a sense of insignificance in light of the sheer size of the vast universe.[9] Timeless questions about its meaning, purpose, and significance become more pressing when the Earth is viewed as an insignificant dot in a vast and still expanding universe of uninhabitable planets.

As early as the sixteenth century, astronomer Nicholas Copernicus, one of the founders of modern science and a deeply religious man, grappled with the Earth's purpose in the universe. He correctly determined that the Earth was not the center of the universe, which was the accepted worldview, but was one of a number of planets orbiting the sun. This apparent "demotion" of the status of the Earth, hence the status of mankind, impacted the worldview of the theological and scientific communities of that time and for future generations.

It would be appropriate to note that Copernicus would still have seen the Earth as central to God's purpose for the entire universe, since this is the planet where God sent His Son to be the

Redeemer of fallen human beings. However, evolutionists eventually invented the so-called "Copernican principle," or *principle of mediocrity*, which infers that if there is nothing special about the astronomical, geological, physical, and chemical circumstances of Earth, then there should be nothing special or unique about its biology either, such as, *mankind*.

This reasoning obscures the purpose for Earth and mankind. The natural result of embracing the "principle of mediocrity" is to think that earthlings are insignificant in the overall scheme of the universe. This thinking made one twentieth-century scientist conclude, "Our planet is a lonely speck in the great enveloping cosmic dark."[10] When you consider the astronomical number of star systems man is capable of viewing with telescopes, you can understand how insignificant that could make one feel.

However, this Copernican mediocrity principle (unfortunately named), which is still embraced by many twenty-first-century scientists, is losing its validity for other scientists, as a result of current studies in astronomy. As early as 1974, ironically, at a conference celebrating the five hundredth anniversary of Copernicus' birth, Cambridge physicist Brandon Carter spoke about the unusual number of "coincidences" that make the Earth actually a *unique and rare planet* in the vast universe of planets. Other scientists, on the basis of actual scientific evidence, have proposed the "Rare Earth Hypothesis." This theory argues that the virtually unique cargo of advanced animals our planet has developed probably come to flourish on a *unique* planet, the likes of which is to be found nowhere else in the visible galaxies.[11]

Many scientists reason that unless there is something extraordinarily unusual, even miraculous, about what has happened on our planet, then what has happened here must have happened many times in the history of the universe. However, from their observation, that is not the case. Since 1995, astrobiologists have been exploring planets beyond our solar system (over one hundred have been identified) for signs of complex life, past or present. Few scientists believe there are conditions on these planets that can sustain *even the simplest form of life.*

Gonzalez and Richards explain that there are many factors necessary to have conditions for a habitable planet like Earth. (See photo on page 220.) The main prerequisite for life is liquid water. The searches being done for life on other planets are based first of all on the presence of water. Another vital factor is the distance of the planet from its main star. If Earth were just 5 percent closer to its sun, it would be subject to the same fate as Venus, which has temperatures rising to one thousand degrees Fahrenheit. Conversely, if Earth were 20 percent farther from its home star, a cycle of ice and cold would destroy any possibility of life. Scientists have compiled a list of over one hundred vital elements necessary for making a planet inhabitable. Some of the items on the lists are:

- An oxygen-rich atmosphere and nitrogen, in correct and consistent amounts necessary for complex life

- A terrestrial planet of soil-rich land

- A global system of plate tectonics which are in constant motion and regulate the interior temperature and shape the continents. We live on a thin crust; if it were thicker, the plate tectonics would not function.

- A correct ratio of liquid water and continents

- A nearly circular orbit

- A moderate rate of rotation

- Protection from meteor or comet impacts provided by nearby gas giant planets

- A large moon orbiting it to stabilize the axis of the Earth, ensuring temperate season changes (see photo on page 222)

- A large magnetic field (if smaller, the planet would be barren)[12]

According to scientists, the complete list of complex factors have to meet at *one time and place* in order to make a planet as habitable as the Earth. They conclude that the probability ratio of that happening is less than one chance in a billion.[13] In other words, it is very unlikely. Yet, these scientists are still asking the question: While these facts make us *rare* in the galaxy, do they make us *significant?*

The entire universe is highly hostile to life. Yet, in the midst of that phenomenal dearth of life, the Earth exists like a giant organism, where systems interact in a way that allows all kinds of life to survive and flourish around the globe. Why did this happen? Is it chance? Coincidence? As we mentioned, the odds are extremely small for that. What if it is designed for a purpose? How can we tell?

Intelligence

Gonzalez and Richards also explore the theory of *intelligent design* as it relates to our planet. They discuss the fascinating fact that, not only does complex human life exist on our planet, but we have the *intelligence* and ability to understand our planet and the universe in which we exist in great depth of detail. This superfluous intellectual ability is not consistent with the Darwinian theory of evolution, which states that a level of intelligence is evolved solely for survival purposes. We don't have to know how the universe functions to live here and to survive. This astonishing reality has led these scientists to conclude: "There is something about the universe that cannot be simply explained by impersonal forces of nature, atoms colliding with atoms. You have to reach to something beyond the universe to account for it."[14]

Gonzalez asks the question, "Why would beings like us be able to observe and understand our universe in such detail?" Our planet is governed by laws and forces that are finely calibrated to allow for complex life as well as scientific discovery. Wipe out one of the laws, for example, gravity, and there is no life. Even increasing the gravitational force slightly would not allow for human or other complex life. A slight difference in the ratio of any of the forces of the universe would make life impossible. Yet, these principles of the universe are as simple as they are beautiful: relativity, gravitational force, electromagnetic force, and so on, can be reduced to simple mathematical equations understood by the human intellect."[15]

Most scientists accept the fact that we live in an ordered universe. Still, it is extraordinary that human beings can understand its complexity. The question arises, Why? In a sense, scientists today feel they are discovering the mind of God as they uncover the secrets of our universe and beyond. They are acquiescing more and more to the greater *probability* of intelligent design, with its implied significance for all of creation

Recognizing the Creator

We have seen that the Bible teaches that God is the Creator of the heavens and the Earth and all that is in them. From the first verse of the Bible to the last, it is clear that those "holy men of God," who "spoke as they were moved by the Holy Spirit" (2 Pet. 1:21) to write the Holy Scripture, accepted as fact the Creator. In the Book of Genesis we read the record of beginnings:

> In the beginning God created the heavens and the earth. The earth was without form, and void; and darkness was on the face of the deep. And the Spirit of God was hovering over the face of the waters.
>
> —GENESIS 1:1–2

This lovely description of the beauty of the Earth God prepared for mankind follows:

> The LORD God planted a garden eastward in Eden, and there He put the man whom He had formed. And out of the ground the LORD God made every tree grow that is pleasant to the sight and good for food.
>
> —GENESIS 2:8–9

Our loving Creator gave us everything we see around us to enjoy and provided us with exquisite senses of sight, hearing, feeling, tasting, and smelling to experience them to the full. He placed the first couple in a garden and gave them the assignment to cultivate and administrate it. They had all they needed to sustain life and to enjoy the presence of their Creator as He walked with them "in the cool of the day" (Gen. 3:8). And even after they disobeyed His command and lost fellowship with Him, creation did not lose all of its beauty and comfort. According to the psalmist, God Himself tends to His garden now:

> You visit the earth and water it, You greatly enrich it; The river of God is full of water; You provide their grain, For so You have prepared it. You water its ridges abundantly, You settle its furrows; You make it soft with showers, You bless its growth.
>
> —PSALM 65:9–10

Delighting in creation

Do you rush madly through the day, the month, the seasons of the year, scarcely noticing anything, except perhaps the inconvenience of a hot, humid summer day, pouring rain, or the bitterly cold wind of a December day? We have suggested that *gratitude* is the proper response to a God who has so abundantly blessed us with the multitudinous facets of nature. Our Creator not only made life possible, but intended it to be enjoyable as well. The psalmist expresses our desired response:

O Lord, how manifold are Your works! In wisdom You have
made them all. The earth is full of Your possessions…I will sing
to the Lord as long as I live; I will sing praise to my God while
I have my being. May my meditation be sweet to Him; I will be
glad in the Lord.

—Psalm 104:24, 33–34

If you have not expressed appreciation for the creation of God
that is all around you, why not start today? Ask the Holy Spirit
to open your eyes to its wonders, its beauties, and the refreshing
relaxation it holds for you. Begin to exercise your senses to focus
on the natural phenomena you encounter every day. Touch the
bark of a tree, or the petals of a delicate flower and allow yourself
to marvel at its feel. When you eat fresh fruit or vegetables, imagine
them growing in their natural habitat, and be thankful. Behold the
stars and planets in the night sky, and be thankful that you have
the ability to do so.

Discovering God

The apostle Paul asserts that men everywhere are without
excuse for not knowing God by observing the things He made:

For since the creation of the world His invisible attributes are
clearly seen, being understood by the things that are made, even
His eternal power and Godhead, so that they are without excuse,
because, although they knew God, they did not glorify Him as
God, nor were thankful, but became futile in their thoughts, and
their foolish hearts were darkened.

—Romans 1:20–21

Paul explains that it is possible to know God's eternal power
and His Person by acknowledging the wonder of the creation around
us, and being thankful to Him for it. According to Scripture, there
is a capacity in the human spirit to grasp the invisible attributes of
God through the visible creation that He has made. St. Francis of

Assisi wrote the words of a beloved hymn to facilitate our acknowledging of God in His creation:

> All creatures of our God and King, Lift up your voice and with
> us sing, Alleluia, Alleluia!
> Thou burning sun with golden beam, Thou silver moon with
> softer gleam, O praise Him!
> Thou rushing wind that art so strong, Ye clouds that sail in
> heav'n along, O praise Him!
> Thou rising morn, in praise rejoice; Ye lights of evening find a
> voice, O praise Him!
> Thou flowing water, pure and clear, Make music for thy Lord
> to hear. Alleluia, Alleluia!
> Thou fire so masterful and bright, That givest man both
> warmth and light, O praise Him!
> And all ye men of tender heart, Forgiving others take your
> part. O sing ye! Alleluia![16]

Of course, we can, and must, get to know God more perfectly through relationship with His Son, Jesus Christ, who came to Earth to become our Savior. Yet, we dare not ignore the wonderful opportunity He has given us to revel in the genius of the Creator— the Maker of heaven and Earth.

For You formed my inward parts; You covered me in my mother's womb. I will praise You, for I am fearfully and wonderfully made; Marvelous are Your works, And that my soul knows very well.

—Psalm 139:13–14

Tracing the Hand of the Creator

To a scientific materialist, there can be no nonmaterial intelligence that created the first life or guided its development into complex form, and no reality such as the supernatural. Dr. Michael Behe, early in his scientific career, began to question this scientific naturalist philosophy, which states that everything real has a material basis and that all teleological conceptions of nature—"we are here for a purpose"—are invalid.[1]

On a break with a colleague, Behe posed the question: "If the first life did arise by random naturalistic processes from a chemical soup, as all textbooks are saying, what exactly are the minimum systems that are required for life?" Together they ticked off a mental list of the minimum requirements: a functioning membrane, a system to build the DNA units, a system to control the copying of DNA, and a system for energy processing. Suddenly, they broke off their speculation, looked at each other, and smiled, jointly muttering, "Naaah—too many systems; it couldn't have happened by chance."[2]

THE DANCE OF DNA

After considering the vastness of the universe, the splendor of the galaxies, the marvels of the oceans and seas, and the majesty of the mountains, surely we must honestly admit to a kind of awe and wonder that their very existence demands. And while observing the immense variety and astounding instincts of the animal kingdom, as well as the startling beauty of the plant kingdoms of the world, our finite minds may simply be overwhelmed by the complexity of created life as we know it. Yet, nothing that is observable in the sphere of scientific knowledge can compare to the genius of creation—mankind.

I like to think of the unfathomable, artistic design and function of your DNA as a joyful "dance," filled with the Creator's divine gift of life, which is unique for every individual. As we consider this "dance" of the DNA, we will concentrate our full gaze upon the wondrous beauty of God's jewels of creation—you and me. The still unfathomable DNA, responsible for every one of more than sixty trillion cells in your body, is designed by the Creator to give every person born a unique identity.

I believe that an intense encounter with your divine *dance of life* will make it impossible for you to live in "your" self-centered world any longer, feeling like you are responsible for life as you know it. As you gain knowledge of the exquisite creation you are, you will learn to appreciate the "dance of life" you have been given.

While it is true that you must take responsibility for the gift of life, it is equally true that you are not the *source* of that life. Learning to know the Source of life, as well as His redeeming power, will awaken you to the purpose of all of life. Only in that perception can you begin to fulfill your divine destiny, which is the longing of every human being.

The Creator's art

Just to think that life is not our idea—that it springs from the heart of the One who designed it—should raise the question in our minds, "For what purpose have I been given the awesome gift of life?" I believe such a question arises from the seed of divine destiny that rests within every human heart. Whether or not destiny is identified and fulfilled in your life depends, in part, on understanding the awesome gift of life you have been given.

Before considering the fascinating DNA molecule, let's discuss in more detail the wonder of your conception. Science understands that each of the estimated sixty trillion cells that comprise your body is derived from the human zygote formed at conception. Jerome Lejeune, the internationally prominent, prize-winning geneticist has testified: "Each of us has a unique beginning—the moment of conception...As soon as the twenty-three chromosomes carried by the sperm encounter the twenty-three chromosomes carried by the ovum, the whole information necessary and sufficient to spell out all the characteristics of the new being is gathered...When this information carried by the sperm and by the ovum has encountered each other, then a new human being is defined which has never occurred before and will never occur again...a very specialized individual, i.e., someone who will build himself according to his own rule.[3]

Some scientists, who want to defend the pro-choice position, declare that this single-cell embryonic human zygote, consisting of forty-six chromosomes (twenty-three from the mother and twenty-three from the father), does not contain all of the "molecular information" needed to be a self-directing, human individual, and therefore it is not a human person.[4] Other scientists refute this idea as faulty biology, stating that "molecular information" is not the same as genetic (chromosomal) information. And, they argue, the "molecular information" itself is coded in the original single-cell human zygote at conception.

The genetic information in the original human zygote determines what "molecular information" will be formed, which in turn determines what proteins and enzymes will be formed, which determines what tissues and organs will be formed. In genetics, this is called the "cascading" effect. That is, the information in the original single-cell embryonic human zygote "cascades" throughout embryological development—each previous direction causing the specific formation of each succeeding direction. Those are simply the correct biological facts.[5]

In simple terms, you existed as the person you are today in the human zygote formed at conception by your mother and father. Within this tiny first cell, measuring mere microns, is the blueprint for building an entire human body with a complexity that is incomprehensible. This first cell of a human being, a single fertilized ovum, is smaller than the period at the end of this sentence. Yet, with apparent ease, it directs the proliferation and differentiation of tens of trillions of cells, as various from each other as the retina is from the toenail. The secret of this differentiation—which will eventually result in over two hundred different kinds of tissue and organ cells—is mysteriously locked up in the DNA.[6] The splendor of this wondrous jewel of creation is not through dazzling our eyes. Here are a few glimpses into the secrets of your DNA.

Unfathomable complexity

The zygote, a single combined mega-chromosome formed at conception, is also referred to as the *human genome*. The centerpiece of each cell is its nucleus. And the primary function of the nucleus is to provide a repository for *deoxyribonucleic acid*—DNA. Now, you begin to observe the microscopic "dance of DNA." Within this tiny human genome, you can envision the DNA as a very, very long twisted strand consisting of two thin pieces of filament. They are wound tightly together in what is called a double helix. (See diagram on page 218.) It was the discovery of this molecular model of twisted-ladder DNA in 1953 that later won Francis Crick and James Watson the Nobel Prize.[7] Since that time, scientists have studied DNA relentlessly, trying to unlock its secrets to all of life.

DNA is the chemical molecule that encodes all necessary instructions for the construction and replication of all living things. The DNA molecule is an exquisite filigree of the Creator's art. It has a spiral-shaped, sugar-phosphate "backbone," and nitrogen bases—only four of them. Yet the sequence of these four bases can be altered in an infinite number of ways, which creates the diversity between you and your sister or brother. Strings of these base combinations are called genes.

Less than 1 percent of genes are unique to you, providing your own special physical attributes and probably many elements of your personality. And there is a complete copy of all that information, locked in your DNA strands in every one of the sixty trillion cells in your body. We have mentioned that if the DNA sequence of the human genome were compiled into thousand-page books, it would require two hundred volumes to hold all the information.[8] From what scientists understand of the DNA, we can conclude the following:

- If you were to take all the DNA out of a single cell and stretch it out, it would be over five feet long.

- If you were to take this single-cell DNA and compress it down, it would be tinier than a speck of invisible dust.

- If you took all the DNA from all the cells in the body and squeezed it together, it would fit inside an ice cube.

- If you were to take this same DNA from all the cells and stretch it out end to end, it would reach ten billion miles (at minimum; the maximum estimated range is one hundred seventy billion miles).[9]

Scientists have discovered the patterns of over thirty thousand complex proteins within living human cells, all of which are formed by the same twenty amino acids into precise shapes depending on their function. They have also determined that the necessary assembly instructions for each protein are found in the separate DNA chains within the cell. No entity in the known universe stores and processes more information as efficiently as the DNA molecule.

This molecular information in the cells has to be copied from the DNA and then "manufactured" to form the proteins necessary for our bodies and minds to function normally. Scottish biologist Sir J. Arthur Thomson exclaims: "The body is a self-building machine; a self-stoking, self-regulating, self-repairing machine—the most marvelous and unique automatic mechanism in the universe."[10]

The DNA replication occurs with remarkable accuracy, making only one error in a billion copy steps. The DNA has its own "spell-checker" of sorts, an enzyme that examines the newly copied DNA for errors. When an error is found, that segment is replaced. If the error is not found and corrected, the resulting flawed DNA then carries a "mutation." This is thought to be the mechanism (at least in part) behind many birth defects, cancer, and aging. However, while nearly 100 percent of us carry genetic defects of some type, only about 10 percent of us has or will develop an inherited genetic disorder. That is due to the incomprehensible accuracy and efficiency of the DNA's functions.[11]

These multitudes of microscopic cellular functions are happening continually *in every cell of your body*. Many of us simply take for granted the fact that we can see, hear, taste, think, and move about as the wonderful creation God made us to be—a human being. Yet it is the knowledge of these *irreducibly complex* cellular functions making all that possible that has led many scientists to conclude that the origin of life is not possible except for the existence of a Designer.

The cell and its DNA, nature's unbounded variation and variety, the eye, the pancreas, consciousness and imagination, and *spirit*—the mechanism of random emergence of traits selected by environment, cannot account for the biology, the chemistry, and the wonder of it all. Only an intelligence would have the adequate, appropriate palette and paints to generate such a masterpiece. The only explanation for both the elm and elk is in design, an intelligent design, a design shrouded in mysterious beauty and predicated on a purpose.[12]

A genetic language

The DNA *code*, as it is called, is made up of four bases that form the *rungs* of a ladder, the double helix. These bases act as the *letters* of a genetic alphabet. They combine in various sequences to form words, sentences, and paragraphs. These base sequences are all the instructions needed to guide the functioning of the cell. The DNA code is a genetic *language* that communicates information to the cell. Because the DNA molecule is exquisitely complex and extremely precise—the *letters* must be in a very exact sequence for the instructions given to the cell. If they were not they would act like a typing error that would garble the instructions to the cell. This DNA code represents "specified complexity."[13]

Scientists' discovery that life in its essence is *information* inscribed on DNA, has greatly narrowed the question of life's origin. The question has now become focused on the *source* of that information. The scientific *information theory* is applied to biology in this way:

> Information in this context [of DNA] means the precise determination, or specification, of a sequence of letters. A code represents "specified complexity." We are now able to understand what *specified* means: The fewer choices there are about fulfilling each instruction, the more highly specified a thing is…Information theory has given us tools to distinguish between the two kinds of order…The first kind of order is the kind found in a snowflake…a snowflake is specified but has a low information content. Its order arises from a single structure repeated over and over…The second kind of order, the kind found in the faces on Mount Rushmore, is both specified and high in information.[14]

There is no convincing empirical evidence that specified order with high information content, such as is found in the DNA molecule, can arise by natural processes. On the contrary, the evidence shows only that it takes intelligence to produce this kind of complex order. In our experience, only human language and human artifacts (books, machines, bridges) match the specified complexity exhibited in the DNA and the proteins it reproduces. Even the simplest forms of life, with their store of DNA, are characterized by specified complexity. Therefore life itself is *prima facie* evidence that some form of intelligence was in existence at the time of its origin.[15]

It is a scientific reality that the essence of all living things is a highly complex information system—a genetic language—DNA. This fact sheds new light on the apostle John's description of origins:

> In the beginning was the Word, and the Word was with God, and the Word was God. He was in the beginning with God. All things were made through Him, and without Him nothing was made that was made. In Him was life, and the life was the light of men.
>
> —JOHN 1:1–4

The Word of God addresses the profound question of the origin and purpose of life. We believe that our Creator-God is at work in unfolding the glorious function of our DNA and the activation of all of our messenger proteins. As we embrace God's rightful place in our lives—first acknowledging Him as Creator, then receiving Christ as Lord and Savior—we receive the anointing of the Holy Spirit on our lives—our DNA. Then the life-giving power of God's Word begins to heal and transform us, changing our thoughts and desires, motivations and goals. As followers of Christ, we discover the joy of living and the peace of His presence. And our hearts are filled with gratitude for the gift of life He has given us.

Let it dance!

Science has confirmed that the DNA given to us in the zygote has a potential for life that is far beyond what we can imagine. We simply need to learn how to live in the anointing of God and let our DNA "dance." That is, we must learn to stop hindering the marvelous design of our DNA through our selfish lifestyles.

When we live stress-filled lives and allow negative thoughts and emotions of anger, self-pity, and bitterness to consume us, we hinder the beautiful expression of our DNA. When we fail to get proper exercise and do not eat properly, we cripple the function of the marvelous DNA we have been given. Every poor lifestyle choices we make drain us of energy and creativity, weakens our physical body, challenges our immune system, and hinders the dance of our DNA. But when we acknowledge our Creator and express our gratitude for the gift of life, we begin to relate to divine purpose and live in such a way that we can enjoy all He has given to us.

Ellen Vaughn describes the sheer pleasure of living in this divine anointing of "radical gratitude:"

> Ah. The habit of giving thanks to God in all things opens our eyes to daily wonders that will waken worship...Gratitude unleashes the freedom to live content in the moment, rather than being anxious about the future or regretting the past. So one's focus is free to have not only a keener awareness of spiritual blessings, but the physical pleasures of everyday things we can taste, touch, hear, see, smell...God has designed us so that senses can serve as powerful [reminders] of His faithfulness, and thereby be triggers of gratitude.[16]

Learning to release the "dance of DNA" is described in the Bible as living an anointed life. What does such a blessed life look like? The New Testament word for *anointing* comes from the Greek word *charisma*, which means a special endowment or charism given by the Holy Spirit. *Charisma*, according to Webster's dictionary, is "an extraordinary power (as of healing) given a Christian by the Holy Spirit for the good of the church."[17] Jesus declared that He was the anointed One of God. In the synagogue one Sabbath, He read from the prophet Isaiah the prophecy which He fulfilled:

The Spirit of the LORD is upon Me, Because He has anointed Me To preach the gospel to the poor; He has sent Me to heal the brokenhearted, To proclaim liberty to the captives And recovery of sight to the blind, To set at liberty those who are oppressed; To proclaim the acceptable year of the LORD.

—LUKE 4:18–19

As you read of the life of Jesus in the Gospels, you cannot help but be moved by His tender compassion, loving and forgiving heart, as well as His hatred of all that is unrighteous. As He blessed little children, healed the sick, fed multitudes, and taught the poor, His anointing of divine love was evident. He lived in perfect unity with His Father, praying often and revealing the Father's heart and purposes in the Earth. Jesus stated plainly to His disciples that as the Father had sent Him into the world, He was sending them also (see John 20:21). He also said they would do "greater works" than He had done after He returned to His Father (John 14:12).

As we learn to abide in Christ and in the Father, He restores the beauty of expression of the gift of life that He created, filling us with His divine love and anointing to know the truth. Jesus declared: "I am the way, the truth, and the life" (John 14:6). To know truth is to know Christ. To know Christ is to be filled with gratitude for His redemption and His anointing on your heart, life, and DNA. Jesus taught clearly that we should abide in Him and let His words abide in us if we want to be fruitful in life:

Abide in Me, and I in you. As the branch cannot bear fruit of itself, unless it abides in the vine, neither can you, unless you abide in Me...If you abide in Me, and My words abide in you, you will ask what you desire, and it shall be done for you. By this My Father is glorified, that you bear much fruit; so you will be My disciples.

—JOHN 15:4, 7–8

Fruitfulness is a description of success in every aspect of our lives. It means manifesting the gifts, abilities, and divine purposes for our life that can only be known and fulfilled through abiding in Christ. It means allowing our DNA to dance the beautiful dance of life. As we read the Word of God, we learn to abide in the truth of God, which transforms our thinking, motivations, and desires. Scripture teaches us why the anointed Word of God has the power to transform our lives. The writer of the Book of Hebrews declares:

> For the word of God is living and powerful, and sharper than any two-edged sword, piercing even to the division of soul and spirit, and of joints and marrow, and is a discerner of the thoughts and intents of the heart.
>
> —Hebrews 4:12

We can enhance the God-intended function of our DNA through proper nourishment of our physical body, our mind, and our spirit. As we fill our minds with God's Word, learn to live in the divine anointing of the Holy Spirit, and embrace the joy and peace of God, we activate the divine blessing on our DNA. In that way we can let it dance, let it dance, let it dance!

The sheer joy of living life as God intended it to be lived will fill us with humble gratitude to Him. Then we will bow in adoration and worship before the great Creator who has designed us to know fulfillment in discovering our divine destiny, for which we can only praise Him.

Do you not know that your bodies are members of Christ? ... Or do you not know that your body is the temple of the Holy Spirit who is in you, whom you have from God, and you are not your own? For you were bought at a price; therefore glorify God in your body and in your spirit, which are God's.

—1 Corinthians 6:15, 19–20

Tracing the Hand of the Creator

The human body provides both microscopic and macroscopic evidence of intelligence, irreducible complexity, and design. Consider these wonderful facts concerning your DNA:

- The adult body's estimated sixty trillion cells are absorbed and replaced at a rate of a trillion a day. This is approximately equivalent to renovating a house the size of Texas by continuously tearing down and rebuilding one million rooms per second! At that rate, skin is entirely replaced every two weeks, and you have an entirely new skeleton every seven years.

- Lungs, with a surface area of half a tennis court, inhale twenty-three thousand times a day (twenty-four pounds of air), or six hundred thirty million times before your last breath.

- Your heart is a fabulous, tireless organ that will squeeze life (over sixty million gallons of blood, in total) throughout and around your body an average of almost three billion times in seventy-five years of life!

- Nothing anywhere in the universe has the complexity of arrangement of matter as the human brain, with each neuron (brain cell) talking to ten thousand others. If you are using 10 percent of your brain at this moment, it is making a thousand trillion computations a second.[1]

ANOINTED DNA

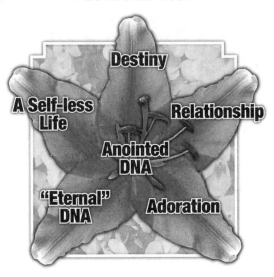

I n the introduction, I discussed four words that express the thesis of this devotional: *appreciation, adoration, anointing,* and *antiquated.* And I want to give you the knowledge you need of empirical scientific discoveries that will spark your *appreciation* of all of creation. This knowledge will help you understand why theories of evolution have become truly *antiquated* in light of the irrefutable evidence of irreducible complexity that points to intelligent design. I believe that as you raise your awareness of the marvels of creation, especially of mankind, your appreciation for the gift of life will increase profoundly.

And as you learn to properly value the gift of life you have been given, your spontaneous response should be to bow in awe before the Creator of life. In that place of humility, the Holy Ghost can work in your heart to reveal the Redeemer. Christ, the Son of God came to Earth to live, die, and be raised from the dead as a sacrifice for the sin that separates every person from their Creator-Redeemer (see Day 12). Becoming reconciled to your Redeemer will result in your *adoration* of Him and in His placing a divine *anointing* on your life. With that anointing comes revelation of your divine purpose—the reason for which you were born. It is in fulfilling destiny that you experience the greatest expression of your unique DNA.

Of course, there is a certain mystery surrounding the gift of life. We do not know precisely the way the soul is related to the body. We understand that the soul-spirit is the spiritual dimension of the person and the body is the physical dimension of the person. DNA is the template for the body, which is joined to the soul-spirit in God's own way. The brain is a physical organ of the body and the mind is the intellectual expression of the soul. All are related integrally in God's design. We ask for the anointing of our DNA so that the beautiful, intricate unfolding and dance of this comprehensive divine design is fulfilled in our lives.

Relationship

It was the "Creator's plan" that our lives be the most beautiful expression of created life known to mankind. Our loving God created mankind to live in harmonious relationship with Him, which would be accompanied by His anointing on our unique expression of the dance of life. There is no instructor that can teach us this spiritual dance like the Word of God can. When we seek forgiveness of sin, and accept salvation through Christ, our life is anointed by the Holy Spirit. Then we begin to express the beauty of our spiritual life through worship, prayer, and spontaneous rejoicing. We drop off the stoic, religious "person" in our life that does not respond sincerely to the living God. And we become filled with spontaneous praise for His divine gift of life. As a result, our lives are characterized by intimate love, joy, peace, patience, kindness— all of the attributes of a loving Creator-God.

Ellen Vaughn writes: "God has designed us so that senses can serve as powerful Ebenezers of His faithfulness, and thereby be triggers of gratitude...Ah. The habit of giving thanks to God in all things opens our eyes to daily wonders that will waken worship. Gratitude is like a pair of glasses that get progressively sharper: the more I thank, the more I see to be thankful for, and the more I end up praising God...All good gifts come from God. Not to enjoy them is to be ungrateful."[2]

It is in this spiritual expression of gratitude that we know purity of thought, action, and motivation, which become a beautiful expression of life. Life becomes a response of appreciation for everything God is, His creation, and His redemption of our lives, past, present, and future. This spiritual dance of life leads us into more intimate relationship with God through every season of our lives. As we progress to deeper and inexpressible adoration, we respond in complete surrender to the redemption of Christ, and are reconciled to the will of our heavenly Father. Our dance of gratitude gives dignity to the human body, declaring that we are made according to a divine plan by a great God who wants to love us and only cares that we love Him in return.

This response to God affects our relationships to others as well. We begin to really care for people, even those who cause us trouble—we simply love them. As we allow our grateful hearts to overcome all other obstacles, ours will become a godly love, which cares more for others than for ourselves. We become aware that our dance of life is not haphazard; it is ordered by God. As we meditate on the Word of God, we feel the presence of His Spirit within us orchestrating our spiritual dance. It may not often be a public expression of worship; it is most evident in a simple lifestyle that is surrendered to God.

Those who have sought God and found His precious anointing of their heart, life, and DNA, guard themselves for their Beloved, Christ alone. As they surrender their lives to the Creator, He pours

His love through them to others. Their life is kept, not for religion, but for relationship—intimate relationship with the Redeemer, Jesus Christ. And His life radiates through their smiles, words, attitudes, and actions.

A selfless life

The apostle Paul fulfilled his destiny in living a selfless life, wholly given to the divine purposes of God in His relationship with Christ. He declared:

> I have been crucified with Christ; it is no longer I who live, but Christ lives in me; and the life which I now live in the flesh I live by faith in the Son of God, who loved me and gave Himself for me.
>
> —GALATIANS 2:20

The apostle Paul acknowledged the pain of his personal crucifixion with Christ and of surrendering his will and all he possessed to the lordship of Christ. While death to our selfish desires causes pain, it also liberates us. Choosing to live a selfless life gives us a capacity to experience the love of God and His love for others. There are flowers that will close up their petals tightly when anything comes to "cause pain" and threaten their beautiful bloom. However, the selfless life does not reject even the pain of denying ourselves and taking up our cross, as Jesus taught us to do (see Mark 8:34). The anointed life does not have "petals" that close up in the face of difficulties and pain. We dare not become angry with God, rejecting Him when pain comes into our lives and despising His ways.

There are many ways to reject God, such as forsaking prayer and worship and neglecting to rejoice in the greatness of our God. When we lack purity, holiness, and a true appreciation of God we are also rejecting Him. Even a lack of appreciation and respect for ourselves and for others, causes us to reject the love of God for us. These grave errors always oppose our spiritual life and hinder God's anointing from defining destiny in our lives.

In order to be recipients of His divine love, we must seek to know Him and call upon Him to anoint our lives by His Spirit. We live in the fact of our salvation, which is a fact of faith, based conclusively on the premise, "We love Him because He first loved us" (1 John 4:19). As we yield our lives to the business of loving God and doing our work in a godly way, we live in constant anticipation of His presence in our life. It is that divine presence that we will enjoy throughout eternity.

"Eternal DNA"

While we cannot know for certain how the eternal expression of our life in heaven will look, it is fascinating to consider our eternal response to God. In the same way that we are products of the DNA of our ancestors, all the way back to the first man formed by God out of the dust of the Earth, we are also made in the likeness of God, who is Spirit. Through our redemption in Christ, God Himself comes to dwell within our spirit, reconciling us to His love (see Day 12).

Because scientists have discovered such elaborate, divine orchestration of human life, beyond our imagination or understanding, it seems reasonable that some of the fundamental life secrets locked into our natural DNA would have their spiritual counterpart in our eternal "body." Admittedly, this is speculation. But we can point to the reality of our hope for the eternal body we will one day possess, as we consider the words of the apostle Paul:

> But someone will say, "How are the dead raised up? And with what body do they come?" Foolish one, what you sow is not made alive unless it dies. And what you sow, you do not sow that body that shall be, but mere grain—perhaps wheat or some other grain. But God gives it a body as He pleases, and to each seed its own body...There are also celestial bodies and terrestrial

bodies; but the glory of the celestial is one, and the glory of the terrestrial is another...So also is the resurrection of the dead. The body is sown in corruption, it is raised in incorruption...It is sown a natural body, it is raised a spiritual body...And as we have borne the image of the man of dust, we shall also bear the image of the heavenly Man [Christ Jesus].

—1 CORINTHIANS 15:35–38, 40, 42, 44, 49

However it occurs, we know that our "eternal DNA" will be beautiful. All God does is exquisite beyond our simple imagination, to such extraordinary heights that we are humbled by His majesty, beauty, wisdom, knowledge, and understanding. To think that this great God desires eternal relationship with each of us, calling us to be believers—walking in divine destiny—is unimaginable to our natural minds. The flower of our "eternal DNA" is a future reality we can only thank God for creating, though we cannot imagine how it will be expressed throughout eternity.

Meanwhile, for our earthly life we have inherited from one human zygote, our own personal DNA, which contains unimaginable potential for development of our human body, in every aspect of life. While we cannot create a single cell, much less make ourselves a living person, we can seek to fulfill the divine design of our DNA by seeking to be filled with exceeding gratitude for the gift of life we have been given. And we can enjoy the satisfying fulfillment of purpose and destiny as we seek God to anoint our lives and our DNA, in the beautiful, intricate unfolding of all that God has designed for our DNA to express. Scripture teaches this marvelous potential for living a godly life:

Grace and peace be multiplied to you in the knowledge of God and of Jesus our Lord, as His divine power has given to us all things that pertain to life and godliness, through the knowledge of Him who called us by glory and virtue, by which have been given to us exceedingly great and precious promises, that through these you may be partakers of the divine nature.

—2 PETER 1:2–4

Redemptive characteristics such as being "partakers of the divine nature," show the unfathomable results of enhancing the life, design, and function of your DNA. These promises actively at work in your life enable you to enjoy an intimate relationship with your Creator. You will be filled with grace, favor, and peace when your unique individuality is conformed to the image of Christ (see Rom. 8:29). In that anointed way of life, the beautiful character of Christ will flow His love, grace, peace, and joy through you to others. As you determine to fulfill your divine destiny, I encourage you to "let it dance!"

Adoration

God is love, and the more you seek His anointing and influence of the Holy Spirit, the greater becomes your spiritual response of love. Because God is love (see 1 John 4:7), and you are made in the image of God (see Genesis 1:26), God's love is the only true source of satisfaction for your heart. Your highest response to the Creator's eternal plan for your life is to bow before Him in humble *adoration* for creating in you a capacity to live in relationship with Him. Webster's Dictionary defines the verb, *adore*, "to worship or honor as a deity or as divine; to regard with reverent admiration and devotion."[3]

Ellen Vaughn suggests that we must be aware of the "difference between sensuality, which connotes self-indulgent preoccupation with fleshly appetites, and the sanctified enjoyment of sensory pleasures within God's good laws... When we are occupied with the Giver, then we can hold His gifts with open hands, relishing them, but being at peace if they are taken away."[4] When we bow in adoration to our Creator and Savior, we are totally occupied with the Giver of life.

Do you readily identify with intense affection inherent in adoration? Reverent admiration? Devotion? Gifts pale in comparison to the treasure of the Person worthy of our adoration. What the Giver does is insignificant in light of who He is. To be with Him is the ultimate pleasure and satisfaction. To please Him is your delight and deep desire.

If you have experienced the rescue of your soul by Christ, your divine Redeemer, there will be a natural (or supernatural) response to your new "owner"—inexpressible gratitude, devotion, and expressed adoration. Not content to just receive the gifts Christ gives to us, we simply want to be with Him, to enjoy the nearness of His presence. That is the essence of adoration. In order to experience the spiritual purpose for which our body and DNA are joined to our soul, we must acknowledge our Creator as the Giver of life as well as the Redeemer of our souls. This is the spiritual expression of our DNA. Without Him there is no dance of life, no hope, no joy, no fulfillment—only a dirge of grief, pain, loneliness, and ultimate death.

We decide whether or not we will adore our Maker. The weight of that choice is amazing to me. That choice—to adore the Creator-Redeemer—is the most important issue of life. Other choices are important, but this is the basic issue that will determine the expression of our DNA and our destiny. It is not enough to give intellectual assent in acknowledging a Creator. Only in cultivating an adoring relationship with our Redeemer can we experience the ultimate satisfaction He ordained for our life—for eternity.

And whatever you do in word or deed, do all in the name of the

Lord Jesus, giving thanks to God the Father through Him.

—COLOSSIANS 3:17

Tracing the Hand of the Creator

All life on Earth, whether bacteria, bee, bear, or boy, is DNA based. Molecular biophysicist Harold Morowitz calculated that if one were to take the simplest living cell and break every chemical bond within it, the odds that the cell would reassemble under ideal natural conditions would be $10^{100,000,000,000}$.[1]

The tiny first cell of a human being, a single fertilized ovum, is smaller than the period at the end of this sentence. Yet, with apparent ease, it directs the proliferation and differentiation of tens of trillions of cells, as various from each other as the retina is from the toenail. The secret of this differentiation—which will eventually result in over two hundred different kinds of tissue and organ cells—is mysteriously locked up in the DNA.[2]

GOD THE FATHER

Perhaps one of the most awesome experiences for a man or woman is to hold their firstborn infant, the fruit of their union, in their arms. Scientists have been fascinated with the study of human genetics for many decades. The wonder of a female ovum uniting with a male sperm to create a human life is an awesome reality, indeed.

The wonder of fatherhood

As we have discussed, there are twenty-three pairs of chromosomes in the first human cell—one half contributed from the maternal egg and one-half contributed from the paternal sperm. If you connect all these twenty-three pairs together (at least figuratively) you will have the total genetic structure of the human body. The purpose of the chromosomes and DNA is to carry the genes—the genetic inheritance from mother and father that will form a unique individual. And the purpose of the genes is to make proteins. And the purpose of the proteins is to... well, to do everything. These proteins are made from twenty different amino acids.[3]

The DNA is responsible for duplicating thousands of different proteins flawlessly in order to create and maintain the life of each particular tissue and organ, which will form a human being. It functions well with these phenomenal demands, working as a super computer, copy machine, and Encyclopedia Britannica combined. The DNA even has its own spell-checker of sorts, an enzyme that examines the newly copied DNA for errors. Should this enzyme not function properly, the resulting flawed DNA would carry a "mutation," which is thought to be the mechanism (at least in part) behind many birth defects, cancer, and aging.[4]

As phenomenal as the DNA task is, it is even more remarkable that only 10 percent of the DNA is involved in coding the proteins, and scientists are not yet sure what role the other 90 percent plays. Such evidence of design simply cannot be reduced to notions of origins of life, from chaos to such exquisite order, through time and chance. Richard Swenson explains in satirical terms the "logic" behind the evolutionists' theory of origins:

> Evolutionists trust—as a matter of fact, they totally rely on—the process of mutation for the development and advancement of all species. The *theory of first things* goes like this: first you start with nothing, which then becomes something. The something then becomes a prebiotic soup with hydrogen, carbon, nitrogen, and water vapor (free oxygen arrives later). The soup bubbles into compounds like methane and ammonia. Lightning strikes periodically, stirring the pot. This frightens various molecules into each other's arms. Eventually, after this happens enough, you get an amino acid. Then several. These get frightened into each other's arms (they don't like lightning either), and you get a protein. Then larger and larger proteins. Then more and more

of them. And pretty soon (well, actually, not so soon) you have an organism with a hundred thousand proteins made by a DNA that has three billion base pairs—all because of random beneficent mutations. When the pot stops bubbling and the smoke clears, out of the cave steps Arnold Schwarzenegger: tens of trillions of cells with a hundred billion neurons, sixty thousand miles of blood vessels, and a retina that in a fraction of a second solves nonlinear differential equations that would take a Cray-2 supercomputer a hundred years to solve.[5]

To the evolutionist the above "reasoning" seems logical, insightful, and astute. But for honest scientists who submit to the established laws of science, which include *information theories* (where there is information there must be an intelligent source), and *design theories* (presence of complex design infers a designer), the evolutionists' theory of the origin of life is, simply put, *antiquated*.

Many evolutionists still refer to the Stanley Miller experiment performed in 1953, in which he shot electricity through an atmosphere like the one on the primitive Earth, creating amino acids, the basic building blocks of life. The clear implication of his experiment was that life could be created naturalistically, without the intervention of a Creator. Obviously, the significance of Miller's experiment—which to this day is still featured in many biology textbooks—hinges on whether he used an atmosphere that *accurately simulated* the environment of the early Earth.[6]

While no one knows for sure, the present-day consensus among scientists is that the atmosphere was not at all like the one Miller used. He chose a hydrogen-rich mixture of methane, ammonia, and water vapor as the elements of the primitive atmosphere, before life existed. Many scientists have abandoned Miller's hypothesis of the early Earth's atmosphere. Two of the leading origin of life researchers, Klaus Dose and Sidney Fox, confirmed that Miller used the wrong gas mixture.[7] The best hypothesis now is that there was very little hydrogen in the primitive atmosphere because it would have escaped into space. The atmosphere probably consisted of carbon dioxide, nitrogen, and water vapor.

So what happens if you produce Miller's experiment with an accurate atmosphere? According to scientists, you don't get amino acids. While some concur that you could link together "organic" molecules, they would not be the life-giving kind. Rather, they would be cyanide and formaldehyde—embalming fluid! Just the fumes from these chemicals are so toxic that they fry proteins and kill embryos. To suggest that formaldehyde and cyanide give you the right substrate for the origin of life is laughable.[8]

Lee Strobel, former atheist journalist, set out on a quest for scientific proof of Darwinian evolution, interviewing leading scientists of our day. He interviewed Jonathan Wells, holder of two Ph.D.'s, one in molecular and cell biology from Berkeley. He later worked as a post-doctorate research biologist there. Strobel asked the question, "If a scientist actually manages to produce amino acids from a realistic atmosphere of the early earth...how far would that be from creating a living cell?" Dr. Wells responded, "Oh, *very* far, *incredibly* far... You would have to get the right number of the right kinds of amino acids to link up to create a protein molecule—and that would still be a long way from a living cell. Then you'd need dozens of protein molecules, again in the right sequence, to create a living cell. The odds against this are astonishing. The gap between nonliving chemicals and even the most primitive living organism is absolutely tremendous."[9]

Dr. Wells continued, speaking authoritatively, "You can't make a living cell. There's not even any point in trying. It would be like a physicist doing an experiment to see if he can get a rock to fall upwards all the way to the moon. In other words, if you want to create life, on top of the challenge of somehow generating the cellular components out of nonliving chemicals, you would have an even bigger problem in trying to put the ingredients together in the right way. The problem of assembling the right parts in the right way at the right time and at the right place, while keeping out the wrong material, is simply insurmountable."[10]

"Our Father"

Strobel also questioned Walter Bradley, a former professor at Texas A&M University, who coauthored the landmark 1984 book, *The Mystery of Life's Origin*, about the origin of life. Bradley demonstrated that none of the various theories advanced by scientists for how the first living cell could have been naturalistically generated—including random chance, chemical affinity, self-ordering tendencies, seeding from space, deep-sea ocean vents, and using clay to encourage prebiotic chemicals to assemble—can withstand scientific scrutiny.[11]

Bradley shares the view of many scientists that the yawning gap between nonlife and life means that there may very well be no potential of ever finding a theory for how life could have arisen spontaneously. That's why he's convinced that the "absolutely overwhelming evidence" points toward an intelligence behind life's creation. Bradley went further, "I think people who believe that life emerged naturalistically need to have a great deal more faith than people who reasonably infer that there's an Intelligent Designer."[12]

The real question becomes, *On what purpose is this intelligent design predicated?* How can we discern the mysterious beauty of the Designer? The answer lies in the divine revelation to our spirit of the Creator Himself—our Father. Even biochemist and spiritual skeptic Francis Crick, who shared the Nobel Prize for discovering the molecular structure of DNA, cautiously invoked the word [miracle] a few years ago. "An honest man, armed with all the knowledge available to us now, could only state that in some sense, the origin of life appears at the moment to be almost a miracle, so many are the conditions which would have had to have been satisfied to get it going."[13]

What could be the purpose of this "miracle," the motive of the "Intelligent Designer" for creating such exquisitely complex life on a planet of apparent insignificance in the limitless scope of the universe? Beloved theologian and Bible teacher, Fuchsia T. Pickett explains the eternal purpose of our heavenly Father for His creation:

> Because God is love, He [wanted] someone to share His love. Because of that longing, [the Godhead] said among Themselves, "Let us make man in our image" (Gen. 1:26). God expressed His longing in His desire for a family, one into whom He could pour His very nature. His purpose in creating mankind was to have someone with whom to fellowship and share His love. He desired a family who would have His "family spirit" and would choose to respond to His love.
>
> The lonely existence of all humanity evokes the five-fold cry: *Who made me? Who is God? What is the purpose of my life? How can I fulfill my destiny? After this life, what?* Until we properly answer these questions we do not know we are people of destiny, born at the exact time God intended that we be born. When we discover answers to these questions, our search for identity is over. We know who God is and who He meant us to be.[14]

It is God's very nature to be a father. He delighted to express that divine nature in creation. Who can fathom the love of God that created mankind because He wanted to express His divine love to them—to relate to them as His children? Our gratitude for the gift of life will be inspired primarily as we experience personal relationship to the Giver of all life—God the Father.

Revealed through Christ

Jesus, the Son of God, came to Earth to reveal the Father to us. He spoke often of His Father, and prayed to Him. And Jesus taught

His disciples to begin their prayer by addressing the Father: "Our Father in heaven, Hallowed be Your name" (Matt. 6:9).

According to Scripture, no one on Earth has seen God the Father. It is true that Moses cried out to see the glory of God. God granted his desire, made a place for him to hide, then allowed His great goodness to pass by him (see Exod. 33:19). That glimpse of God transformed Moses and caused His face to shine so brightly that he had to cover it with a veil because the children of Israel could not look upon it.

Yet, the New Testament Scriptures declare plainly, "No one has seen God at any time. The only begotten Son, who is in the bosom of the Father, He has declared Him" (John 1:18). And when Philip, Jesus' disciple, asked Him to show them the Father, Jesus answered Him:

> Have I been with you so long, and yet you have not known Me, Philip? He who has seen Me has seen the Father; so how can you say, 'Show us the Father'? Do you not believe that I am in the Father, and the Father in Me?
>
> —JOHN 14:9–10

It was John who described the eternal essence of Christ so vividly for us: "And the Word became flesh and dwelt among us, and we beheld His glory, the glory as of the only begotten of the Father, full of grace and truth" (John 1:14). Jesus showed us the character of our heavenly Father, reflected in the phrase, "full of grace and truth." Yet, even Old Testament saints understood that God was a Father to them. Isaiah the prophet declared:

> Doubtless You are our Father, Though Abraham was ignorant of us, And Israel does not acknowledge us. You, O LORD, are our Father; Our Redeemer from Everlasting is Your name.
>
> —ISAIAH 63:16

Eternal love

Because the first couple, Adam and Eve, chose to disobey God and walk independently from Him, God has sacrificially sought to redeem mankind from his sin so that those who seek relationship with Him could enjoy the Father's love. John, the beloved disciple, explains:

> In this the love of God was manifested toward us, that God has sent His only begotten Son into the world, that we might live through Him. In this is love, not that we loved God, but that He loved us and sent His Son to be the propitiation for our sins... We love Him because He first loved us.
>
> —1 JOHN 4:9–10, 19

So, through Christ's sacrifice on Calvary, God restored the possibility of any man or woman to be redeemed from sin and reconciled to relationship with God as their Father. Our eternal Father offers His loving care, protection, provision, purpose, and much more to all who call Him "Father." As we are reconciled to our heavenly Father, through accepting the sacrifice of His Son for our sins, we can look forward to living and reigning with Him eternally in His wonderful kingdom.

Father's forgiveness

One of the most endearing portraits of our loving heavenly Father was painted by Jesus in His parable that we call "the prodigal son." The youngest of his father's two sons, this "prodigal," asked for his inheritance before the customary time and then left the father's house and went to a far country where he "wasted his possessions with prodigal living" (Luke 15:13). Then there arose a famine in the land and the boy had nothing to eat. This young man, once accustomed to fine living, got a job feeding pigs and was so hungry he tried eating the "pods that the swine ate" (v. 16). Then he "came to himself" and began to consider the abundance of his father's house, where even the servants had plenty to eat. Filled with remorse, he decided to return home and repent to his father, saying, "I have sinned against heaven and before you" (v. 18). He reasoned that he could ask to be made a hired servant at least, and escape hunger. Listen to the words of Jesus, as he describes the tender love of the father for his wayward son:

> And he arose and came to his father. But when he was still a great way off, his father saw him and had compassion, and ran and fell on his neck and kissed him. And the son said to him, "Father, I have sinned against heaven and in your sight, and am no longer worthy to be called your son." But the father said to his servants, "Bring out the best robe and put it on him, and put a ring on his hand and sandals on his feet. And bring the fatted calf here and kill it, and let us eat and be merry; for this my son was dead and is alive again; he was lost and is found." And they began to be merry.
>
> —Luke 15:20–24

Such forgiving love that runs toward a repentant prodigal is what we can expect from our heavenly Father when we make one step toward Him. His loving heart restores to us our position into the "family" of God that mankind lost in the Fall through our waywardness. It is an unfathomable source of gratitude to consider that God Himself loves all of humanity with such intense desire to do good for us, in spite of our failures. As you meditate on the love of God, the Father, be quick to express your love and praise to Him. He will enlarge your capacity to know Him and to sense His presence and purpose in your life. And He will forgive any wrongs you have done in life. Such love causes us to bow in adoration before our God, declaring, "Our Father in heaven, hallowed by Thy name."

Simon Peter answered and said, "You are the Christ, the Son

of the living God."

—MATTHEW 16:16

Tracing the Hand of the Creator

There are still some scientists who do not accept the validity of a divine origin of life and insist on invoking "chance" as a causal explanation for the origin of biological information. However, few serious researchers still regard life as originating through chance, according to Dr. Stephen C. Meyer, who earned his Ph.D. in the history and philosophy of science from Cambridge University:

> Since molecular biologists began to appreciate the sequence specificity of proteins and nucleic acids, many calculations have been made to determine the probability of formulating functional proteins and nucleic acids at *random*...Such calculations have invariably shown that the probability of obtaining functionally sequenced biomacromolecules at random is, in [Nobelist Ilya] Prigogine's words, "vanishingly small"...*Chance* is not an adequate explanation for the origin of biological complexity and specificity.[1]

DAY 7

JESUS CHRIST, THE SON OF GOD

For scientists who do not accept the growing evidence of a Designer who is responsible for the origin of mankind, as well as every other form of life, there are no answers to purpose for life. If our origin resulted from random organization of biological materials, time, and chance, or in accord with another naturalistic theory, there is no reason to try to understand the purpose of the Creator for His creation.

It follows, that without acknowledging the existence of a Creator, it would be impossible to conceive the wonder of mankind's eternal relationship with God. This godless worldview could never understand why God would send His Son, Jesus Christ, to Earth to save mankind from his sinful destructions. Those who embrace such a perspective of life, denying the existence of their Maker, are hopelessly hindered from true appreciation for the gift of life.

Thankfully, more and more serious-minded scientists are refuting the possibility of a godless worldview, declaring that the complexity of every form of life, even the simplest one-cell bacterium, demands the skills of "an Organizer." Gerald L. Schroeder, in his book, *The Science of God: The Convergence of Scientific and Biblical Wisdom*, states: "Randomness just doesn't cut it when it comes to generating meaningful order out of chaos. Direction is required. Always."[2]

John Horgan, in *Scientific American*, similarly concludes: "Some scientists have argued that, given enough time, even apparently miraculous events become possible—such as the spontaneous emergence of a single-cell organism from random couplings of chemicals. Sir Fred Hoyle, the British astronomer, has said such an occurrence is about as likely as the assemblage of a 747 [jet] by a tornado whirling through a junkyard. Most researchers agree with Hoyle on this point."[3]

For true science to prevail, it is required that traditional "dogma" be set aside in the face of scientific discovery based on the simple application of the logic of scientific laws. For example, scientists can calculate mathematically the unlikely probability of certain events, including the random organization of the cell, as we have mentioned. To cling to the dogma of "chance organization" and "random selection" in the face of such extreme odds is less than scientific.

Neither time nor chance can solve the naturalist's *probability* problem. Everywhere we see life—from simple to highly developed forms—we see order. And this order involves sophisticated, coded information in the form of DNA. Any serious thinker is confronted with the question: How did life encode immensely complex amounts of information on every microscopic strand of DNA? Time and chance cannot answer these questions. Randomness is a nonstarter; not a solution.[4] "Our experience with information-intensive systems indicates that such systems always come from an intelligent source—i.e., from mental or personal agents, not chance," explains Dr. Meyer.[5]

Consider a few facts concerning the "information-intensive" systems of the body, some of which are much smaller than the cell, as described by Richard A. Swenson:

> The human body contains 10^{28} atoms (1 followed by twenty-eight zeros)...According to isotope studies, 90 percent of our atoms are replaced annually. Every five years, 100 percent of our atoms turn over and become new atoms. Of course there are additional organizational units other than atoms. Each level is miraculous in its own right. From the smallest to the largest, we are constructed of:
>
> Subatomic particles > atoms > molecules > cells > tissues > organs > systems
>
> When we first discovered the subatomic particles of the proton, neutron, and electron, we thought we had identified the fundamental building blocks of all of nature...[But] since then we have identified more than two hundred subatomic particles smaller than the initial proton, neutron, and electron.[6]

Scientists often refer to the creating and recreating of the subatomic particles, atoms, molecules, and cells as the "dance of DNA," as we have discussed. "Not only are the *subatomic particles* flashing in and out of existence faster than a New York cabby changes lanes; not only are the *atoms* turning over at a rate exceeding a billion trillion per second; and not only are the *molecules* continuously rearranging themselves in a dance we might call the nanosecond shuffle...but, you guessed it, the *cells* are doing the same thing."[7]

Such complex mysteries have caused one scientist to observe:

> "We speak of the body as a machine, but it is hardly necessary to say that none of the most ingenious machines set up by modern science can for a moment compare with it," observes Scottish biolo-

gist Sir J. Arthur Thomson. "The body is a self-building machine; a self-stoking, self-regulating, self-repairing machine—the most marvelous and unique automatic mechanism in the universe."[8]

The way, the truth, and the life

In the face of a large body of scientific discovery, we are challenged to consider what we will accept as truth regarding the origin of life. That consideration will determine how we relate to Christ, the Son of God, who declared plainly: "I am the way, the truth, and the life. No one comes to the Father except through me" (John 14:6). Such a claim demands that every honest seeker of truth weigh in on its validity.

The religious leaders of His day declared Christ a blasphemer, a mere man falsely declaring Himself to be the Son of God, the Messiah. They judged Him guilty and took Him to Pontius Pilate, the Roman procurator of Judea, who asked Him, "What is truth?" (John 18:38). This same confusion reigns today in the minds of many who have not accepted Christ as the Messiah, the long-awaited Savior who would "save His people from their sins" (Matt. 1:21). Many people today openly deny Christ; others have not heard of Him; and still others are seeking truth in many other places. Yet, when Jesus walked the Earth, He went quietly about, proving His divinity in His life, His death, and His resurrection.

Full of grace and truth

One of His disciples who had observed Him closely declared: "And we beheld His glory, the glory as of the only begotten of the Father, full of grace and truth" (John 1:14). Scripture declares: "For the law was given through Moses, but grace and truth came through Jesus Christ" (John 1:17) While the devil is characterized as the Father of lies (see John 8:44), God the Son lived His life in juxtaposition to every lie. We must conclude that it is not possible to know truth without knowing the One who embodies all truth.

Again, using picture language, Jesus explained how grace and truth provide security to the believer. He said that one who does not enter the sheepfold by the door, climbing up some other way is a thief and a robber. It is the shepherd who enters by the door and the sheep hear his voice. He calls His sheep by their names and leads them out (see John chapter 10). In other words, Christ is so intimate with His own that He does not have to drive them; they follow Him, trusting the Good Shepherd when they hear Him calling their name. Christ, who engenders trust, security, and deep affection, has become the way, through relationship with His sheep.

And Jesus assured His disciples: "He who has seen Me has seen the Father" (John 14:9). Christ is the only way to the Father. Our heavenly Father is the essence of love as revealed in Christ. The beloved apostle, John, declared in his Gospel:

> No one has seen God at any time. The only begotten Son, who is
> in the bosom of the Father, He has declared Him.
>
> —John 1:18

For over three years the disciples walked with Jesus, talked with Him, received His instruction about the kingdom of God, and watched Him perform all kinds of miracles. They saw His compassion for the multitudes as He taught them, fed them, and healed them. Grace and truth were not just words to them; they had become a Person. Jesus Christ, the Messiah, had won their affection, their admiration, and their loyalty.

Redeemer

Though the disciples failed Him in His hour of agony, after Jesus' resurrection they became recipients of His wonderful redemption. And as the founders of the church for which Jesus died, tradition tells us that most of them died martyrs' deaths because of their devotion to their Lord. Some gave to us the New Testament Scriptures, and all were empowered by the Holy Spirit to preach the gospel to a completely pagan world. Years later, an aged John wrote:

> That which was from the beginning, which we have heard, which we have seen with our eyes, which we have looked upon, and our hands have handled, concerning the Word of life—the life was manifested, and we have seen, and bear witness, and declare to you that eternal life which was with the Father and was manifested to us.
>
> —1 John 1:1–2

The lives of these apostles were transformed because they had touched the Christ, who was "full of grace and truth." And our lives can undergo that same transformation, as millions can testify, who have received the wonderful grace and truth of Christ's salvation.

Jesus faithfully taught His disciples that He must suffer many things, be rejected by the religious rulers, and be killed, and that after three days He would rise again (see Mark 8:31). But His disciples could not stand the thought of His death, and on one occasion, Peter even rebuked the Christ for speaking of it (Mark 8:32), which brought him a stern rebuke from the Lord.

John the Baptist was baptizing in the river Jordan, when he looked up one day and saw Jesus coming toward him. He declared: "Behold! The Lamb of God who takes away the sin of the world!" (John 1:29). Through His death on the cross, Christ fulfilled every Old Testament "type" of the justice for mankind's sin required by a holy God. Jesus Christ became the spotless Lamb of God. A blood sacrifice was required to atone for sin. And the Book of Hebrews tells us that the blood of bulls and goats was not enough to provide a complete remedy for sin (see Heb. 9:13–14). That would require the death of the sinless Son of God.

Our humanistic culture declares: "There are many ways to God. It is not important what you believe or in whom, but only *that* you believe." To that errant philosophy Scripture responds power-fully, declaring redemption through Christ alone:

> Nor is there salvation in any other, for there is no other name under heaven given among men by which we must be saved.
>
> —Acts 4:12

The risen Messiah

Only through the death of Christ could He fulfill His divine mission as the Messiah, the anointed One, sent to redeem all of mankind from the darkness and death of sin. Yet, if He had not been raised from the dead, all of His suffering would have been in vain. The apostle Paul explains:

> If in this life only we have hope in Christ, we are of all men the most pitiable. But now Christ is risen from the dead, and has be-come the firstfruits of those who have fallen asleep. For since my man came death, by Man also came the resurrection of the dead. For as in Adam all die, even so in Christ all shall be made alive.
>
> —1 Corinthians 15:19–22

Historians declare that there is more evidence of the resurrection of our Lord, Jesus Christ, than for many other events lost in antiquity. Through the resurrection of Christ, we have hope of eternal life with God. Death, which entered through sin (death was not God's design for Adam), was overcome through Christ, so that we could be raised from death to live with Him forever. Scripture is full of comfort for believers, teaching us that we will be given a glorified body to live in heaven with God and with all the saints who have gone on before.

We conclude our brief look at the wonderful Son of God, who became our resurrected Lord, by pausing to appreciate the wonder and love revealed in the Scripture verse most often quoted:

For God so loved the world that He gave His only begotten Son, that whoever believes in Him should not perish but have everlasting life.

—JOHN 3:16

Gratitude and joy flood the heart as we ask Him to redeem us from our sin. Christ forgives, cleanses, heals, and delivers the seeking soul from the destructive power of sin and gives us eternal life.

When He, the Spirit of truth, has come, He will guide you into all truth; for He will not speak on His own authority, but whatever He hears He will speak; and He will tell you things to come.

—John 16:13

Tracing the Hand of the Creator

Darwinism claims that all living creatures are modified descendents of a common ancestor that lived long ago. According to his theory, every new species that has ever appeared can be explained by descent with modification. Neo-Darwinism claims these modifications are the result of natural selection acting on random genetic mutations.[1] And genetic studies show humans and apes share 98 or 99 percent of their genes, which appears to support the theory that humans descended from apes.

However, to accept that theory, you have to believe that the dramatic differences between us and chimpanzees are due to 2 percent of our genes, because the so-called body-building genes are in the 98 percent. And the two percent of genes that are different are really rather trivial genes that have little to do with anatomy. According to some scientists, there is no more evidence of *common ancestry* between humans and apes than there is *common design*. A designer might very well decide to use common building materials to create different organisms, just as builders use the same materials to build different bridges that end up looking very dissimilar from one another.[2]

GOD THE HOLY SPIRIT

Theologians refer to God the Holy Spirit as the third Person of the Trinity. While we must be careful not to err in separating God into three distinct Gods for our discussion of the Holy Spirit, it will be helpful to focus on His *function* as God. According to Scripture, the Spirit of God was present in creation: "In the beginning God created the heavens and the earth. The earth was without form, and void; and darkness was on the face of the deep. And the Spirit of God was hovering over the face of the waters" (Gen. 1:1–2). When God spoke, "Let there be light" (v. 3), it seems that it was the Spirit of God who "performed it." The psalmist refers to the Holy Spirit in creation as well:

> You send forth Your Spirit, they are created; And You renew the face of the earth.
>
> —Psalm 104:30

God is Spirit

Jesus declared to the woman at the well: "God is Spirit, and those who worship Him must worship in spirit and truth" (John 4:24). So, while we discuss the Holy Spirit as a part of the Trinity, and endeavor to learn how to relate to Him in a biblical way, we need to understand that God *is* Spirit. Again, we are confronted with the reality of the transcendent, divine mystery of the Trinity—a Triune Godhead.

When God decided to create mankind, He said: "Let Us make man in Our image, according to Our likeness" (Gen. 1:26). Scripture acknowledges both a plurality in the Godhead—"Let Us"—as well as consensus of purpose among them. To be created in the image of God, who is Spirit, necessarily implies that we are in essence spiritual beings. That is to say, we are more than a biological phenomenon made of chemicals. The apostle Paul referred to this reality when he prayed:

> Now may the God of peace Himself sanctify you completely; and may your whole *spirit*, *soul*, and *body* be preserved blameless at the coming of our Lord Jesus Christ.
>
> —1 THESSALONIANS 5:23, EMPHASIS ADDED

Though this spiritual side of human life has been neglected by many, and is completely rejected by naturalists and secularists, it is taught throughout Scripture as an eternal reality. Accepting this biblical truth will determine much of your worldview. The Genesis account of the origin of mankind says simply:

> And the LORD God formed man of the dust of the ground, and breathed into his nostrils the breath of life; and man became a living being.
>
> —GENESIS 2:7

In light of the awesome scientific data we are discussing regarding the complexity of our unique DNA and the cellular structure of our bodies, the simplicity of this description of mankind's creation is striking. God formed man from the dust of the ground and breathed His breath of life into him. Scientists now know that our bodies are indeed composed of the same elements that form the dust of the Earth. Yet, the structure of every microscopic cell of the human body is incredible in its form and function. Consider these scientific facts about the human body:

- Every one of the estimated sixty trillion cells that make up a human body, unimaginably complex, must live in community with their surrounding neighbors, flawlessly doing their own specialized part in the whole.

- Each cell is surrounded by a membrane thinner than a spider's web that must function precisely, or the cell will die.

- Each cell generates its own electric field, which at times is larger than the electric field near a high-voltage power line.

- Each cell contains specialized energy factories called biofires that use adenosine triphosphate (ATP). Every cell contains hundreds of these miniature ATP motors embedded in the surfaces of the mitochondria. Each motor is two hundred thousand times smaller than a pinhead.

- Cells don't stockpile ATP energy, but instead make it as needed from food consumed. Active people can produce their body weight in ATP every day.

- Each cell has its own internal clock, switching on and off in cycles from two to twenty-six hours, never varying.[3]

After God formed man, He breathed life into his nostrils. As we mentioned, Scripture declares that God is a Spirit (see John 4:24). The Hebrew word translated *spirit* in Genesis chapter one is *ruwach*, which is also translated "wind" or "breath." Another Hebrew word, *neshamah* is used to describe God breathing His breath into the first man's body, who "became a living being" (Gen. 2:7). *Neshamah* can be translated as "wind, vital breath, divine inspiration, and intellect." From this biblical account of the creation of mankind, which shows mankind receiving the breath of life from the Spirit of God, we can conclude that the essence of mankind's life is *spiritual*.

As an ophthalmologist, I see a lot of people who are near-sighted, which means they only see the things that are up close. All of us can be considered nearsighted spiritually when we fail to see the overall view of God's purpose for creating mankind. We focus too often on our personal plans and desires, failing even to consider the concerns of those around us whom we love. And we are not aware many times of God's desire for us.

The apostle James describes the brevity of our lives: "Why, you do not even know what will happen tomorrow. What is your life? You are a mist that appears for a little while and then vanishes" (James 4:14, NIV). In the grand scheme of things, our lives seem insignificant. Only as we focus on God with the help of the Holy Spirit can we begin to appreciate the eternal realities of life. When we believe in His promises, our focus is no longer shortsighted and placed on the things of this world. We see the distant view—the eternity, the greatness of all reality. That is when we begin to comprehend who God really is.

A divine "Person"

Perhaps the most misunderstood "Person" of the Godhead is the Holy Spirit. Maybe because we have difficulty relating to "spirit," and can more easily identify with the natural relationships of a Father and Son. Many tend to regard the Holy Spirit as an influence, a force, or other intangible being. However, the Holy Spirit is revealed in Scripture as a divine Personality.

Perhaps considering other names given to the Holy Spirit in Scripture will help us to understand Him better. In the Gospel of John, He is called the *Comforter*, which can also be translated Counselor, Helper, Advocate, Intercessor, Strengthener, and Standby (see John 16:7, AMP.) Jesus declared the Holy Spirit to be the "Spirit of truth" (John 14:17) and the Helper who teaches (see John 14:26, NAS). The New Testament epistles confirm these wonderful facets of the work of the Holy Spirit in the lives of believers.

Fuchsia T. Pickett, in her book, *Presenting the Holy Spirit*, describes the divine Personhood of the Holy Spirit:

> Being a person involves the power of intellect or the mind; the power of volition, or the will; and the power of emotional response. Only as we learn to recognize and properly relate to these three aspects of the personality of the Holy Spirit can we intimately fellowship with Him as a divine Person. As the Third Person of the Godhead, the Holy Spirit reveals the *mind* of God as He fulfills the *will* of God for mankind. He also expresses the *emotions* of God in His loving and holy relationship to mankind.[3]

There are many Scriptures exhibiting the "personal" responses of the Holy Spirit to our attitudes and actions. The Old Testament prophet, Isaiah, declared that God's people *vexed* His Holy Spirit (Isa. 63:10, KJV). The apostle Paul warned believers not to *grieve* Him: "And do not grieve the Holy Spirit of God, by whom you were sealed for the day of redemption" (Eph. 4:30). And he admonishes them not to *quench* the working of the Holy Spirit in their midst (1 Thess. 5:19).

Perhaps one of the saddest responses of the human heart to the Holy Spirit is to *resist* Him, which is actually refusing the love of God and His desire to redeem us. In Peter's sermon on the Day of Pentecost, he rebuked the people as "stiff-necked and uncircumcised in heart and ears! You always resist the Holy Spirit" (Acts 7:51). In contrast, Scripture urges believers to believe, obey, and honor the Holy Spirit by allowing Him to fill their lives and to guide them into holiness.

There are at least fourteen emblems of the Holy Spirit used to describe Him in Scripture, each portraying an aspect of His nature and work. For example, He is typified as oil, fire, rain, wind, and the breath of God.[4] But perhaps the gentle dove best captures for us the personality of the Holy Spirit. He is a sensitive, divine Person, who can be grieved, quenched, and vexed. He can also be entreated.

When Jesus went to the Jordan River to be baptized by John the Baptist, the Holy Spirit appeared in the form of a dove, and the Father spoke from heaven:

> When all the people were baptized, it came to pass that Jesus also was baptized; and while He prayed, the heaven was opened. And the Holy Spirit descended in bodily form like a dove upon Him, and a voice came from heaven which said, "You are My beloved Son; in You I am well pleased."
>
> —LUKE 3:21–22

The work of the Holy Spirit

What a wonder it is that the Holy Spirit can be entreated to reveal the love of God to our hearts and to do His precious, divine work in our lives. Jesus made it clear that our heavenly Father wants to give to us the Holy Spirit:

> If a son asks for bread from any father among you, will he give him a stone? Of if he asks for a fish, will he give him a serpent instead of a fish? Or if he asks for an egg, will he offer him a scorpion? If you then, being evil, know how to give good gifts to

your children, how much more will your heavenly Father give the
Holy Spirit to those who ask Him!

—Luke 11:11–13

Jesus declared that when He ascended into heaven to the
Father, He would send the Holy Spirit to do His divine work in the
Earth. He then described the work of the Holy Spirit on Earth:

And when He has come, He will convict the world of sin, and
of righteousness, and of judgment: of sin, because they do not
believe in Me; of righteousness, because I go to My Father and
you see Me no more; of judgment, because the ruler of this world
is judged.

—John 16:8–11

It is the work of the Holy Spirit first to convict our hearts and
show us our need of a Savior. Then He teaches us and gives us wisdom for life, revealing our purpose and destiny that God intended
for us. It is His divine unction that transforms us and enables us
to do the will of God. He gives us divine abilities, gifts of the Holy
Spirit, to empower us to fulfill our divine destiny.

The fruit of the Holy Spirit

As we mentioned, we are dependent on the precious Holy
Spirit to show us that we are sinners in need of a Savior, and then
to guide us into the truth of righteous living in every area of our
lives. We need Him to give us power over the evil one, the devil,
who was defeated through Christ's death on Calvary. In order to
grow in our faith, the New Testament epistles admonish believers to "Walk in the Spirit" (Gal. 5:16), to "live in the Spirit" (Gal.
5:25), and to "be filled with the Spirit" (Eph. 5:18). And the
apostle Paul declares plainly that believers are the temples of the
Holy Spirit who indwells us (1 Cor. 3:16). What will our lives
look like if we live and walk in the Spirit? Scripture describes the
beauty of such a life:

But the fruit of the Spirit is love, joy, peace, longsuffering, kindness, goodness, faithfulness, gentleness, self-control. Against such there is no law...If we live in the Spirit, let us also walk in the Spirit.

—GALATIANS 5:22–23, 25

Carefully consider this list of the fruit of the Spirit to determine how much your life looks like them. Learning to yield to the Holy Spirit in every situation of life will cause you to grow in grace, displaying a godly character filled with love, joy, peace, longsuffering, kindness, goodness, faithfulness, gentleness, and self-control. While none of us can produce such godly qualities ourselves, we can trust the Holy Spirit to fill us with the love of God and live His life through us. The apostle Paul declared, "The love of God has been poured out in our hearts by the Holy Spirit who was given to us" (Rom. 5:5).

The anointing of the Holy Spirit

Even Old Testament saints were characterized as people in whom the Spirit of God dwelt. When Pharaoh listened to Joseph interpret his dreams, he said to his servants:

"Can we find such a one as this, a man in whom is the Spirit of God?" Then Pharaoh said to Joseph, "Inasmuch as God has shown you all this, there is no one as discerning and wise as you."

—GENESIS 41:38–39

When Moses needed skilled craftsmen to do the elaborate work of building the tabernacle, he called for those who were filled with the Spirit of God:

See, the LORD has called by name Bezalel the son of Uri, the son of Hur, of the tribe of Judah; and He has filled him with the Spirit of God, in wisdom and understanding, in knowledge and all manner of workmanship, to design artistic works, to work in gold and silver and bronze, in cutting jewels for setting, in carving wood, and to work in all manner of artistic workmanship.

—EXODUS 35:30–33

The work of God in all ages has been attributed to the Spirit of God. Christ Himself accomplished His work on Earth by the anointing of the Holy Spirit. He stood in the synagogue one day and declared that the Word He read was fulfilled in Him:

The Spirit of the LORD is upon Me, Because He has anointed Me To preach the gospel to the poor; He has sent Me to heal the brokenhearted, To proclaim liberty to the captives And recovery of sight to the blind, To set at liberty those who are oppressed; To proclaim the acceptable year of the LORD.

—LUKE 4:18–19

As we bow our hearts in humble gratitude for the gift of the Holy Spirit, He will accomplish His divine work in our lives. He will give to us the things of Jesus (John 16:14), help us to pray (Rom. 8:27), transform us (2 Cor. 3:18), and fill us with the love of God (Rom. 5:5). To be filled with the Spirit means to be yielded to Him, obeying Him as He changes us into the image of Christ. This is what the kingdom of God is all about: "Righteousness and peace and joy in the Holy Spirit" (Rom. 14:17). When the Holy Spirit is present in our lives, we must remember that He is not the resident—He is the President. As He mediates the presence of God to us, our minds and souls are opened so that it seems we are standing in the very courts of heaven.

I love Him for His companionship, and because He chose to dwell in my heart, though greatly plagued with sin. And when I think I will fail because of my sinfulness, He whispers the Word of God to my heart: "He who is in you is greater than he who is in the world" (1 John 4:4). As we learn to yield to the power of the Holy Spirit within us, we can defeat every enemy of our soul and rest in the wonderful redemption of our Lord.

By the word of the Lord the heavens were made, And all the host of them by the breath of His mouth ... Let all the earth fear the Lord; Let all the inhabitants of the world stand in awe of Him. For He spoke, and it was done; He commanded, and it stood fast.

—Psalm 33:6, 8–9

By faith we understand that the worlds were framed by the word of God, so that the things which are seen were not made of things which are visible.

—Hebrews 11:3

Evolutionists consider that the human DNA is only partially functional. They refer to the major part of the DNA as "junk." However, most recent findings suggest that designating DNA as "junk" merely cloaks our current lack of knowledge about its function. The theory of intelligent design encourages scientists to look for function where evolution discourages it.[1]

There are broad moral implications for society involved in the acceptance of irrefutable evidence of *intelligent design*. If humans are in fact designed, then we can expect psychosocial constraints to be hardwired into us. Transgress those constraints, and we, as well as our society, will suffer. The basic concepts with which science has operated these last several hundred years are no longer adequate in an information age, and certainly not in an age where design is empirically detectable. To admit design into science is to liberate science from its crisis of contradiction, freeing it from restrictions that can no longer be justified.[2]

THE WORD OF GOD

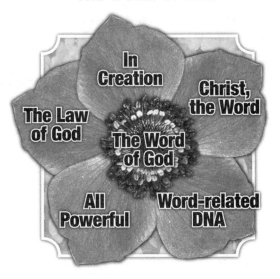

Scientists who are convinced of the empirical evidence of intelligent design seen in all of creation conclude that "if humans are in fact designed, then we can expect psychosocial constraints to be hardwired into us."[3] In others words, the One who designed us knows what makes us function at optimum for all spheres of life—body, soul, and spirit. If we violate the hardwired "psychosocial constraints" He ordained for our optimal function, not only will we suffer individually, but also the entire human society will suffer. "There is plenty of empirical evidence to suggest that many of the attitudes and behaviors our society promotes undermine human flourishing."[4] For answers to what will make your DNA reach its highest fulfillment, we must turn to the "owner's manual" given to us by the Designer—the Word of God.

Omnipotence—all powerful

The biblical account of the beginnings of our world simply declares, "Then God *said*, 'Let there be...'and there was" (Gen. 1–3, emphasis added). According to Scripture, God created everything we see through the omnipotent power of His Word. And the New Testament declares that He *upholds* everything by the power of His Word (see Heb. 1:3).

We understand that the *written* Word of God comprises the Old and New Testaments of the Bible. It was recorded when "holy men of God spoke as they were moved by the Holy Spirit" (2 Pet. 1:21). Scripture teaches that the *living* Word is Jesus Christ. Jesus declared that He is the living bread that came down from heaven (see John 6:51). He explained, "The words that I speak to you are spirit, and they are life" (John 6:63). He is God incarnate who was made flesh and dwelt among us (see John 1). As we embrace the divine mystery of the eternal truths written in the Word of God, we understand they cannot exist apart from Christ, the living Word of God. It is precisely this mystery, the exquisite blending of fragrances of every aspect of divinity in creation, that evokes awe, deep worship, and appreciation for our Maker.

Pursuing God through study of His Word is one of the greatest pursuits in life. If we hope to know the God of the Bible, it is vital that we read the Word of God from beginning to end, not once, but many times. Continual study of Scripture will produce great benefits, planting living truth into our hearts and minds and enabling us to fulfill our eternal purpose in life. Great modern heroes of faith such as John Wesley, George Whitfield, and others loved the Word of God. And they were used mightily by God to bring great revivals and transformations of their societies. It was their insatiable pursuit of God through His Word that made them great worshipers of God as well.

The law of God

Even Old Testament saints learned to know God and to love and obey Him through surrendering in obedience to His law. The psalmist understood the omnipotent power contained in the law of God:

> The law of the LORD is perfect, converting the soul; The testimony of the LORD is sure, making wise the simple; The statutes of the LORD are right, rejoicing the heart; The commandment of the LORD is pure, enlightening the eyes; The fear of the LORD is clean, enduring forever; The judgments of the LORD are true and righteous altogether.
>
> —Psalm 19:7–9

Have you ever received a birthday card that said just the words of love you wanted to hear and made you want to cry with gratitude and joy? That card was written by someone unknown to you. But it was purchased by someone who loves you and wants to express that love to you. The Bible is like that. It is God's love letter to you, uniquely applied to your life situation. As you allow the Holy Spirit to quicken the Word of God to your mind and heart, you will have that sense, that though written long ago, it is applicable for your personal situation right now. God is speaking through it to you—out of the love of His heart.

The psalmist also expressed an insatiable love for the Torah—the Law of God. He declared: "The law of Your mouth is better to me Than thousands of coins of gold and silver…Oh, how I love Your law! It is my meditation all the day" (Ps. 119:72, 97). If you feel like the Bible is just words on a page, I encourage you to begin to pray, *Lord, this is your Word. Please help me to love it and meditate on its truths and apply it to my life.* Ask, as the psalmist did, for your eyes to be opened to the beauty of God's law:

Open my eyes, that I may see Wondrous things from Your
law...Let Your mercies come also to me, O Lord—Your salvation according to Your word.

—Psalm 119:18, 41

The Word of God itself will produce awe and reverence in the
serious student. Again, the psalmist declared: "Let all the earth
fear the Lord; Let all the inhabitants of the world stand in awe of
Him" (Ps. 33:8). As you meditate on its eternal truths, ask the Holy
Spirit to make them a reality in your life. The more you meditate
on the wonder of your Creator and the beauty of His creation, the
more you will begin to appreciate the omnipotence of your sovereign God.

As I discussed earlier in the text, true appreciation of someone
involves a sensitive *awareness* as well as an *expression* of admiration
and gratitude for them.[5] To truly *appreciate* requires that we grasp
the nature, worth, and significance of a person and that we view
them with heightened perception or understanding. That is what
happens as we read the Word of God—we become keenly aware of
and utterly grateful to our loving Creator for His gift of life to us.

In creation

God first revealed the omnipotent power of His Word when
He spoke the worlds into existence in creation. And His voice
continued speaking to His highest creation—mankind. The first
couple, Adam and Eve, heard His voice in the cool of the day in that
beautiful garden where He placed them. Even after they disobeyed
His voice and brought calamity on the entire human race, He came
to them.

The patriarchs, Noah, Abraham, Isaac, Jacob, Moses, Joshua,
and others, had dramatic encounters with the voice of God. They
understood the power of His Word to them in that they obeyed it
and received divine promises. To the Old Testament prophets, priests,
and kings, God continued speaking His Word to guide the course of

humanity. In His pursuit of them, divine love—God is love—continued to reveal Himself through His Word to His people.

The Bible is self-vindicating in its declaration that "prophecy never came by the will of man, but holy men of God spoke as they were moved by the Holy Spirit" (2 Pet. 1:21). Of course, there were long periods of time when, because of mankind's rejection of the Word of God, the Scriptures lament: "The word of the LORD was rare in those days; there was no widespread revelation" (1 Sam. 3:1). And there were the terribly dark four hundred years between the close of the Old Testament era and the New Testament Gospels, during which there seems to have been complete silence from God.

Even in our day, there are entire cultures and nations who have not received the truth of the Word of God. The question must arise, "Why do men hate the truth?" Early church fathers, like Saint Augustine, wondered at this sad reality:

> But why does truth generate hatred, and why does Your servant, preaching the truth, become their enemy, since a happy life is loved, which is nothing else but rejoicing in the truth? How is this so unless the truth is loved in such a way that those who love something else want what they love to be the truth? And because they do not want to be deceived, they do not want to be convinced that they are. Therefore they hate the truth, for the sake of the thing they love instead of the truth...Thus does the mind of man—blind, sick, foul and ill-behaved—wish to be hidden, but does not want anything hidden from it. But the very opposite happens. The mind is not hidden from the truth, while the truth remains hidden from it.
>
> —FROM *THE CONFESSIONS OF ST. AUGUSTINE*[6]

Christ, the Word

The breaking of that desperate, dark silence of hundreds of years, after the Old Testament prophets ceased speaking, must have made the words of John's Gospel exquisitely beautiful to the hearers of his day. He described Jesus as the incarnate Word of God:

> In the beginning was the Word, and the Word was with God, and the Word was God. He was in the beginning with God. All things were made through Him, and without Him nothing was made that was made. In Him was life, and the life was the light of men...And the Word became flesh and dwelt among us, and we beheld His glory, the glory as of the only begotten of the Father, full of grace and truth.
>
> —John 1:1–4, 14

In reading those verses, we have just buried our faces in the exquisitely fragrant "bouquet" of the Creator, the Word, the Christ, the revelation of the Father, the glory of God, grace and truth, peace, and every redemptive attribute of God. How can we ever comprehend the "Word" as a divine Person? How can we really fathom the infinitely divine when we are so finite? Yet, until we pursue that divine mystery, we cannot appreciate, admire, and esteem the Word, the written Word, or the Christ, as we should. Years later, John was given a vision of the eternally reigning Christ as the Word of God:

> Now I saw heaven opened, and behold, a white horse. And He who sat on him was called Faithful and True, and in righteousness He judges and makes war. His eyes were like a flame of fire, and on His head were many crowns. He had a name written that no one knew except Himself. He was clothed with a robe dipped in blood, and His name is called *The Word of God*.
>
> —Revelation 19:11–13, emphasis added

When we behold Christ as the King of kings, our sovereign Lord, it is difficult to imagine the humility that accompanied His incarnation. Yet, the Word of God had to become man, humbling

Himself to become a servant of men in order to redeem mankind and then be exalted to His rightful place as Lord of all. The apostle Paul explains this humbling of divinity, when he instructs believers to "Let this mind be in you which was also in Christ Jesus" (Phil. 2:5):

> Who, being in the form of God, did not consider it robbery to be equal with God, but made Himself of no reputation, taking the form of a bondservant, and coming in the likeness of men. And being found in appearance as a man, He humbled Himself and became obedient to the point of death, even the death of the cross. Therefore God also has highly exalted Him and given Him the name which is above every name, that at the name of Jesus every knee should bow, of those in heaven, and of those on earth, and of those under the earth, and that every tongue should confess that Jesus Christ is Lord, to the glory of God the Father.
>
> —Philippians 2:6–11

Jesus taught us how to live humbly in right relationship to the Word of God. He declared that He was completely dependent on the words of His Father, doing nothing He did not hear from His Father: "I am able to do nothing from Myself [independently, of My own accord—but only as I am taught by God and as I get His orders]" (John 5:30, AMP). Filled with the Spirit of God, Christ fulfilled His divine destiny, walking in complete obedience to the Father's will.

Scripture teaches that the Word of God is "living and powerful, and sharper than any two-edged sword, piercing even to the division of soul and spirit, and of joints and marrow, and is a discerner of the thoughts and intents of the heart" (Heb. 4:12). And the apostle Paul instructs us in how to wage war against the enemies of our souls, using the "sword of the Spirit, which is the word of God" (Eph. 6:17). As the written Word fills our minds and hearts with illumination—spiritual understanding—by the power of the Holy Spirit, we can truly know Christ, the living Word, and grow in grace in our personal relationship with Him.

Word-related DNA

It is this supernatural power of the Word of God working in believers' hearts that can cause our DNA to dance. As Christians, we can learn to declare the Word of God over our situations, and the enemy has to admit defeat; in that way we prevail over negative spiritual forces that are stronger than we are. And we conquer our own negative thinking patterns and attitudes, fears, and other unhealthy lifestyles by believing and expressing the truth of the Word of God.

According to Scripture, the Word of God has the power to transform our minds and heal our bodies (see Ps. 107:20; Rom. 12:2). Scripture also teaches that the words we think and speak have profound influence on our quality of life—body, soul, and spirit—and the outworking of our entire DNA. The Holy Spirit revealed this truth to the writer of the Proverbs: "For as he thinketh in his heart, so is he" (Prov. 23:7, KJV). And the apostle James describes the tongue as a fire, which can defile the whole body and which no man can tame (James 3:5–8). He explained: "If anyone does not stumble in word, he is a perfect man, able also to bridle the whole body" (James 3:2). Only the power of the Holy Spirit can transform our lives to such a state.

The Word of God reveals the character of God, the power of God, and the love of God. As believers, when we seek to renew our minds by meditating on the Word of God, we enjoy the eternal life Christ came to give to us. Eternal life is that quality of life that results from knowing God as we live on Earth; and it will allow us to live forever with God in heaven (see John 17:3). We need the Word of God to be a lamp unto our feet and a light to our path (see Ps. 119:105), influencing our DNA with its transforming power.

Yet, Jesus warned of forces in life that would choke out the Word of God and make it of no effect in our lives. In His parable of the sower and the seed, Jesus explains that the Word of God is the seed. The seed is good, but there are "kinds of soil"—attitudes of life—onto which it falls where it cannot grow. He used the analogy of seed being sown among the thorns to explain this tragedy:

> And the ones [seed] sown among the thorns are others who hear the Word; Then the cares and anxieties of the world and distractions of the age, and the pleasure and delight and false glamour and deceitfulness of riches, and the craving and passionate desire for other things creep in and choke and suffocate the Word, and it becomes fruitless.
>
> —MARK 4:18–19, AMP

It is vital that we consider what "thorns" may be in our lives that would choke and suffocate the divine influence of the Word of God, making us unfruitful. Let me encourage you to ask God to prepare your "soil" and cleanse your heart of any distractions or attitudes that would keep you from producing the fruit of the Word in your life—transforming the expression of your DNA. Then you will know the fulfillment of this precious promise in your life:

> And all of us, as with unveiled face, [because we] continued to behold [in the Word of God] as in a mirror the glory of the Lord, are constantly being transfigured into His very own image in ever increasing splendor and from one degree of glory to another; [for this comes] from the Lord [Who is] the Spirit.
>
> —2 CORINTHIANS 3:18, AMP

Now it shall come to pass, if you diligently obey the voice of the LORD your God, to observe carefully all His commandments which I command you today, that the LORD your God will set you high above all nations of the earth. And all these blessings shall come upon you and overtake you, because you obey the voice of the LORD your God.

—DEUTERONOMY 28:1–2

Tracing the Hand of the Creator

The capacity of the brain is such that it can hold information equivalent to that contained in twenty-five million books, enough to fill a bookshelf five hundred miles long. In contrast, the Library of Congress has seventeen million volumes. Yet, even though we know that the brain generates both electrical and chemical activity, we still do not know precisely what thinking is, or intuition, or consciousness, or what distinguishes the mind from the brain.

—Richard A. Swenson, M.D.[1]

THE COMMANDMENTS OF GOD

The three-pound brain within your skull is, as far as we know, the most complex and orderly arrangement of matter in the universe, according to scientist and author Isaac Asimov.[2] It is so complex that in spite of our modern scientific research, we are only beginning to penetrate the brain's secrets. The basic cell of the brain is called the *neuron*, of which, according to some estimates, there may be as many as one hundred billion. Each neuron has ten thousand tiny branching fibers and filamentous projections called *dendrites*, from a Greek derivative, meaning "tree." Each neuron is thus in contact with ten thousand other neurons, for a total of one hundred trillion neurological interconnections.[3] (See illustration of human brain on page 217.)

If you stretched out all the neurons and dendritic connections from one brain and laid them end to end, they would reach one hundred thousand miles, circling the Earth at the equator four times. It is no wonder that the potential capacity of a brain is such that it can hold information equivalent to that contained in twenty-five million books, enough to fill a bookshelf five hundred miles long. Assuming that 10 percent of the brain cells are firing at any given time, this implies a rate of a thousand trillion computations per second. And unlike the parts of a computer, nerve cells are highly individual. No two cells are exactly the same, nor do they respond to the same incoming information in the same way; each neuron is unique in all the universe.[4]

This astounding scientific knowledge of your physical brain gives new significance to the biblical assertion that your thinking dramatically influences your life. The Book of Proverbs states: "Be careful what you think because your thoughts run your life" (Prov. 4:23, NCV). Your thoughts determine who you are and what you do. They are intertwined with what I call "imaginations of the mind." Imagination is an ability God has given you that can be used for your good or for your harm.

In my book, *Imaginations: More Than You Think*, I give this simple definition of imagination: "the image-making faculty of the mind." These mental images or pictures powerfully influence your thoughts, your ideas, and your attitudes. Imaginations form a pattern of thinking and develop a whole mind-set toward life, which helps to determine your creativity, your outlook, your self-discipline, your ability to solve problems, and your ability to handle the choices we make every day.[5]

Divine absolutes

Enter now, the commandments of God. The Creator of all gave us a comprehensive "Designer's manual," in which He clearly indicates how we are to think, and then act, in every situation of life. The Word of God delineates His divine principles to us for the optimal function of our DNA. These divine principles for life should be considered absolute truth because the Maker of all things has "hardwired" into us, for our well-being, the necessary constraints they imply.

Unfortunately, we live in a world today that scoffs at "absolutes" in any realm. The "doctrine of relativism" has spawned phrases like "If it feels good, do it," and "Do whatever is right for you." While those attitudes reflect a convenient way to rationalize our selfish behavior, the Word of God does not affirm those views. Instead, God, the "manufacturer" of mankind, has communicated to His people divine absolutes, which are meant to govern us for the well-being of all humanity.

Consider for a moment the practicality of a civic ordinance that determines the flow of traffic. A red light means for motorists to stop; a green light indicates a right to continue. If that ordinance were continually violated by motorists, motivated by their momentary "feelings," death and carnage would result from the chaos. Or, if one city used a red light to indicate the rights of traffic to proceed, and a green light to indicate their need to stop, motorists from other cities would cause accidents because of the confusion the change in that ordinance would create for them. Similarly, the commandments of God, which have been given to us for our well-being and blessing, when broken, create chaos that results in much harm and misery.

The human life is fragile; it can be severely damaged physically, emotionally, mentally, and spiritually if anything other than divine "specification" is adopted as an accepted norm. Though some consider the commandments of God to be limiting, out-dated, or completely undesirable, the fact remains that they have been given to us to insure our potential success in life. When obeyed, God's divine absolutes spark the lovely spiritual dance of our DNA.

For our blessing

The brain holds 10^{14} bits of information, and thus has a storage capacity one thousand times that of a Cray-2 supercomputer.[6]

What kind of information does your mind contain? How do your imaginations affect your quality of life, your relationships, and your peace of mind?

The first step in obeying the commands of God to receive His favor on your life is to know what those commands are specifically. While this may be stating the obvious, in our culture today more and more people confess to being completely ignorant of the Word of God. They have not considered it relevant to their lives in this modern society. People have given children surveys, asking them to identify some of the Bible heroes such as Abraham, Moses, and Noah, with disappointing results. While they can readily name characters from Star Wars and give statistics of their favorite sports hero, many have never heard of what previous generations considered "familiar Bible stories." It is to this generation that we must reiterate the commandments of God, which He gave to order our lives and protect us from destruction. Otherwise, they will never gain a satisfying sense of purpose for life.

Death was never God's intent for mankind, His jewel of creation. According to Scripture, death entered the world because of the disobedience of Adam and Eve: "For since by man came death, by Man [Christ] also came the resurrection of the dead. For as in Adam all die, even so in Christ all shall be made alive" (1 Cor. 15:21–22). While Adam and Eve did not physically die immediately after they violated the command of God, their lives were tragically changed for the worse. Their intimate communion with God was broken. They were expelled from their beautiful garden home. Adam had to toil for a living and Eve would now have to suffer in childbearing. Their son committed the first murder out of envy for his brother. And, ultimately, they did die a physical death as well.

But the greatest "death" Adam and Eve experienced was their estrangement from God, which inevitably became the sad plight of all of mankind. Throughout the ages, God has been drawing mankind back to Himself, communicating His will to them through His prophets, and promising great blessing for those who trust Him and obey His commands. There are also terrible consequences for those who do not obey them. When God delivered His people from the slavery of Egypt, He instituted a national Law that would preserve them. We call the short version the "Ten Commandments."

Obedience required

When Moses was used by God to deliver over two million Israelites from the misery of slavery under the oppressive rule of Pharaoh in Egypt, this great multitude of people began moving toward the Promised Land, leaving all that had been familiar to them for over four hundred years. It was absolutely necessary that they be governed by specific social restraints to prevent potential chaos. So God gave Moses the laws and social ordinances that would order the lives of the Israelites in every situation they faced as a nation.

The Ten Commandments are still relevant to society today, and are responsible for much of the peace, tranquility, and order we enjoy as Americans. Many of the divine principles they teach, especially regarding human dignity and respect for others, are embedded in the rule of law established by our national Constitution. Consider this abbreviated version, which outlines God's requirements for our relationship with God and with others:

- You shall have no other gods before me.

- You shall not make for yourself a carved image.

- You shall not take the name of the LORD your God in vain.

- Remember the Sabbath day, to keep it holy.

- Honor your father and your mother.

- You shall not murder.

- You shall not commit adultery.

- You shall not steal.

- You shall not bear false witness against your neighbor.

- You shall not covet.

These commandments of God cannot be broken without grave consequences, both to the human psyche and to society. Yet, in His mercy, God knew that mankind was helpless to keep His Law because of the power of sin that had entered the world. So, He prescribed a system of sacrifices to teach them of the need for atonement for their sin. Through this means, those who sincerely wanted to obey God, but failed, could repent and offer a blood sacrifice. This would result in their sin being covered.

It is in that context that Christ came to Earth to become the spotless "Lamb of God" (John 1:29), and shed His blood as a supreme sacrifice for the sins of the whole world. He made it possible for us to be restored to right relationship with God, as we have discussed (see Day 6). His sacrifice for sin also made it possible for us to become obedient children of God, filled with the blessings of God.

The blessing of obeying the commandments of God is not limited to the benefits of social order they provide. The wonderful power of keeping God's commandments is reflected in communion with God that we enjoy through obedience as well. Even Old Testament saints discovered the reality of this divine relationship based in obedience to God's commandments:

> Blessed is the man Who walks not in the counsel of the ungodly, Nor stands in the path of sinners, Nor sits in the seat of the scornful; But his delight is in the law of the Lord, And in His law he meditates day and night. He shall be like a tree

Planted by the rivers of water, That brings forth its fruit in its
season, Whose leaf also shall not wither, And whatever he does
shall prosper.

—Psalm 1:1–3

It was very clear from the time Moses received the
Commandments on the Mount, that God intended for the people
to obey them. And these laws were never to be rejected, substituted,
or replaced by future generations with different "values" and "mind-
sets." On the contrary, Scripture teaches clearly that they were to be
taught very carefully to succeeding generations:

And these words which I command you today shall be in your
heart. You shall teach them diligently to your children, and shall
talk of them when you sit in your house, when you walk by the
way, when you lie down, and when you rise up.

—Deuteronomy 6:6–7

These instructions were followed by warnings not to forget the
Lord and serve other gods, "Lest the anger of the Lord your God
be aroused against you and destroy you from the face of the earth"
(Deut. 6:15). Of course, the history of the nation of Israel records
not only the blessings of their obedience but also the consequences
of their disobedience.

The law of love

There are those who believe that because we are living during the
centuries following the death of Christ, we are not subject to the Law
of God. They conclude that we are living under "grace" now, since
Christ died for our sins. However, Christ Himself taught that He did
not come to do away with the law, but to fulfill it (Matt. 5:17). And
when a lawyer asked Jesus, "Teacher, which is the great commandment in the law?" Jesus quoted from the Book of Deuteronomy:

"You shall love the LORD your God with all your heart, with all your soul, and with all your mind." This is the first and great commandment. And the second is like it: "You shall love your neighbor as yourself." On these two commandments hang all the Law and the Prophets.

—MATTHEW 22:37–40

Of course, the entire New Testament confirms the reality of walking in the redemption of God through obedience to His commandments. Yet, it is not an obedience of duty that is required, but a relationship of love. And we do not obey in order to be saved from our sin, but out of love, because we have received His great grace that has forgiven our sin. Out of love for our Redeemer, we pursue an intimate relationship with our Creator and Savior that is absolutely satisfying. This divine relationship motivates us to love our neighbor, which Jesus defined as anyone we see in need and wounded along the road of life (see Luke 10:25–37.) As we truly fall in love with Christ, we will say with the psalmist: "I delight to do Your will, O my God, And Your law is within my heart" (Ps. 40:8).

Beloved, let us love one another, for love is of God; and everyone who loves is born of God and knows God...For God is love. In this the love of God was manifested toward us, that God has sent His only begotten Son into the world, that we might live through Him.

—1 JOHN 4:7–9

This is My commandment, that you love one another as I have loved you.

—JOHN 15:12

Tracing the Hand of the Creator

Powering the circulatory system is a formidable task, unforgiving of errors. But the heart is remarkably effective. Every day, uncomplaining, this ten-ounce muscle contracts 100 thousand times...Over a lifetime of faithful service, these two self-lubricating, self-regulating, high-capacity pumps beat two and one-half billion times and pump sixty million gallons of blood without pausing to rest...This circulatory effort is so dynamic that each blood cell returns back to its cardiac starting place every minute...Even though the four-chambered heart is remarkably effective, as with all engines it is not mechanically very efficient (typically less than 10 percent efficiency rating)...Any lack of efficiency is more than made up for by a commensurate faithfulness. I stand in awe.

—Richard A. Swenson, M.D.[1]

LOVE

God is Love.

Storge: Affection

Phileo: Friend

Love

Eros: "In Love"

Agape: Charity

L ove—that powerful four letter word that is, perhaps, one of the most misused and misunderstood words in the human language—haunts, tantalizes, fills with hope, dashes to despair, and creates the greatest pursuit in all of life. In the final analysis, love eludes the hearts and minds of many, leaving them feeling unloved and alone in life. At least, their *concept* of love has not been fulfilled, which causes them to suffer feelings of discontent and an ache of unbearable emptiness. They fail to find satisfaction despite their mad pursuit of the thing they call "love."

It seems a cruelty of fate that a quality of life so necessary to happiness as love should so easily elude us. Ask any brokenhearted lover, or listen to the moaning of the pop song artists, and you will hear the pain inflicted on the human psyche through broken promises of love. Yet, this emotional pain is not limited to failed, adult romance; it stalks children, the elderly, and everyone who experiences circumstances that make them feel "alone" and unloved.

Where does one go to find the love that will satisfy the deepest yearnings of the human heart? Are those desires even legitimate, or are they selfish? Why do some people seem to "have it all together" and others feel neglected and lonely, even though they enter into relationships of marriage, parenting, community and church activities, friendship, and employment?

These are just a few of the questions people ask relating to their quest for love. Children wonder why Daddy or Mommy didn't love them enough to keep their home together. Parents wonder where they went wrong when, in old age, their children don't want to spend time with them. An estranged spouse wonders why their marriage partner could have been seduced by "that man" or "that woman." We cannot hope to find answers for the painful questions of life without first discovering the source of love.

God is love.

The Bible doesn't simply say that God *loves* or that He *has* love; it states plainly: "God *is* love" (1 John 4:8, emphasis added). His very essence is divine love, which He desires to infuse into all of His creation. Is it any wonder that the human heart craves love so deeply, and on so many levels? We were made by love to walk in relationship with God, who is love. Seeking God, who *is* love, to come into our lives and "dwell" there is one of the most awesome spiritual realities we can experience. Learning to appreciate God's presence in our lives is the first step in knowing true satisfaction for our deepest desire for love. Blaise Pascal (1623–1662), the famous French physicist, mathematician, and philosopher wrote:

> There is a God-shaped vacuum in the heart of every man which cannot be filled with any created thing, but only by God, the Creator made known through Jesus [Christ].[2]

The Hebrew verb for *love* used in this verse is *ahab* and means "to have affection for as for a friend." Our whole being—heart, soul, and strength—is to be engaged in cultivating friendship with God. Only in that divine relationship can we expect to find ultimate satisfaction in life. We mentioned that when Jesus was asked which was the greatest commandment in the law, He responded: "'You shall love the LORD your God with all your heart, with all your soul, and with all your mind.' This is the first and great commandment. And the second is like it: 'You shall love your neighbor as yourself'" (Matt. 22:37–39). Love is to be the motivating force for humanity.

The Bible is filled with revelation of the kind of intimacy God desires to have with mankind. The writer of the Proverbs declared: "For the devious are an abomination to the LORD; But He is intimate with the upright" (Prov. 3:32, NAS). In the Hebrew, the word *intimate* means "to sit down together, to counsel and instruct, to establish, to settle, and to share inward secrets. To think of sitting down with God and receiving His counsel, and even hearing His secrets, may seem almost irreverent to some. But for those who are learning to appreciate the Creator, and who have felt His divine presence even as they observe His awesome creation, it is the most deeply satisfying experience they have known. Ellen Vaughn writes:

> We cannot yet see God. For now, He hides, in light inaccessible. But He lavishes His presence upon our world in the clues of His creation. In this, even the smallest hint of God's immanence, even the tiniest shadow of the reflection of His glory, is cause for holy fear: awe mingled with thanks.[3]

Agape: charity

The deep craving we have for intimacy involves the innate need to be fully known, fully loved, and fully accepted. The psalmist described the profound wonder of the relationship he revered in being known by God:

O Lord, You have searched me and known me. You know my sitting down and my rising up; You understand my thought afar off. You comprehend my path and my lying down, And are acquainted with all my ways…Such knowledge is too wonderful for me; It is high, I cannot attain it…How precious also are Your thoughts to me, O God!

—Psalm 139:1–3, 6, 17

When the Bible declares that God is love, the Greek word translated *love* is *agape*. It means affection, benevolence, and charity. C. S. Lewis, in his classic book, *The Four Loves*, calls this divine love of God "charity." He describes man's original relationship to God in creation:

When God planted a garden He set a man over it and set the man under Himself. When He planted the garden of our nature and caused the flowering, fruiting loves to grow there, He set our will to "dress" them.[4]

Lewis explains that the source of all love is God, and that only as we properly relate to His *divine* love—charity—will we be able to enjoy the three *natural* loves: storge (affection), phileo (friendship), and eros ("falling in love").

Some have tried, however unsuccessfully, to make the rules of language dictate what we can "like" and what we can "love." We have been taught that we cannot love inanimate objects, in expressions such as "I love ice cream." However, Lewis disdains that idea, saying that there is a correlation between our "likes" and our "loves." And in other languages, such as French, there is only one word for both concepts. He suggests that since "the highest does not stand without the lowest" we had better begin at the bottom, with mere *likings*; and since to "like" anything means to take some sort of pleasure in it, we must begin with pleasure. Lewis then describes four elements present in love, admitting that they are seldom experienced apart from each other:

- Gift love, which longs to serve

- Need love, which cries to God from our poverty

- Need pleasures, preceded by desire

- Pleasures of appreciation, the starting point for our whole experience of beauty[5]

Gift love/need love

It will be helpful to briefly discuss these four elements of love from Lewis' classic work, *The Four Loves*, in order for you to evaluate your own experience of them.

Gift love

God implants in us both natural gift loves and need loves. The gift loves are natural images of Himself, relating most closely to *agape*. Gift love moves a person to work and plan and save for the future well-being of his family, even after he is gone and will not benefit personally from it. It also enables him to love what is not naturally lovable: lepers, criminals, enemies. Through this divine love, he is able to give his will and heart to God for His glory.[6]

It was God's divine gift love that caused Him to create all of us. He designed us and everything around us with unbelievable genetic make-up. He allows us to enjoy the "dance of our DNA" for seven or eight decades, from our birth to our death—then we return to Him. However, that return ultimately depends on whether or not we received God's love in Christ and trusted Him to anoint our lives here on Earth. Did we ask for His anointing on our DNA throughout our lifetime? It is God's desire to enjoy fellowship with us throughout eternity—never ending. He issued the invitation through His Son, Jesus: "Come to Me, all you who labor and are heavy laden, and I will give you rest" (Matt. 11:28). He is a giving God.

And according to Scripture, as astonishing as it may seem, we can give to God in very meaningful ways. For example, when we give to strangers whom we feed or clothe or visit in prison, we are expressing gift love to God Himself. Jesus declared:

> For I was hungry and you gave Me food; I was thirsty and you gave Me drink; I was a stranger and you took Me in; I was naked and you clothed Me; I was sick and you visited Me; I was in prison and you came to Me...I say to you, inasmuch as you did it to one of the least of these My brethren, you did it to Me.
>
> —MATTHEW 25:35–36, 40

True appreciation of God will allow His gift love to flow through us to those we consider "the least of these." We will appreciate the privilege we have of being a channel of God's agape love to those who are needy. Instead of a sense of revulsion or even a wrong sense of superiority, we will experience the compassion of a loving Savior, and reach down to allow His giving love to flow through us to touch hurting humanity wherever we find it. Charity toward others is a result of appreciating the divine love of God that has been given to us.

Need love

Need love is that love which sends a frightened child to his mother's arms. It is the accurate reflection in consciousness of our actual nature: born helpless; as soon as we are fully conscious we discover loneliness; we need others physically, emotionally, and intellectually. The craving to be loved is complicated. Though it is not mere selfishness, it can be selfishly indulged. However, no one calls a child selfish because he turns for comfort to his mother, nor an adult who turns to his fellow for company.[7]

And man's love for God, from the very nature of the case must always be very largely, and must often be entirely, a *need* love. This is obvious when we implore forgiveness for our sins or support in our tribulations. We should be growing in our awareness that our whole being is one vast need, incomplete, preparatory, empty yet cluttered, crying out for Him who can untie things that are now knotted together and tie up things that are still dangling loose. Our need love for God is unique, because our need of Him can never end. However, if our awareness of our need for God dies, then our need love dies with it.[8]

Need pleasures

There are pleasures preceded by desire, such as the need for a drink of water. A cool drink brings pleasure, but it was not done just for the fun of it. These pleasures represent the need loves. We must always be aware, however, that personal absorption with our own needs is an unhealthy mental and emotional state.

According to many experts in human behavior, selfishness stands alone as the most common mental illness. O. Quentin Hyden, M.D., supports this concept in his book, *A Christian's Handbook of Psychiatry*: "Selfishness is the root cause of all sin, and the result of sin may sometimes lead to personality or adjustment problems and some neurotic, psychosomatic or even psychotic conditions."[9] Of course, Dr. Hyden assures us that sin alone doesn't cause all mental breakdowns or emotional disturbances, but it plays a key role. "We could presume, then, that the opposite is true. The soundest state of mind—in an individual or a nation—is selflessness... for sound mental health, [we must] develop the desire to *give* rather than *take*."[10]

Appreciation in love

One of the indications of a healthy mind is the expression of appreciation expressed by that person. In order to appreciate anything in life you have to be focusing on the good that is around you.

Pleasures of appreciation

These pleasures differ from need pleasures, in that they often come unexpectedly, gratifying our senses in such a way that they claim our appreciation by right. For example, a man goes for a walk and passes a field of sweet peas. He is delighted with the fragrance of the plants that gratifies his senses unexpectedly. He would be insensitive and unappreciative if he did not acknowledge his enjoyment of the moment, which he may remember for years to come. Pleasures of appreciation somehow give us the sense that we owe it to them to savor, to attend to and praise them.[11]

Appreciative pleasure is the starting point of our whole experience of beauty. We cannot appreciate the Creator if we choose to ignore the wonderful beauty that delights our vision, our hearing, and all of our senses daily. It is as we learn to express appreciation that all of the loves become meaningful and flourish in our lives in the way they were meant. While *need* love cries to God from our poverty, and *gift* love longs to serve or even to suffer for God, *appreciative* love says: "We give thanks to thee for thy great glory."[12]

At every stage of life, we encounter different need loves, pleasures of appreciation, and expressions of gift love. The very young have need loves that can be fulfilled by those who are more mature, expressing gift love toward them. And the elderly once again experience some of the need loves of children, which can be fulfilled by young people sharing their love for them. There must be a balance in all of life for expressing the natural loves, which, of course, must be submitted to God's divine love—charity. As we allow God to anoint our lives with His love, the natural loves will take on godly character and will help us fulfill the destiny for which we were ordained.

Lewis concludes that we do injustice to love to dissect it too exactly. In actual life, all of these elements of love mix and succeed one another moment by moment. Yet, it is helpful to articulate the characteristics of love analytically, so that we can learn to intentionally express our appreciation to God for every revelation of His love.[13]

Hindrances to love

C. S. Lewis warns of the dark side of natural loves, with their propensity to become rather complicated forms of hatred. Love begins to be a demon the moment he begins to be a god. There must be a balance in our understanding of love, which allows for the truth that *God is love*, without perverting it to mean that *love is God*. Every human love, at its height, has a tendency to claim for itself a divine authority, sounding as if it were the will of God Himself. Hence, we derive the philosophy that if anything is done "for love's sake," it is acceptable. We clearly understand the error of this claim in erotic love, which demands a person's infidelity to a spouse. But family affection may also make inordinate demands in a "godlike" claim on family members. Some have even made "friendship" love into a god as well.[14]

Lewis also cites the sinful condition of mankind as a hindrance to enjoying any kind of love. He uses the analogy of a garden to represent the fruit of our love. We are the gardeners who must labor to keep weeds out, to feed, and to prune the plants as needed, in order to have a beautiful garden of love. But our position as gardener does not make us the source of any of the loves; that would be like saying we were the creator of the flowers. No matter the "realm" of love we experience, we must reflect on its true source: the heart of the Creator. That reality is simply stated in Scripture: "God *is* love."

Charity is the divine love of God that we can experience in our own lives. Only as we become centered in God's love can we learn to love others, to forgive others, and to become loving people even in difficult situations. Left to ourselves, our own idea of love is sinful, inordinate, and selfish. Regarding these natural loves, Lewis states, "they are unworthy to take the place of God by the fact that they cannot even remain themselves and do what they promise to do without God's help."[15]

Even with the "gardener's" human help, it is still the inherent divine nature of love created in the "flower" that causes it to bloom.

The garden of love would cease to exist without the divine source of love that created it. Only as we learn to rest in the redemption of God will we begin to display the fruit of the Spirit of God in our own "gardens"—our personal lives and relationships. The apostle Paul describes the loveliness of this supernatural fruit:

> The fruit of the Spirit is love, joy, peace, longsuffering, kindness, goodness, faithfulness, gentleness, self-control. Against such there is no law.
>
> —GALATIANS 5:22–23

A brief discussion of the three natural loves articulated by C. S. Lewis may serve to help you understand how to love more effectively in your "natural" relationships.

Storge: affection

Storge (pronounced stor-gay), is defined simply as *affection*, but especially as it applies to parents' feeling for their children and vice-versa. While this is the central meaning of the word, affection extends far beyond the relation of parents and children. Storge depicts the warm comfortableness, the satisfaction in being together, of all kinds of relationships. C. S. Lewis writes:

> It is indeed the least discriminating of loves…Almost anyone can become an object of affection…there need be no apparent fitness between those whom it unites…It ignores the barriers of age, sex, class and education. It can exist between a clever young man from the university and an old nurse, though their minds inhabit different worlds. It ignores even the barriers of species. We see it not only between dog and man but, more surprisingly, between dog and cat.[16]

Lewis describes affection as the humblest of all the loves. It does not put on airs. People can be proud of being "in love" (eros) or of friendship, but affection is modest. It almost slinks or seeps through our lives. It lives with humble undress and private things such as soft slippers, old clothes, and the thump of a sleeping dog's tail on the kitchen floor. It can exist apart from the other loves. And it can enter into all the other loves, coloring them all through and becoming the very medium in which they operate from day to day.[17]

The lasting benefit of this broadest of loves, according to Lewis, is that it liberates us to get beyond our own idiosyncrasies and learn to appreciate goodness in any person we find it, not according to our preferences. "In my experience," writes Lewis, "it is Affection that creates a [wide] taste [in humanity], teaching us first to notice, then to endure, then to smile at, then to enjoy, and finally to *appreciate*, the people who 'happen to be there.'"[18] We can take this as a lesson in helping us "love our neighbor as we love ourselves," knowing that they are as special to God as we are. It is storge—Affection—that will help us to fulfill the biblical instruction: "In lowliness of mind let each esteem others better than himself" (Phil. 2:3).

Lewis gives a final warning regarding affection, which causes us to reflect again on the source of all love—the Creator: "You need 'give and take;' that is, you need justice, continually stimulating mere Affection when it fades and restraining it when it forgets or would defy the art of love. You need 'decency.' There is no disguising the fact that this means goodness; patience, self-denial, humility, and the continual intervention of a far higher sort of love than Affection, in itself, can ever be. That is the whole point. If we try to live by Affection alone, Affection will 'go bad on us.'"[19] As important as storge love is to our lives, we must consciously allow it to be energized by charity—the divine love of God. As we cultivate His divine love in our lives, storge will be sanctified to God's purposes and will make our lives and the lives of those around us sweeter.

Phileo: friendship

C. S. Lewis defines friendship as the least *natural* of the loves; "the least instinctive, organic, biological, gregarious and necessary...Without Eros none of us would have been begotten and without Affection none of us would have been reared; but we can live and breed without Friendship."[20] He describes friendship love as "that luminous, tranquil, rational world of relationships freely chosen...Friendship is a relation between men at their highest level of individuality."[21] Lewis continues his discussion of friendship love by asserting that true friendship is not possessive or jealous. "Two friends delight to be joined by a third, and three by a fourth...In this, Friendship exhibits a glorious 'nearness by resemblance' to Heaven itself where the very multitude of the blessed (which no man can number) increases the fruition which each has of God."[22]

How reminiscent are his thoughts regarding friendship to our Lord's declaration to His disciples:

> This is My commandment, that you love one another as I have loved you. Greater love has no one than this, than to lay down one's life for his friends [philos].
>
> —John 15:12–13

The Greek word translated *friends* in this passage is *philos*, from which we derive names like Philadelphia, the city of "brotherly love." Even the love of God is referred to on occasion as *philanthropia* in Scripture: "But when the kindness and the *love* of God our Savior toward man appeared...He saved us" (Titus 3:4–5). God is the original philanthropist, a lover of mankind, full of goodwill toward His creation.

Friendship is a relationship between equals where openness and sharing of mind and heart are the norm. In friendship there is respect for individuality and an inclusive atmosphere that appreciates a person's intrinsic worth. How humbling it is to consider that the Son of God wants to call us friends. The patriarch, Abraham, is called in Scripture "the friend of God" (James 2:23). The divine love of God wants to embrace His creation in the bonds of friendship, raising us to "sit together in the heavenly places in Christ Jesus" (Eph. 2:6). Of course, we will never be His equal; yet, He desires to call us "friends." Jesus said to His disciples: "No longer do I call you servants, for a servant does not know what his master is doing; but I have called you friends, for all things that I heard from My Father I have made known to you" (John 15:15).

The characteristics Jesus taught of friendship involve a sharing of heart and mind as well as a willingness to "lay down one's life for his friends" (v. 13). There are no perfect people in friendship. Yet, between friends there is a bond that demands loyalty and respect. Jesus laid down His life for His friends, literally. And there is in true friendship a willingness to expend ourselves for another, to give time to listening, caring, giving, and praying for specific needs.

Eros: "falling in love"

C. S. Lewis differentiates between the terms *sexuality* and *eros*, preferring to refer to eros as "sexuality which develops within 'love.' Sexuality may operate without Eros or as part of Eros. Eros makes a man want, not any woman, but a particular woman. In some mysterious but quite indisputable fashion the lover desires the Beloved herself, not the pleasure she can give...Without Eros, sexual desire, like every other desire, is a fact about *ourselves*. Within Eros, it is rather about the Beloved"[23].

If we allow the pleasures of appreciation to be expressed in eros, married love will not be selfish. Though eros qualifies as a need love, it can become a gift love as we learn to truly appreciate the worth and beauty of our mate as a gift of God to us. Need love says to a woman, "I cannot live without you," while gift love longs to give her happiness, comfort, protection, and if possible, wealth. Appreciative love gazes and holds its breath and is silent, rejoicing that such a wonder should exist, even if not for him. In expressing that appreciation, a man will desire to give to his spouse in ways that will truly satisfy *her* needs, as well as his own, within eros love.[24]

Lewis outlines the seriousness of entering into eros love, giving several reasons to consider it carefully:

- First, theologically, because this is the body's share in marriage, which, by God's choice, is the mystical image of the union between God and man

- Secondly, on the moral level, in view of the obligations involved and the incalculable momentousness of being a parent and ancestor

- Thirdly, it has a great emotional seriousness in the minds of the participants.[25]

Again, we are reminded of the scriptural standard for eros love: "Marriage is honorable among all, and the bed undefiled; but fornicators and adulterers God will judge" (Heb. 13:4). Those who submit their marriages to God can enjoy the blessing of God on their lives. All of the "natural" loves must be submitted to the divine love of God—charity— if they are to express the beauty for which they were intended. C. S. Lewis concurs:

Only those into which Love Himself has entered will ascend to Love Himself. And these can be raised with Him only if they have, in some degree and fashion, shared His death; if the natural element in them has submitted—year after year or in some sudden agony—to transmutation...In my love for wife or friend the only eternal element is the transforming presence of Love Himself...We were made for God. Only by being in some respect like Him, only by being a manifestation of His beauty, lovingkindness, wisdom or goodness, has any earthly Beloved excited our love...By loving Him more than them we shall love them more than we now do.[26]

C. S. Lewis ends his classic volume on love by revealing the greatest gift God can give to a man or woman: a supernatural *appreciative* love:

> He [God] can awake in man, towards Himself, a supernatural Appreciative love. This is of all gifts the most to be desired. Here, not in our natural loves, nor even in ethics, lies the true centre of all human and angelic life. With this all things are possible.[27]

That divine gift love that desires only to give glory to the Creator in all of life is truly a state to be coveted. It takes the Christian beyond the relationship of need love with His God. Lewis admits his own inability to describe such divine love or to even know if he has ever tasted it himself. Yet, even to imagine its existence makes the beauty of all other loves pale in comparison.

Religious affections

Jonathan Edwards, noted theologian and preacher of the eighteenth century, wrote a two hundred-page treatise called "Religious Affections." This classic work expresses the essence of Christianity. In it, he answers the question, "What are the distinguishing qualifications of those that are in favor with God and entitled to His eternal rewards?" He puzzles over the fact that there is so much good and so much bad in the church; even in a good Christian, observing the divine and precious as well as corruption and hypocrisy in individual saints. To answer this enigma, he shows that the Bible teaches that religious affections pertain to the heart and go deeper than mere decisions and inclinations of the mind and soul. And he concludes that religious affections are more important than decisions because affections determine decisions.[28]

For example, resolutions made at the beginning of a New Year may be good decisions, but often fail to affect the life for very long. But when your affections are changed, through a genuine change of heart, there is an inner resource of life that dramatically transforms the expression of your life. God declared through the prophet Ezekiel: "I will give you a new heart and put a new spirit within you; I will take the heart of stone out of your flesh and give you a heart of flesh. I will put My Spirit within you and cause you to walk in My statutes, and you will keep My judgments and do them" (Ezek. 36:26–27). A heart of stone is insensitive and unresponsive; a heart of flesh is sensitive and inclined toward God. That change of heart results in religious affections that transform the mind and express the love of God in every situation of life.

True religious affections desire to obey the Ten Commandments out of a transformed heart filled with God's love, not from a mere decision of the mind and will to do what is right. Often the religious spirit supplants religious affections, demonstrating self-righteousness, exclusivity, and pride. These sinful attributes are opposed to the classic Christian walk, which is to be characterized by humility, servanthood, and stewardship of every gift of God. Classic Christians don't follow 613 rules; we respond from our hearts to the love of God with exceeding gratitude and deep appreciation for who Christ is and the work of the Holy Spirit in our lives.

Jesus, conversing with the Samaritan woman at the well, explained to her that the living water He gives becomes "a fountain of water springing up into everlasting life" (John 4:14). And He also declared on one occasion, "Out of the abundance of the heart the mouth speaks. A good man out of the good treasure of his heart brings forth good things, and an evil man out of the evil treasure brings forth evil things" (Matt. 12:34–35). When you choose to go beyond the natural, mental assent in regard to your faith in God, and to "love the Lord your God with all your heart, with all your soul, and with all your mind" (Matt. 22:37), you engage the religious affections that express eternal life. This heart desire makes you hunger to read the Word of God, to delight in prayer, to desire to commune with God, and to serve Him in everyday life.

Jesus taught that all the commandments of God hinge on this one great commandment. Loving God "with all your heart, with all your soul, and with all your mind" speaks of the depth of your being, the fountain of your life, the deepest passions, greatest desires, and inclination of life being motivated by love for God. To experience that depth of religious affection requires a profound work of the Holy Spirit in a heart to change its stony, insensitivity into sensitive responsiveness. That work is promised to one who comes to God, believing "that He is, and that He is a rewarder of those who diligently seek Him" (Heb. 11:6).

God's love is so compelling that throughout history men and women have been martyred for love of Him. They have sailed to distant lands and suffered all manner of hardship to share His love with heathen tribes. They have left every other love to pursue the divine love of God. One of the most profound descriptions of love I have found was written in the late 1600s by Scotsman Henry Scougal to a friend. He concluded that the nature of wholeness lies in union of the soul with God. We must be branches joined to the Vine, which is Christ, and draw our life and strength from Him (see John 15:5). The capacity of love is so immense that it can only be satisfied with an infinite, perfect object.[29]

There is an exchange of hearts in love. In that exchange you are refreshed and enlivened by the joy God possesses and the delight He shows in you. God's love to you far exceeds the love you can offer Him, yet even the tears of repentance and its sorrows have a sacred sweetness when you pour them out before the divine Beloved. Once your soul finds its satisfaction in God, then you can live from the strength of that felicity. You are renewed and healed.[30]

Your love to others becomes an overflow of this love and delight in God. If you start at the wrong place and do not seek love and satisfaction in God first, you will experience perpetual frustration, because no human being can bring this satisfaction. When God Himself is your first love and chief portion, then you find overflowing joy and love within to channel to others, independent of their appreciation. This is the new life![31]

Perhaps the songwriter captures best the tenacious, seeking love of God that draws hearts to Himself:

O Love that wilt not let me go,
I rest my weary soul in thee;
I give thee back the life I owe,
That in Thine ocean depths its flow may richer, fuller be.[32]

I encourage you to seek agape, the divine love of God, by reading His Word and surrendering yourself and your relationships (or the lack of them) to Him. As you set yourself to seek His face in prayer, He will answer your heart cry and satisfy your "love-starved" soul with a love that will not let you go. And He will anoint your DNA to express all the natural loves in a redemptive, godly way.

Jesus said... "for the Son of Man has come to seek and to save

that which was lost."

—LUKE 19:10

TRACING THE HAND OF THE CREATOR

Although the universe seems to measure between ten and twenty billion light-years across, it is not possible for us to locate its center. We are floating somewhere in the middle of a pretty big cosmic bubble. The universe contains a trillion trillion trillion trillion tons of matter (10^{56} grams). In addition, the observable universe contains a hundred million trillion trillion trillion trillion trillion trillion elementary particles (10^{80}).[1]

SALVATION OF MANKIND

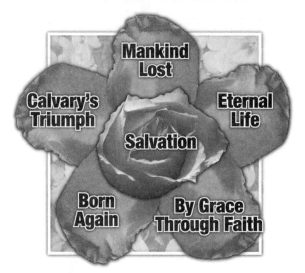

Mankind Lost

Calvary's Triumph

Eternal Life

Salvation

Born Again

By Grace Through Faith

Our galaxy, the Milky Way, is one of the smaller galaxies of the universe. Besides our small galaxy, the universe contains at least a hundred billion other known galaxies. Each is peppered with about a hundred billion stars. Galaxies come in all shapes and sizes. Most are either elliptical (shaped like a racetrack) or irregular (no distinct shape). The Milky Way galaxy is an example of a spiral galaxy, which is flat and round like a pancake. The spiral spins rapidly around the center nucleus like a pinwheel in a hurricane. Our Earth, located on a distant arm of the spiral, spins rotationally at a half-million miles an hour.[2]

Nobel laureate physicist, Charles Townes, believes that intelligence must have been involved in creating the laws of the universe. He concludes: "As a religious person, I strongly sense...the presence and actions of a creative being far beyond myself and yet always personal and close by."[3] Dr. Swenson concludes: "God has allowed us the privilege of living in a time when great mysteries are being uncovered. No previous era knew about quantum mechanics, relativity, subatomic particles, supernovas, ageless photons, or DNA. They all reveal the stunning genius of a God who spoke a time-space-matter-light universe into existence, balanced it with impossible requirements of precision, and then gifted it with life. Does it not stir your heart to realize that in a millionth of a second, a trillion atoms in your body turn over—and yet somehow God makes it work? Does it not deepen your reverence to realize that God is more impressive than a magnetic cloud thirty million miles in diameter careening through space at a million miles an hour, or a neutron star that weighs hundreds of millions of tons per teaspoon? Does it not give you pause to think that of the ten thousand trillion (10^{16}) words spoken by humans since the dawn of time, God heard every one, remembers every one, can recite them all backwards from memory, and even knew them before they were spoken?...The truths of Scripture, the life of Christ, the discoveries of science—all should combine to lift us heavenward."[4] Charles Townes observes: "People of faith often tend to fear science or even dread it. My feeling, however, is quite different. Science is thrilling. True science is a friend of Truth. Truthful science always tells us much about the power, precision, design, and sovereignty of God—details we learn nowhere else."[5]

Mankind lost

God created everything we see around us. He is the creative Genius of all that scientists are only recently discovering in astounding detail under high-powered microscopes and through powerful telescopes. We have mentioned that when God created mankind He placed them in a beautiful garden. They were given dominion over all of creation and the task to tend the garden. Their greater purpose was to enjoy communion with God continually.

Tragically, through man's determined disobedience to the "laws" of creation given him by his Creator, mankind suffered the loss of that intimate relationship he enjoyed with God. As a result, this alienation from our Creator-God became a tragic reality, not just for that first couple, but for all people who would be born to them.

In our everyday lives, we often take for granted those relationships or possessions we consider most precious to us. Sadly, we often do not appreciate their value until they are taken from us by tragic circumstances. However, God knew before He formed man that He would lose the precious relationship He delighted in and enjoyed with the first couple, Adam and Eve. Scripture clearly states that God's remedy for mankind's disobedience was already in place at the time of creation.

In the Book of Revelation, Christ is called "the Lamb slain from the foundation of the world" (Rev. 13:8). In order to enjoy the "family" He wanted, God knew, even before He created mankind, that He would have to sacrifice His only begotten Son. Yet, so great was His desire to express His love in a reciprocal manner with mankind, that He chose to endure the suffering our redemption would require.

Throughout the Old Testament, God can be understood through types and shadows of this ultimate redemption, which He revealed through the patriarchs and the prophets. It was only a matter of time in the sovereignty of God that He would make His redemption complete—buying back the treasure He had lost in mankind through the death of His only begotten Son, Jesus Christ. The Book of Hebrews explains:

> God, who at various times and in various ways spoke in time past to the fathers by the prophets, has in these last days spoken to us by His Son, whom He has appointed heir of all things, through whom also He made the worlds.
>
> —HEBREWS 1:1–2

Calvary's triumph

It will perhaps require all of eternity for us to appreciate the profound sacrifice that Christ, the Son of God, became for us at Calvary. The fact of His crucifixion and the unimaginable suffering and agony in the manner of His death is terrible enough. Yet, we must consider that this was the Lamb of God, the perfect One, who had never known the terrible curse of sin. Yet, He *became* sin for us so that we could be freed from its curse: "For He made Him who knew no sin to be sin for us, that we might become the righteousness of God in Him" (2 Corinthians 5:21). The deep horror of having the sin of all of mankind laid on the sinless Christ to satisfy the justice of God simply cannot be fathomed by our human spirit. We can only bow our heads and our hearts at the foot of the cross and worship in deep gratitude for the peace of God we enjoy, as believers, because Christ loved us enough to lay down His life for us.

Scripture indicates that the prophets of old could not grasp the magnitude of this redemption, and that even angels desire to know the things that pertain to our salvation (1 Pet. 1:12). Yet, God made His plan of redemption so simple that it is possible for a child to receive the gift of salvation.

Born again

Religious leaders of the day did not understand the salvation that Jesus came to bring. Nicodemus, a religious leader and teacher came to Jesus by night to ask honest questions regarding the kingdom of God. Jesus led him to the real question for which he wanted an answer: "Most assuredly, I say to you, unless one is born again, he cannot see the kingdom of God" (John 3:3). When Nicodemus questioned how a grown man could be born again, Jesus explained:

> Jesus answered, "Most assuredly, I say to you, unless one is born
> of water and the Spirit, he cannot enter the kingdom of God.
> That which is born of the flesh is flesh, and that which is born

of the Spirit is spirit. Do not marvel that I said to you, 'You must be born again.' The wind blows where it wishes, and you hear the sound of it, but cannot tell where it comes from and where it goes. So is everyone who is born of the Spirit."

—JOHN 3:5–8

At the risk of losing his influence and possibly even his position as leader among the Jews, Nicodemus had sought a secret audience with Jesus. And Jesus astonished this spiritual leader by explaining the essence of salvation, which means being born again. He explained that this new birth was a spiritual birth, which would allow one to enter into the kingdom of God. And he taught that relationship with God could only be restored through this new birth experience.

By grace through faith

Salvation is not accomplished by doing good works or religious activities; it is received by placing your faith in the Son of God. After the resurrection of Jesus, the apostles understood more fully the way of salvation and preached it to the people. When the multitudes asked Peter on the Day of Pentecost what they must do to be saved, he replied, "Repent, and…be baptized in the name of Jesus Christ for the remission of sins; and you shall receive the gift of the Holy Spirit" (Acts 2:38). Later, when addressing the Sanhedrin, the Jewish religious leaders, Peter asserted: "Nor is there salvation in any other, for there is no other name under heaven given among men by which we must be saved" (Acts 4:12).

And the apostle Paul explained how to be forgiven and enter new life with God: "If you confess with your mouth the Lord Jesus and believe in your heart that God has raised Him from the dead, you will be saved. For with the heart one believes unto righteousness, and with the mouth confession is made unto salvation" (Rom. 10:9–11). It is of ultimate importance that you understand salvation is through faith in the grace of God alone; it does not depend on your good works.

Even some early Christians became confused on this point, and the apostle Paul wrote an entire letter to the church of the Galatians to correct their theology. They were so accustomed to "practicing" their religion according to the Law of Moses, that they were trying to add their "faith" in Christ to the legal practices they had known. It simply cannot be done. While Scripture teaches that we are saved to do good works, those good works do not save us. Our good works could never redeem us back to relationship with God. That redemption was much too costly, requiring the death of His only begotten Son. According to Scripture, we are restored to relationship with God for eternity by grace, through faith in Jesus Christ:

> For by grace you have been saved through faith, and that not of yourselves; it is the gift of God, not of works, lest anyone should boast. For we are His workmanship, created in Christ Jesus for good works, which God prepared beforehand that we should walk in them.
>
> —Ephesians 2:8–10

We are born again in the moment we repent of our sin and confess Christ as our Lord and Savior. Our spirit becomes alive to the Spirit of God, who comes to do His work in us, revealing to us the wonderful life and truth of God. It is a spiritual reality that the power of God comes into our lives in the new birth to begin our deliverance from the power of sin.

However, salvation is also an ongoing work of the Spirit in our lives. Our soul, which is our intellect, will, and emotions, must be continually transformed by the power of the Holy Spirit as we yield to the truth He reveals to us. The sanctification, or ongoing deliverance of our souls from the power of sin, requires that we become disciples of Christ, obeying His commands. The apostle Paul teaches this doctrine of salvation:

> For the grace of God that brings salvation has appeared to all men, teaching us that, denying ungodliness and worldly lusts, we should live soberly, righteously, and godly in the present age, looking for the blessed hope and glorious appearing of our great God and Savior Jesus Christ, who gave Himself for us, that He might redeem us from every lawless deed and purify for Himself His own special people, zealous for good works.
>
> —Titus 2:11–14

Of course, we cannot live righteous lives in our own strength. It is the Holy Spirit who convicts us of sin. As we obey the Word of God, He cleanses us and gives us a new heart of obedience to Him. He changes our old patterns of thinking and doing, and sheds the love of God abroad in our hearts (Rom. 5:5). The apostle Peter explains:

> Since you have purified your souls in obeying the truth through the Spirit in sincere love of the brethren, love one another fervently with a pure heart, having been born again, not of corruptible seed but incorruptible, through the word of God which lives and abides forever.
>
> —1 Peter 1:22–23

Eternal life

All of Scripture reveals the heart of our eternal Father who longs to enjoy fellowship with His highest creation, mankind, forever. Perhaps the poignancy of Jesus' words in His high priestly prayer just before His crucifixion best expresses this longing of the Godhead:

> Father, the hour has come. Glorify Your Son, that Your Son also may glorify You, as You have given Him authority over all flesh,

that He should give eternal life to as many as You have given Him. And this is eternal life, that they may know You, the only true God, and Jesus Christ whom You have sent.

—John 17:1–3

Simply stated, eternal life is *knowing* God. To know Him involves properly appreciating who He is, who He made you to be, and all that He has given you for life. As we continually yield our lives to Christ, we can enjoy the quality of eternal life now, in this troubled world, which will prepare our hearts to live with God forever. These desirable qualities of eternal life are described in Scripture as peace, joy, righteousness, strength, and rest for our souls. Love, patience, perseverance, and every other named characteristic of God are worked in us as we yield our souls to His redemptive process, seeking Him to anoint our hearts and lives.

There are those who dare not assert that they will live with God forever; they cling to a vague hope that, if they are a good person, everything is all right between them and God. That is not the teaching of Scripture. Being born again into relationship with God is a decisive experience, followed by cultivating a new lifestyle of obedience to the Word of God. For the believer, life becomes an adventure into truth, and a satisfying relationship with the One who made them. It was John who made it supremely clear that we can know that we have eternal life: "These things I have written to you who believe in the name of the Son of God, that you may know that you have eternal life, and that you may continue to believe in the name of the Son of God" (1 John 5:13).

The supreme love of our heavenly Father permeates every facet of redemption. John Piper writes, "Every one of us desires forgiveness and an escape from hell to heaven, but heaven without Jesus is no salvation. Love is not a deed. Love is a reflex of the newly born heart responding to the beauty of God in Christ. A deed of love can be imitated, but a reflex of the heart cannot be. Love arises from the cell of the heart to the beauty of God in Christ. To truly love God we must delight in a relationship with God that satisfies. Loving God is delighting in, cherishing, savoring, treasuring, revering, and admiring God beyond any gift—life and health notwithstanding."[6] So great is the gift of His salvation of our souls that Scripture declares even angels desire to look into it (1 Pet. 1:12).

In [Christ] we have redemption through His blood, the forgiveness of sins, according to the riches of His grace which He made to abound toward us in all wisdom and prudence.

—Ephesians 1:7

And be kind to one another, tenderhearted, forgiving one another, even as God in Christ forgave you.

—Ephesians 4:32

Tracing the Hand of the Creator

Charles Darwin expressed doubt regarding his own theory of origins when he considered the marvel of the human eye. He said: "To suppose that the eye with all its inimitable contrivances for adjusting the focus to different distances, for admitting different amounts of light, and for the correction of spherical aberration, could have been formed by natural selection, seem, I confess, absurd in the highest degree"[1] The human eye, which mystified Darwin, is so sophisticated that it still eludes full explanation by modern science. All of the separate components of the body, as observed by twenty-first century scientists, would now be equally surprising to him as indications of deep design and divinely inspired complexity.[2]

FORGIVENESS

When Christ was crucified on the cross at Calvary, enduring unfathomable agony, He uttered these astounding words about those responsible for His death: "Father, forgive them for they do not know what they do" (Luke 23:34). Our first question might be, "What kind of love could forgive such undeserved cruelty?" Then we might wonder, "What did He see that others did not, that He could say, 'They do not know what they do'?"

Jesus could hear and feel the cruel mocking, cursing, and hatred being expressed by those who perpetrated His death. As "eyewitnesses" after the fact, we would conclude readily that His enemies did know exactly what they were doing. Yet, Jesus pleaded their ignorance and asked the Father to forgive their murderous intent. Obviously, He was "seeing" lost humanity from a higher perspective than we are able to do. He understood that in the darkness of their hearts, they were blinded to the spiritual realities that He came to restore to mankind through forgiveness.

In fact, Jesus had spoken of the blindness of the religious leaders of His day: "Let them alone. They are blind leaders of the blind. And if the blind leads the blind, both will fall into a ditch" (Matt. 15:14). Of course, He was not referring to a physical blindness, but to the inability to see spiritual truth. Later, the apostle Paul would identify the cause of the blindness of people's spiritual eyes: "If our gospel is veiled, it is veiled to those who are perishing, whose minds the god of this age has blinded, who do not believe, lest the light of the gospel of the glory of Christ, who is the image of God, should shine on them" (2 Cor. 4:3–4).

There are many people today who do not see the invisible attributes of a loving God through the visible manifestation of His creation, as God intended (see Rom. 1:18–32). Their spiritual eyes are darkened by what they *think* they know. Jesus explained this phenomenon of spiritual blindness:

> The light of the body is the eye: therefore when thine eye is single, thy whole body also is full of light; but when thine eye is evil, thy body also is full of darkness. Take heed therefore that the light which is in thee be not darkness. If thy whole body therefore be full of light, having no part dark, the whole shall be full of light, as when the bright shining of a candle doth give thee light.
>
> LUKE 11:34–36, KJV

Jesus connected our natural sight with our spiritual understanding, admonishing us to avoid having an "evil eye." He declared that He is the light of the world: "I am the light of the world. He who follows Me shall not walk in darkness, but have the light of life" (John 8:12). Hundreds of years earlier, the psalmist cried out: "Open my eyes, that I may see Wondrous things from Your law" (Ps. 119:18). He was reading the law of God with his physical eyes, desiring to gain spiritual sight in order to know God.

In similar ways, all of our senses should be employed in knowing God. Ellen Vaughn, in her captivating book, *Radical Gratitude*, comments on the lavish "sensuality" of God revealed in nature and our desired response:

> The Scriptures are full of descriptions of what He sees, smells, hears, feels, tastes...[and] creation itself reflects the glory of God. The world quivers with sensory beauty of every kind, just as His nature pulses with truth, beauty, joy...As a great friend of ours has said, a thankful heart gives a greater sensitivity to beauties both divine and mundane. He often finds himself sitting still in the moment and looking at what's around him, processing it all with different gradations of appreciation, but using the same word throughout: 'Oh, Lord! I love my family. I love my house. I love the sky. I love this cup of coffee. I love You! Thank You!' That's not only gratitude, and love, and worship. It's called joy.[3]

Scripture confirms that every good gift comes from God (James 1:17). For example, one of the most precious gifts of God is your eyesight. Have you taken time to appreciate the wonderful gift of your eyesight? Have you considered how altered your lifestyle would be if you were unexpectedly blinded? The physical eye is one of the most complex marvels of creation known to man. Even Charles Darwin had to admit from his observations of the eye that his theory of origins, the evolution of life based on time and chance, could not adequately explain the complex functions of the human eye. (See eye sketch on page 215.)

Consider these awesome characteristics of your blue, brown, hazel, or green eyes:

- The eye makes one hundred thousand separate motions a day, and the eyelids will blink over four hundred million times in an average lifetime.

- The cornea is the initial light-focusing structure of the eye. The balance of corneal clarity—and, therefore, sight—is highly dependent upon the ability of each highly specialized corneal cell to control its own absorption of water, nutrients, and oxygen.

- The iris contracts and dilates to control passage of light to the back of the eye. It is the most data-rich structure in the body. An iris possesses 266 identifiable characteristics, compared to the rather scant thirty-five displayed by the hand's fingerprint, which is currently used for identification.

- After the focusing accomplished by the lens, light and images strike the retina, which blankets the back of the eye. The cells of the retina—rods for dim and peripheral vision, and cones for color and fine detail perception—translate light photons into electrical impulses for the brain. The retina's continuous "exposure" and "development" of its pictures would take a Cray supercomputer one hundred years to simulate what is occurring in the eye every second.[4]

These simple facts do not begin to describe the complexity of the eye, in terms of its potential for healing itself. The cornea itself consists of five layers. Within one layer, the endothelial cells are able to recognize disease and trauma at relative distances that would be equivalent to a mother in New York City responding to her child crying in San Diego. These forewarned cells then begin producing a new protective barrier at the Descemet's membrane near the back surface of the cornea as a preemptive repair mechanism that prevents perforation. With such a system in place, the cornea, the whole eye, and sight may be saved.

Yet, with such potential that our eyesight gives for precise perception of life, many grope blindly through life, almost as if they were physically blind. They do not see the towering oak tree as the sublime work of their Creator. They do not perceive their fellow man as precious, filled with the same potential for loving life as themselves. Their focus is on personal pleasure or other selfish pursuits, which deny appreciation for life on a higher level, according to the way Christ lived His life on Earth.

From Christ's spiritual perspective He could honestly pray, while suffering the agony of crucifixion and death for mankind on the cross, "Father, forgive them, for they do not know what they do" (Luke 23:34). He was filled with compassion to forgive the darkness, the spiritual blindness, in which they lived. Some Bible students believe Jesus' prayer was answered at Pentecost when many, perhaps even of those who mocked Him, were converted.

God's forgiveness for sin

Although it is true that we receive forgiveness of our sins through the shed blood of Jesus Christ, forgiveness is not first introduced to New Testament believers. Forgiveness is taught clearly in the Old Testament as well. Ever since Adam and Eve sinned in the Garden of Eden, which "blinded" them to relationship with God, God has been offering His forgiveness to those who have sinned against Him.

The first recorded blood sacrifice was made by God Himself, when He slew animals to make coats of skin to cover Adam and Eve's nakedness after they had disobeyed His command (see Gen. 3:21). Because of their sin, they began to experience the mystery of good and evil. They were expelled from the beauty and perfection of the garden in which He had placed them. Yet, even then, God Himself came to "cover" their nakedness and to atone for their sin.

For some, forgiveness of sin simply seems more than they can hope for. There are people who believe in Christ and His sacrifice on the cross but feel they are "too bad," their sin is too awful, and they don't deserve to be forgiven. The wonder of divine grace is that no one deserves to receive it; it is unmerited favor. Grace is a divine gift given by a loving God to a sinful world. The good news of the gospel is that "while we were still sinners, Christ died for us" (Rom. 5:8). Such is the unfathomable love of God. It is no wonder that when we experience salvation, we can only bow in worship before Him.

The apostle Paul lays claim to being the worst sinner: "This is a faithful saying and worthy of all acceptance, that Christ Jesus came into the world to save sinners, of whom I am chief" (1 Tim. 1:15). Yet, he also declared, "By the grace of God I am what I am, and His grace toward me was not in vain" (1 Cor. 15:10). He was not boasting in his sin, but rejoicing in the forgiveness he had received that transformed his life and revealed his destiny in life.

Some have not entered into the spiritual freedom that forgiveness brings because they cannot forgive themselves. R. T. Kendall, the pastor of Westminster Chapel in London, England for twenty-five years, wrote a powerful book called *Total Forgiveness*, in which he states:

> Forgiveness is worthless to us emotionally if we can't forgive ourselves...It certainly isn't *total* forgiveness unless we forgive ourselves as well as others. God knows this. This is why He wants us to forgive ourselves as well as to accept His promise that our past is under the blood of Christ...He wants to make it easy for us to forgive ourselves. That is partly why He gave us what is possibly Paul's most astonishing promise:

> And we know that all things work together for good to them that love God, to them who are the called according to his purpose.
> —Romans 8:28, kjv

God doesn't want us to continue to feel guilty, so He says, "Just wait and see. I will cause everything to work together for good to such an extent that you will be tempted to say that even the bad things that happened were good and right." Not that they were, of course, for the fact that all things work together for good doesn't mean necessarily that they were right at the time. But God has a way of making bad things *become* good.[5]

Each time we pray we can ask the Father to forgive us for our sin. And we must expect that He will be true to His Word and do it. Even the Old Testament psalmist understood the greatness of God's forgiving power:

> Bless the Lord, O my soul; And all that is within me, bless His holy name!…Who forgives all your iniquities, Who heals all your diseases, Who redeems your life from destruction…As far as the east is from the west, So far has He removed our transgressions from us.
>
> —Psalm 103:1, 3–4, 12

If you have difficulty forgiving yourself or others, I encourage you to begin to thank God in faith for the promise of His Word. As you do, the power of the Holy Spirit will be manifest in your life to make forgiveness a reality to your heart, cleansing you and filling you with His peace and joy.

Forgiveness for the offense of others

Another reason people sometimes do not enjoy the spiritual freedom of total forgiveness is because they have not forgiven others who have hurt them. Do you remember the phrase in the model prayer: "Forgive us our debts, As we forgive our debtors"? (See Matt. 6:9–13.) In order to enjoy spiritual freedom, you must choose to forgive those whom you consider "your debtors." People who offend you, who hurt and wound you deeply, must receive your forgiveness for you to be free. R. T. Kendall explains:

When everything in you wants to hold a grudge, point a finger and remember the pain, God wants you to lay it all aside. You can avoid spiritual quicksand and experience the incredible freedom found in total forgiveness.[6]

After Jesus taught the disciples to pray the model prayer, He continued to talk to them about their need to forgive others:

> For if you forgive men their trespasses, your heavenly Father will also forgive you. But if you do not forgive men their trespasses, neither will your Father forgive your trespasses.
> —Matthew 6:14–15

Some may say that they have tried to forgive, but cannot rid themselves of the bad feelings and negative thoughts they have toward a person. Forgiveness, like any other godly act, must be done by the grace of God through faith. Forgiveness is a choice, not a feeling. After the right choice is made, feelings will begin to change. As believers, we can be sure that God will not ask us to do something that cannot be done. He is a gracious Father who provides all we need to become Christlike.

As we accept the truth of God's Word that promises, "all things work together for good" (Rom. 8:28), it will be easier to release others from our resentment, grudges, and bitterness. These negative emotional responses will do much more harm to ourselves than to anyone else.

Spiritual freedom

One example of a man who learned to walk in spiritual freedom by releasing the offenses of those against him was the Old Testament hero, Joseph. The second youngest son of Jacob, Joseph, was sold into slavery in Egypt by his own brothers. As a young man, he was his father's favorite son, the firstborn of Rachel, whom Jacob loved. However, Jacob's special treatment of this boy provoked bitter jealousy from his other sons. Then, to make matters worse,

Joseph had some dreams that he shared with his family, which made it look like he would rule over them. This evoked deep hatred from his brothers. Joseph's impudence could not be tolerated, so when they had a chance, the brothers sold him to a traveling caravan and lied to their father, telling him an animal had devoured his beloved son.

For years Joseph lived in exile, separated from his family and his homeland. Yet, God was with him and made him to prosper in his captivity. Then, the wife of his owner tried to seduce him, and when Joseph refused her, she lied about him. As a result, his owner had him thrown into prison. One can only imagine the anguish of a young man, intent on living a noble life that honored God, finding himself a prisoner in a foreign land. Betrayed by his brothers and maligned by his employer's wife, Joseph had good reason to become bitter.

Yet, God worked in Joseph's life and situation in such a powerful way that he was made ruler over Egypt, second only to Pharaoh. And God worked integrity into Joseph's heart in such a way that when his brothers came down to buy grain from him, he wept over them, treated them with respect, and was reconciled to them. He did not heap guilt upon them for their betrayal and the years of torment they had caused him. Instead, he forgave them and released them from guilt by telling them the real reason for his exile in Egypt:

> "But as for you, you meant evil against me; but God meant it for good, in order to bring it about as it is this day, to save many people alive. Now therefore, do not be afraid; I will provide for you and your little ones." And he comforted them and spoke kindly to them.
>
> —Genesis 50:20–21

Unforgiveness will destroy you, your relationship with the Lord, and your relationship with those around you. It is comforting to know that even the most hurtful thing that has happened to you can work for your good, if you choose to forgive. From his own painful experience, R. T. Kendall shares candidly how he lost his inner peace for many years because of unforgiveness for the offenses of others. He said he tried to pay more tithes, to pray two hours a day, to have others pray for him—all to no avail. The only way he found his peace restored was to forgive those he felt had wronged him. In his book, *Total Forgiveness*, Kendall lists seven steps to practicing total forgiveness, which should become a lifetime commitment for the believer:

- Make the deliberate and irrevocable choice not to tell anyone what they did (Prov. 17:9).

- Be pleasant to them should you be around them (John 20:19).

- If conversation ensues, say that which would set them free from guilt (Gen. 45:5).

- Let them feel good about themselves (Gal. 6:1).

- Protect them from their greatest fear (Gen. 45:9–14).

- Keep it up today, tomorrow, this year, and the next (Luke 6:37).

- Pray for them (Matt. 5:44).[7]

The Scriptures demonstrate that it is possible to face bitter experiences of life without becoming bitter, negative people. The grace of God will keep you in perfect peace as your mind is continually meditating on His love. As you choose to forgive, you will enjoy the complete forgiveness of the Father. And He will manifest His divine power in your soul to cleanse your heart from all negative feelings and thoughts toward others as well.

For I am not ashamed of the gospel of Christ, for it is the power of God to salvation...For in it the righteousness of God is revealed from faith to faith; as it is written, "The just shall live by faith."

—ROMANS 1:16–17

Tracing the Hand of the Creator

The statement, "The life is in the blood," is not only good theology, but also good biology. The body has sixty thousand miles of blood vessels, a distance nearly two and one-half times around the Earth at the equator. Red blood cells (RBCs) are of critical importance to life. Red blood cells are tiny but plentiful. We each make over two million RBCs every second. If we took them all out of our body and laid them side by side, they would go around the Earth at the equator four times.

The necessary element to healthy RBCs is oxygen. All fires require oxygen, including the energy-releasing fire within our cells. The body has an ingenious mechanism to transport oxygen into the tissues. When oxygen is inhaled into the respiratory tract, it snuggles up against the thinner-than-paper lining of the lung wall. Immediately on the other side of this wall are capillaries. The favorable diffusion coefficient attracts the oxygen molecule across the lining and into the capillary blood stream, where other mechanisms are needed to finally use the oxygen efficiently for sustaining life.[1]

IMPUTATION

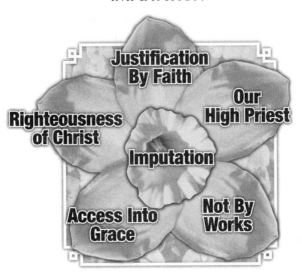

Perhaps you are not familiar with the theological significance of the term *imputation*. To *impute* means simply "to charge or credit to one's account."[2] The beauty of imputation, a major Christian doctrine, can only be understood as we look at the redemption Christ accomplished at Calvary. As we discussed in our devotional regarding salvation (Day 12), Jesus became sin for us when He hung on the cross to forgive our sin. God charged all our sin to His "account." Jesus paid the penalty for sin so that all who believe in Him would not have to suffer the penalty of eternal death for their sin. In that way, He credits—imputes—His righteousness to the account of all who receive Christ as their Savior.

The apostle Paul gives us a human example of imputation when he appealed to Philemon for mercy regarding Onesimus, his runaway slave. While Paul was a prisoner in chains, he had won Onesimus to Christ, calling him "my son Onesimus, whom I have begotten while in my chains" (Philem. 1:10). Now he was sending him home. He appealed to Philemon to receive Onesimus again, "no longer as a slave but more than a slave—a beloved brother" (v. 16), and if he owed him anything, Philemon was to charge it to Paul's account. (v. 18). The willingness of Paul to become liable for the debt of this runaway slave, imputing his guilt to himself reflects the grace of imputation—the undeserved favor—that we receive in salvation.

A scientific illustration of imputation may be derived from understanding the role of the white blood cells in your body. (See illustration on page 217.) Richard Swenson explains that while the red blood cells are superstars, the real heroes are the white blood cells and platelets. Red blood cells are tiny but plentiful. Under normal resting conditions, the RBC releases only about 25 percent of its oxygen to the tissues. It reserves the other 75 percent for strenuous work and exercise or unexpected emergencies.[3]

However fantastic the function of these red blood cells, the white blood cells and platelets are the real heroes because they die for us. They were born ready to die. Platelets are half the size of erythrocytes (red blood cells) and survive only a matter of days. This is why we must continually produce five million new platelets every second. They are critical for the clotting of the blood, rushing to the site of injury and heroically throwing their tiny bodies into the hole. The white blood cells are no less self-sacrificing. They are a vital link in our quest for daily survival against the billions of microbes continuously seeking to do us harm.

The body must have ready fifty billion white blood cells standing guard as active duty forces with a backup force hiding in the bone marrow of one hundred times as large to be activated in emergencies. These cells have one mission, one purpose—to give their lives in defense of ours.[4] In that sense they "impute" life to us, through no merit of our own doing, defending us continually against harmful microbes.

The righteousness of Christ

Similarly, God imputed life to us through the sacrifice of His Son: "But God demonstrates His own love toward us, in that while we were still sinners, Christ died for us. Much more then, having now been justified by His blood, we shall be saved from wrath through Him" (Rom. 5:8–9).

Our debt of sin and guilt, which we cannot atone for, was imputed to Christ, the sinless Lamb of God, who willingly paid the penalty for our sin through His death on Calvary. Just as the imputation of sin from one man, Adam, fell upon the whole human race, so the imputation of righteousness is applied through the sacrifice of the Son of God, Christ Jesus, to everyone who believes in Him. The apostle Paul explains:

> Therefore, as through one man's offense judgment came to all men, resulting in condemnation, even so through one Man's righteous act the free gift came to all men, resulting in justification of life. For as by one man's disobedience many were made sinners, so also by one Man's obedience many will be made righteous.
>
> —ROMANS 5:18–19

If we do not grasp this beautiful reality of imputed righteousness, we cannot fully appreciate the sacrifice of Christ that was necessary for our salvation. Not only that, but we will try to "save ourselves" by our own goodness, our works, or another human standard for "earning" eternal life. If you have been involved in this erroneous way of thinking, I urge you to consider the wonder of the divine grace that is offered to you by Christ. Your own efforts can never save you or change your sinful ways. Only by yielding to the power of the precious Holy Spirit and receiving the imputed righteousness of Christ can you be changed into His likeness.

Before Christ came, Old Testament saints understood that to be righteous in the eyes of God, they had to bring a blood sacrifice of a spotless lamb to atone for their sins and show their trust in the coming Messiah. The New Testament explains that these sacrifices could not really forgive sin. They only "rolled it back" until the time when the Lamb of God, the sinless One, would come and satisfy the justice of God against sin once and for all. When Christ came, He lived in perfect obedience to His Father, being filled with the Spirit, and then lay down His life so that our sin and guilt before a holy God would be imputed to Him. Only in that way could mankind be redeemed from the curse of sin. Scripture declares:

> For all have sinned and fall short of the glory of God, being justified freely by His grace through the redemption that is in Christ Jesus, whom God set forth as a propitiation by His blood, through faith, to demonstrate His righteousness, because in His forbearance God had passed over the sins that were previously committed, to demonstrate at the present time His righteousness, that He might be just and the justifier of the one who has faith in Jesus.
>
> —ROMANS 3:23–26

Justification by faith

Martin Luther nailed his ninety-five theses on the door of the church in Wittenberg, Germany in 1517 and reclaimed for the church the lost truth of "justification by faith." The Catholic church had become corrupt in its approach to forgiveness for sin, charging large sums of money (indulgences) to its parishioners in order for their sins to be remitted. As a sincere priest seeking for divine truth, Martin Luther read Scripture to find peace for his own soul. As he read the apostle Paul's epistle to the Romans, suddenly he understood that true righteousness was possible through faith in Christ alone. Martin Luther wrote of his wonderful revelation of the mercy and grace of God:

> I greatly longed to understand Paul's Epistle to the Romans, and nothing stood in the way but that one expression, 'the righ-

teousness of God,' because I took it to mean that righteousness whereby God is righteous and deals righteously in punishing the unrighteous. Night and day I pondered until...I grasped the truth that the righteousness of God is that righteousness whereby, through grace and sheer mercy, he justifies us by faith. Thereupon I felt myself to be reborn and to have gone through open doors into paradise. The whole of Scripture took on a new meaning, and whereas before 'the righteousness of God' had filled me with hate, now it became to me inexpressible sweet in greater love. This passage of Paul became to me a gateway to heaven.

—Martin Luther[5]

In 1520, Martin Luther wrote a lengthy treatise, "Concerning Christian Liberty," which he delivered as an address to the German nobility. In it he explained clearly how true faith results in the highest worship of the soul:

Thus the soul, in firmly believing the promises of God, holds Him to be true and righteous; and it can attribute to God no higher glory than the credit of being so. The highest worship of God is to ascribe to Him truth, righteousness, and whatever qualities we must ascribe to one in whom we believe. In doing this the soul shows itself prepared to do His whole will; in doing this it hallows His name, and gives itself up to be dealt with as it may please God. For it cleaves to His promises, and never doubts that He is true, just, and wise, and will do, dispose, and provide for all things in the best way. Is not such a soul, in this its faith, most obedient to God in all things? What commandment does there remain which has not been amply fulfilled by such an obedience? What fulfilment can be more full than universal obedience? Now this is not accomplished by works, but by faith alone.[6]

Through his rebirth experience, Martin Luther understood that true righteousness was imputed by God to man through the death and resurrection of Christ. Faith in Christ alone could make a man righteous, and that faith would evoke the most complete obedience possible for a believer.

Access into grace

The apostle Paul explains that Abraham was considered righteous in God's eyes because of his faith. God told Abraham that he and Sarah would have a son, even though they were past the years of childbearing. Paul declares: "[Abraham] did not waver at the promise of God through unbelief, but was strengthened in faith, giving glory to God, and being fully convinced that what He had promised He was also able to perform. *And therefore 'it was accounted to him for righteousness'*" (Rom. 4:20–22). Then Paul explains that all believers are counted righteous by faith in Christ alone:

> Now it was not written for his sake alone that it was imputed to him, but also for us. It shall be imputed to us who believe in Him who raised up Jesus our Lord from the dead, who was delivered up because of our offenses, and was raised because of our justification. Therefore, having been justified by faith, we have peace with God through our Lord Jesus Christ, through whom also we have access by faith into this grace in which we stand.
> —ROMANS 4:23–25; 5:1–2

Martin Luther declared: "Either sin is with you, lying on your shoulders, or it is lying on Christ, the Lamb of God. Now if it is lying on your back, you are lost; but if it is resting on Christ, you are free, and you will be saved. Now choose what you want."[7] Those who do not "choose" to receive the imputation of Christ's righteousness by faith in Him alone find themselves "trying harder" to live a Christian life—and failing miserably.

Not by works

We have seen that righteousness is not imputed to us because of our good works. The apostle Paul declared: "For by grace you have been saved through faith, and that not of yourselves; it is the gift of God, not of works, lest anyone should boast" (Eph. 2:8–9). Even the faith we need to be saved is a gift of God, according to Scripture. Theologians explain imputation as our only hope of the Christian's acceptance by God:

> The great theme of the book of Romans has to do with the doctrinal expression of imputation of the righteousness of God to the believer as it pertains to his salvation. It is quite obvious, therefore, that this truth is of great consequence to the Christian's salvation. The Pauline epistles in general clearly show that this phase of imputation is the groundwork of the Christian's acceptance and standing before an infinitely holy God. Only this righteousness can find acceptance for salvation, and through it alone one may enter heaven.
>
> The pregnant phrase "the righteousness of God" (Rom. 1:17; 3:22; 10:3) signifies not merely that God Himself is righteous but that there is a righteousness that proceeds from God. Since no human being in God's eyes is righteous (3:10), it is clear that an imputed righteousness, the righteousness of God Himself, is sinful man's only hope of acceptance with the Holy One. Possessing this righteousness is the only thing that fits one for the presence of God (Phil. 3:9; Col. 1:12). By the believer's baptism by the Spirit "into Christ" this righteousness is made a legal endowment by virtue of the death of Christ.[8]

The righteousness of God is revealed in the perfect life of obedience that Jesus lived, which has been put to our account in God's courtroom. The apostle Paul explained: "By one Man's obedience many will be made righteous" (Rom. 5:19). Jesus is God, so it is God's righteousness that we receive as a divine gift through imputation. Paul concluded, "Those who receive abundance of grace and of the gift of righteousness will reign in life through the One, Jesus Christ" (Rom. 5:17).

> The beauty of imputation is that it reveals the unfathomable divine love of God. Because of God's love for His errant creation, mankind, He wanted to redeem us—buy us back—from the alienation caused by sin. C. S. Lewis says there is a divine parallel between creation and redemption. God didn't need to create us. He did it for His own enjoyment, to have a loving relationship with us. The same is true of redemption. He didn't need to give us Jesus as a Savior. He did it because He wanted to restore relationship with His people. God's free and giving heart made Him first create us and then later redeem us.[9]

As we meditate on the wonder of being reborn into newness of life through Christ Jesus and enjoying this justification with God through His imputed righteousness, our hearts can't help but overflow with gratitude and love. One songwriter expressed that love this way:

> My Lord has garments so wondrous fine,
> And myrrh their texture fills;
> Its fragrance reached to this heart of mine,
> With joy my being thrills.

> His life had also its sorrows sore,
> For aloes had a part;
> And when I think of the cross he bore,
> My eyes with tear-drops start.

> *Refrain:*
> Out of the ivory palaces,
> Into a world of woe,
> Only His great, eternal love,
> Made my Savior go.[10]

Our High Priest

Christ became our great High Priest, offering Himself as the sacrifice for our sin in order that we might have peace with God. We have mentioned that Scripture teaches the requirement of blood sacrifice for the forgiveness of sins. The Book of Hebrews declares: "And according to the law almost all things are purified with blood, and without shedding of blood there is no remission" (Heb. 9:22). For that reason, Christ had to shed His innocent blood for our sin. Scripture calls His sacrifice a "better" sacrifice than that of the blood of bulls and goats. Those sacrifices had to be offered by the high priest in the most holy place every year until Christ came and became the perfect High Priest:

> Seeing then that we have a great High Priest who has passed through the heavens, Jesus the Son of God, let us hold fast our confession. For we do not have a High Priest who cannot sympathize with our weaknesses, but was in all points tempted as we are, yet without sin. Let us therefore come boldly to the throne of grace, that we may obtain mercy and find grace to help in time of need.
>
> —Hebrews 4:14–16

There are many reasons why we worship our God and Creator, but for me the greatest reason is the realization of forgiveness of my sin. As I turn to Him in repentance, the shalom of God—His divine peace—that floods my soul with His forgiveness fills me with unutterable gratitude. Seeking to express that deep gratitude, I can only bow in humble worship and adoration of my Savior. He causes me to rest in His redemption, imputing His righteousness to my account by the power of the Holy Spirit. In that divine relationship with God Himself, my soul is filled with deep satisfaction.

For by grace you have been saved through faith, and that not of

yourselves; it is the gift of God, not of works, lest anyone should

boast.

—Ephesians 2:8–9

Tracing the Hand of the Creator

We breathe about twenty-three thousand times per day and six hundred thirty million times over an average life span. With each inhalation we breathe in 10^{22} molecules, more than a billion trillion with each lungful. This amounts to twenty-two pounds of air per day. After the air enters the lungs, the next step is to get it into the bloodstream. To accomplish this, the lungs first divide the breath into smaller portions and send each down a series of dividing wind tunnels. Finally the air arrives into different peripheral rooms where each molecule of oxygen can receive individual attention. A lack of oxygen leads to death, whether for individual cells, organs, or the entire body. The brain is heavily dependent on oxygen, and catastrophic consequences can happen after even a few minutes of oxygen deprivation.[1]

GRACE

Paleoanthropology is a branch of anthropology dealing with fossil man—the historical evidence of the evolution of humanity left in the fossils of ancient life. One of the major problems with paleoanthropology is that compared to all the fossils we have, only a minuscule number are believed to be of creatures ancestral to humans. Often, the fossils that do exist, purported to be of ancient human remains, are only a skull fragment or teeth. This fact gives a lot of elasticity in reconstructing the specimens to fit evolutionary theory. Hen Gee, the chief science writer for *Nature*, was quite candid in talking about this problem: "The intervals of time that separate fossils are so huge that we cannot say anything definite about their possible connection through ancestry and descent. Each fossil is an isolated point, with no knowable connection to any other given fossil, and all float around in an overwhelming sea of gaps."[2]

Gee admitted that all the fossil evidence for human evolution between ten and five million years ago—several thousand generations of living creatures—can be fitted into a small box. He concluded that the conventional picture of human evolution is "a completely human invention created after the fact, shaped to accord with human prejudices." Darwinists assume the story of human life is an evolutionary one, and then they plug the fossils into a preexisting narrative where they seem to fit. Some have even accused that "paleoanthropology has the form but not the substance of a science."[3]

Such shadows of scientific reasoning have made scientists like Jonathan Wells declare bluntly, "My conclusion is that the case for Darwinian evolution is bankrupt. The evidence for Darwinism is not only grossly inadequate, it's systematically distorted. Darwinism is merely materialistic philosophy masquerading as science, and people are recognizing it for what it is. I believe science is pointing strongly toward design. To me, as a scientist, the development of an embryo cries out, 'Design!'"[4]

From that conclusion of the origin of life, there is only one small step to discovering the Designer—a God of love who desires to make His creation a recipient of His divine grace. There are biblical terms that describe the work of God in our lives, which many believers never truly understand. They accept these words as part of their religious experience, perhaps echoing other believers, without ever fully appreciating their significance. *Grace* may be one of those ill-defined biblical terms.

Grace is divine favor

The divine grace of God, which can be translated as "favor," was first revealed in the Old Testament to the people of God. For example, Scripture declares, "Noah found grace in the eyes of the LORD" (Gen. 6:8). When the patriarch, Abraham, was visited by the Lord, he said, "My Lord, if I have now found favor [grace] in

Your sight, do not pass on by Your servant" (Gen. 18:3). In these and other passages in the Old Testament, the Hebrew word *chanan* (khaw-nan`) gives a wonderful word picture of the grace and favor of God. It means literally "to bend or stoop in kindness to an inferior; to favor, to bestow good upon."

As created beings, we are "inferior" to, even infinitely below, the Creator who made us. Yet, in His great kindness, He stoops down to give us His favor, to bestow His divine grace and kindness upon us. The goodness of God is beyond anything we can even imagine. Nothing compares to His love, His peace, His prosperity—the total well-being of body, mind, and spirit that He wants His children to experience.

Unfortunately, our human minds often cannot conceive of God without, inadvertently, "pulling Him down" to our size, making Him one of us. Ellen Vaughn captures the essence of this tendency to "humanize" God, diminishing His greatness, when she wrote:

> Far too often we trivialize the holy, perceiving God as an extension of ourselves. God is white, just like us. Or black, or Asian, or Hispanic, or whatever. He's from North America. Or not. God must be a Republican. Or a Democrat. Or most assuredly an Independent. We unconsciously assume He's whatever *we* are, just bigger, though He shares our little biases, quirks, and opinions. No. God is huge. Mysterious. Multidimensional... We live in a land that has largely lost a sense of holy reverence, let alone the transcendent. Most everything is assessed by the criterion, "how does it affect me?" In a supremely self-referential culture it's hard to conceive of anything that is so wholly Other.[5]

When we consider the grace of God, we must understand it is unlike any *human* characteristic we have observed or experienced. Meditating on the divine favor of God can fill our hearts with wonder and gratitude for His love for us. In the New Testament, the Greek word *charis* is translated "grace." It means "favor, joy, pleasure, and the divine influence upon the heart and its reflection in the life." A life that is filled with the grace of God will reflect all of these wonderful qualities of life.

Beloved pastor and author, David Jeremiah, described the grace of God:

> In Christ, the grace of God is made manifest. If love is the attribute that describes God the best, grace is the one that makes that love obtainable for us. Grace is the most radical concept ever to be introduced into this world. It is counterintuitive to human nature, challenging every human tendency and providing the solution for every human problem.
>
> Grace changes people as nothing else can do. It cleanses the sins of the past. It enables righteousness in the present. And one thing it does for certain: it constantly surprises us. For the essence of grace is surprise. There is nothing shocking about giving people exactly what they deserve. Grace subverts the rules and gives people what they *don't* deserve. It is motivated by the warmth of love rather than by cold calculation. Therefore, grace is always doing something we didn't expect.[6]

People did not expect the coming Messiah to be the apparent son of a carpenter. Yet, Jesus is described in Scripture as coming to us full of "grace and truth" (John 1:17). His life reflected the love of God as He revealed the grace of God, the Father, to the world. The apostle Paul would write to believers: "For you know the grace of our Lord Jesus Christ, that though He was rich, yet for your sakes He became poor, that you through His poverty might become rich" (2 Cor. 8:9). The riches of God's grace are not something we can ever earn; they are to be received by faith in Christ: "Through whom also we have access by faith into this grace in which we stand" (Rom. 5:2). David Jeremiah explains:

The word *access* is only used three times in the New Testament, and it always refers to the believer's access to God through Jesus Christ. Grace is God's riches lavished upon those of us who, only moments before, stood accused. The prisoner on death row, of all people, has won the grand sweepstakes: the unsought, undeserved, and unconditional love of God.[7]

Jesus taught that whoever committed sin was a slave to sin (John 8:34). Then He declared, "Therefore if the Son makes you free, you shall be free indeed" (John 8:36). "Free indeed" is a wonderful description of a life filled with the grace and favor of God. For believers, remembering our rescue from slavery to sin should fill us with continual gratitude. Ellen Vaughn wrote:

> We do well to meditate on the cross. Not the small, tasteful gold jewelry we might wear, but the big, bloody one on which Jesus died. The cross that delivered us from unending agony, flame, regret beyond imagining, dark terrors beyond comprehension. Christ's blood and His own torture saved us from our sin…Psalm 107 tells us that thankfulness to God should constantly be on the lips of those whom He has saved. It begins with these words: "Let the redeemed of the Lord say so, whom He has redeemed from the hand of the adversary" (Ps. 107:2).[8]

As finite human beings, we cannot expect to fully grasp the profound grace that caused Christ to come to Earth as a man and lay down His life for us. Yet, we can revel in the wonder of His coming and be filled with gratitude for the saving grace He has made available to us.

Saved by grace

In our devotional on *Faith*, we discussed the spiritual reality that we are saved by grace through faith: "For by grace you have been saved through faith, and that not of yourselves; it is the gift of God, not of works, lest anyone should boast" (Eph. 2:8). In light of the biblical definition of *grace*, we could paraphrase that verse: "For by the *divine influence working in our lives and the kindness of God to bestow His goodness on us*, you have been saved through faith." Scripture explains clearly that grace is also a gift of God given to us without merit.

Every conflict and destructive influence of sin has been defeated by the wonderful sacrifice of Christ on the cross in order to bestow salvation on us (see Day 12). All we have to do is trust Christ and receive His saving grace to know freedom from sin. In return, He gives to us His Father's kingdom of righteousness, peace, and joy in the Holy Ghost (Rom. 14:17). As we gratefully receive the kingdom of God into our lives, we recognize a different spirit in us toward life. We begin to experience the rest and peace—shalom—of God. And instead of being cynical and uncaring, we begin to sense the love of God for others as well.

Growing in grace

Not only does the grace of God save us from sin, it also keeps us in the love of God, protecting us from the destructive forces that come into our lives through life's daily challenges. The apostle Peter understood that we are "kept by the power of God through faith" (1 Pet. 1:5). And the apostle Paul declared: "by the grace of God I am what I am" (1 Cor. 15:10). He wrote to Titus of the keeping power of that grace: "For the grace of God that brings salvation has appeared to all men...that He might redeem us from every lawless deed and purify for Himself His own special people, zealous for good works" (Titus 2:11, 14).

The immune system of our physical body provides an excellent analogy of the protecting power of divine grace over our spiritual lives. It performs its many roles, including an advance warning system, guard and barrier, and a war machine, with more precision than an atomic clock. It is difficult to fathom the complexity, harmony, intricacy, and integration on multiple levels demonstrated in even the "simplest" feat of your body's triumph over infection and disease. Yet, it is absolutely clear to scientists that a healthy immune system is the definition of survival in the world in which we live.[9] Receiving the grace of God daily for our spiritual health is just as necessary to our survival. The threats against our spiritual life are as real as those against our physical bodies, and can be even more destructive.

To continue the analogy, the human organism faces attack from a wide variety of infectious agents from the moment of conception. From the very first instructions in the zygote's DNA, the fully developed immune system mounts a warfare that includes defensive structures at macroscopic and microscopic levels. The infectious agents that concern us, and can kill us, are nearly innumerable. Pathogens, which are microbes that invade and cause disease, fall into four categories: bacteria, fungi, parasites, and viruses. Protecting the body from pathogens or harmful foreign substances is a complicated war for life and health. It means constant battling in a search-and-destroy mode. The immune system's twin goals are to clearly identify its enemy and then to destroy it without harming the body.[10]

In this rescue mission, the immune system functions similarly to the divine grace of God that identifies sin as the enemy of the soul and comes into your life to destroy its power. As you surrender your life to God, His divine grace enters with one primary goal—to save you from the power of sin. The grace of God becomes your "spiritual immune system," providing supernatural help for every facet of your life.

Your natural immune system exhibits unparalleled complexity and intelligence of design in several significant areas. On the molecular level, it has profound *recognition* capabilities, reacting against a foreign antigen, while permitting the normal cells to function. It exhibits *specificity* in its ability to discriminate between self and foreign, killing foreign without attacking self. It has a *memory*, which builds a resistance or immunity to known invaders so that on subsequent attacks, you will not get sick again. And your immune system displays *diversity*, in its ability to produce more than one hundred million different antigen receptors, each recognizing a different foreign antigen. Of course, the primary attribute and functioning principle for the immune system is *balance*—the appropriate response to injury—in order to maintain optimum health.[11]

Similarly, the grace of God works to protect your spiritual life from the moment you experience the new birth until your death, which ushers you into the presence of God for eternity. Of course, your cooperation is required to maintain physical as well as spiritual health. For physical health, you must aid the strength of your immune system by proper eating, exercise, and other practices vital to health. For spiritual health, you must "eat" the Word of God, exercise the attitude of gratitude, and obey the law of God. Yet, none of this would be possible if God did not take the initiative in our lives. David Jeremiah explains:

> Compare our Lord to the gods of all the world's religions and you'll find that grace is the difference maker. It is the x-factor that radically sets Him apart. Our God is "the God of all grace" (1 Peter 5:10). He is kind, benevolent, and longsuffering. We need not beg Him, bribe Him, or appease Him. He actually longs to bless us every single moment, every single day. He comes down to us rather than demanding that we climb the impossible ladder to infinity to reach Him. Grace is God taking the initiative.[12]

Whatever the temptations or trials we face in life, the Word of God promises that God's grace is sufficient to help us conquer it (see 2 Cor. 12:9). Still we need to understand that there is a servant stewardship required to nurture, not only our physical, but also our spiritual health.

I believe that one of the most important qualities of the Christian life is servant stewardship. The apostle Paul referred to himself often as a servant of God, as did the other apostles. And he wrote to other Christians "Having been set free from sin, you became slaves of righteousness" (Rom. 6:18). Scripture teaches that we are to be good stewards of the gift of eternal life, renewing our minds with the Word and keeping our body pure, as a temple for the presence of God. And we are not only to serve God with grateful hearts, but also to serve one another in the same manner.

Expressing gratitude to God provides a strong spiritual defense—an immunity—against the negative attitudes that tear down our spiritual, as well as our physical, health. Cultivating a grateful heart enables us to grow in grace and enjoy living in serenity rather than stress. How is this growth in grace accomplished? The apostle Peter explains:

> Therefore, laying aside all malice, all deceit, hypocrisy, envy, and all evil speaking, as newborn babes, desire the pure milk of the word, that you may grow thereby, if indeed you have tasted that the Lord is gracious.
>
> —1 Peter 2:1–3

Scripture is referred to as the Old and New *Testaments*. Testament literally means the "will" of God. As we read these divinely-inspired writings, we receive the revelation of God, His will, and His kingdom. And the Holy Spirit empowers us to do the will of God for our lives. While growing in the favor of God also requires prayer and fasting and other spiritual disciplines, without knowledge of the Word of God, none of these other "means of grace" can be effective. The psalmist declared: "Your word I have hidden in my heart, That I might not sin against You" (Ps. 119:11).

The apostle Paul instructs believers: "Walk in the Spirit, and you shall not fulfill the lust of the flesh" (Gal. 5:16). God gives us grace to walk in growing strength against sin as we daily choose His will for our lives. The apostle Paul also admonishes believers to walk in unity (Eph. 4:1–3), to walk in love (Eph. 5:2), to walk in the light (Eph. 5:8), and to walk in wisdom (Eph. 5:15). This divine grace of "walking" in the will of God will cause us to grow into maturity in our relationship with God.

Grace for the humble

Expressed gratitude for the grace of God leads to submission to His will in thought, word, and action. As we have seen, Christ humbled Himself to become our Savior, to a degree of humility we cannot fathom. And He was filled with the grace of God, reflecting the divine influence of God the Father in all He did. This divine grace of the condescension of the Godhead is witnessed throughout Scripture. A holy God is continually reaching out in grace—stooping in kindness to an inferior—to a lost and sinful human race. Scripture admonishes believers to cultivate this godly virtue:

> Be clothed with humility, for "God resists the proud, But gives grace to the humble." Therefore humble yourselves under the mighty hand of God, that He may exalt you in due time, casting all your care upon Him, for He cares for you.
>
> —1 Peter 5:5–7

While we cannot expound on all the evils of pride, it is important to at least note its destructive effect in the life of a person. The psalmist declared: "The wicked in his proud countenance does not seek God; God is in none of his thoughts" (Ps. 10:4). It is important to realize that a lack of appreciation for God and gratitude for His gift of life is rooted in the ugliness of pride. Pride that feels self-sufficient, needing nothing, will not desire to seek God, much less express gratitude and appreciation for Him.

The psalmist understood God's intolerance for the proud: "For You will save the humble people, But will bring down haughty looks" (Ps. 18:27). And he knew that God helps those who humble themselves before Him: "The humble He guides in justice, And the humble He teaches His way" (Ps. 25:9). Divine grace is given to those who recognize their need for divine favor and humble themselves to seek God. There is no fear to those who seek God, for He has promised to draw near to those who draw near to Him (see James 4:8).

Throne of God

Scripture teaches that there is a place to receive the grace of God—the throne of God. The Book of Hebrews encourages us:

> Let us therefore come boldly to the throne of grace, that we may obtain mercy and find grace to help in time of need.
>
> —HEBREWS 4:16

While we are not accustomed as Americans to relating to royalty, in biblical times people were quite aware of the awesome presence of kings, who ruled with absolute power from their thrones. The reigning monarch had authority to do what he would with his subjects, which often caused them to live in fear. In the days of Queen Esther, for example, as she approached the throne of her husband, the king, she feared for her life (Esth. 4:16; 5:1–2). She knew that, according to custom, if he did not hold out the golden scepter to welcome her, she would be killed.

Thankfully, we don't have a King who threatens us with possible death when we come into His presence. On the contrary, Jesus Christ, who is called the King of kings, is sitting at the right hand of the throne of God, making intercession for us (Rom. 8:34). He welcomes us into His presence, telling us to cast all of our care on Him because He cares for us (see 1 Pet. 5:7). And He assures us that as we come to His throne of grace we will find help in our time of need (Heb. 4:16). The words of the old hymn, *Majestic Sweetness Sits Enthroned*, capture some of the exquisite wonder of God's throne of grace and the favor given to His children:

> Majestic sweetness sits enthroned
> Upon the Saviour's brow;

His head with radiant glories crowned,
His lips with grace o'er-flow,
His lips with grace o'er-flow.

No mortal can with Him compare
Among the sons of men;
Fairer is He than all the fair
Who fill the heav'nly train,
Who fill the heavenly train.

He saw me plunged in deep distress
And flew to my relief;
For me He bore the shameful cross
And carried all my grief,
And carried all my grief.

To Him I owe my life and breath
And all the joys I have;
He makes me triumph over death
And saves me from the grave,
And saves me from the grave.[13]

As you meditate on the grace of God, dear reader, I encourage you to approach His throne of grace boldly to receive His divine favor for whatever your need is this day. There you will find the answer to the longing of your heart. And the peace that only God can give will bless your life—spirit, soul, and body.

Therefore, having been justified by faith, we have peace with God through our Lord Jesus Christ, through whom also we have access by faith into this grace in which we stand, and rejoice in hope of the glory of God.

—Romans 5:1–2

So then faith comes by hearing, and hearing by the word of God.

—Romans 10:17

Tracing the Hand of the Creator

The assumption ever since the ancient Greeks has been that the material world is eternal. Christians have denied this on the basis of biblical revelation that states clearly, "In the beginning, God created" (Gen. 1:1). However, secular science always assumed the universe's eternality. The significance of that assumption is that if the Earth is eternal, it had no beginning and there is no need to assume a Creator.[1]

So the discovery in the twentieth century that the universe is *not* an unchanging, eternal entity was a complete shock to secular minds. As early as 1915, Albert Einstein's theory of relativity did not allow for a static universe, much to his chagrin. According to his mathematical equations, the universe should either be exploding or imploding; it was not static. Then in 1929, the American astronomer Edwin Hubble concluded that the universe is literally flying apart at enormous velocities; his observations were among the first empirical evidence of what scientists refer to as the "Big Bang" theory—the beginning point of the universe. To many, empirical evidence strongly suggests that the Big Bang was not a chaotic, disorderly event. Instead, it appears to have been fine-tuned for the existence of intelligent life with a complexity and precision that literally defies human comprehension. This phenomenon is strong evidence to many scientists that the Big Bang was not an accident, but that it was designed.[2]

In light of these scientific discoveries, it is the atheist who has to maintain, by faith, despite all the evidence to the contrary, that the universe did not have a beginning a finite time ago but is in some inexplicable way eternal after all. The Christian can stand confidently within biblical truth, knowing it is in line with mainstream astrophysics and cosmology in declaring "In the beginning"—pointing to a moment of creation, which inevitably infers the existence of a transcendent Mind that caused the beginning.[3]

FAITH

When scientists talk about the *fine-tuning* of the universe, they are generally referring to the extraordinary balance of the fundamental laws and parameters of physics and the initial conditions of the universe. Over the past thirty years, scientists have discovered that just about everything about the basic structure of the universe is balanced on a razor's edge for life to exist. The result is a universe that has just the right conditions to sustain life. The oxygen ratio is perfect; the temperature is suitable for habitation of all forms of life; the humidity is adequate; there's a system for replenishing the air; there are systems for producing food, generating energy, and disposing of wastes.

Even the energy density of empty space around the Earth, called the *cosmological constant,* is crucial to the sustenance of life on planet Earth as we know it. Combining the precise properties of just two of these life-sustaining factors, gravity and the cosmological constant, would make the fine-tuning ratio be to a precision of one part in a hundred million trillion trillion trillion trillion trillion trillion, concluded one scientist. That would be the equivalent of one atom in the entire known universe! This would be totally unexpected under the theory that random chance was responsible. However, it is not unexpected at all under the hypothesis that there is a grand Designer.[4]

In their book, *The New Story of Science*, Robert Augros and George Stanciu sum up the inferences of the amazing confluence of "coincidences" that make life possible in the cosmos: "A universe aiming at the production of man implies a mind directing it," they said. "Though man is not at the physical center of the universe, he appears to be at the center of its purpose."[5]

Now, more than ever, Scripture resonates the truth that "since the creation of the world His invisible attributes are clearly seen, being understood by the things that are made, even His eternal power and Godhead, so that they are without excuse, because, although they knew God, they did not glorify Him as God, nor were thankful" (Rom. 1:20–21). As scientists broaden their understanding of creation, placing their faith in God—a Creator-Designer—is becoming much more reasonable. This conclusion is based strictly on scientific evidence of design. It has become more logical than the enormous "leap of faith" required to believe in Darwinian evolution.

To fully address such a magnificent theme as *faith* would fill volumes, and require the study of most of the Old and New Testaments. Our goal here is to highlight the essence of personal faith so that we can learn to walk in new appreciation of our faith. As we give thanks to God for His wonderful gift of life, we will learn how to grow in faith also. For a definition of faith, Scripture speaks for itself:

> Now faith is the substance of things hoped for, the evidence of things not seen...By faith we understand that the worlds were framed by the word of God, so that the things which are seen were not made of things which are visible.
>
> —Hebrews 11:1, 3

Bible commentaries help to explain this biblical definition of faith. As the "substance of things hoped for," faith substantiates God's promises, the fulfillment of which we look forward to in hope; faith embraces them as present realities. It is the evidence, the convincing proof or demonstration of things not seen. Faith accepts the truths revealed on the testimony of God (not merely on their intrinsic reasonableness), that testimony being given to us in Scripture.[6]

In its essence, faith is simply crediting or accepting God's testimony. According to Scripture, if we do not believe the witness of God, we make Him a liar (1 John 5:9–13). And if we believe God's testimony, essentially it means that we believe and trust in the Son of God, for He and salvation in Him alone form the grand subject of God's testimony. The Holy Spirit alone enables any man to accept God's testimony and accept Jesus Christ as his divine Savior. Faith is receptive of God's gratuitous gift of eternal life in Christ.[7]

Gift of God

Scripture is given to us to work faith in our hearts (Rom. 10:17). Jesus taught His disciples that, if they would drink in His words, the Spirit would send rivers of water through their soul (John 7:37–39). This gift of the faith-creating Word of God is to be embraced by us wholeheartedly. The Holy Spirit uses Scripture by attending God's words with demonstration and power so that our faith is not in the wisdom of men, but in the power of God (1 Cor. 2:4–5).

The apostle Paul states this truth emphatically in Romans 10:8–9: "'The word is near you, in your mouth and in your heart,' (that is, the word of faith which we preach): that if you confess with your mouth the Lord Jesus and believe in your heart that God has raised Him from the dead, you will be saved." Faith for salvation is a gift of God to all who call upon Him to receive eternal life through Christ. We simply have to open our minds and hearts to receive this divine gift of God—saving faith by His great grace:

> For by grace you have been saved through faith, and that not of yourselves; it is the gift of God, not of works, lest anyone should boast.
>
> —EPHESIANS 2:8–9

According to the apostle Paul, the divine power necessary to receive salvation from sin, and the faith required to receive it, is inherent in the gospel message sent to us by the Spirit:

> For I am not ashamed of the gospel of Christ, for it is the power of God to salvation for everyone who believes, for the Jew first and also for the Greek. For in it the righteousness of God is revealed from faith to faith; as it is written, "The just shall live by faith."
>
> —ROMANS 1:16–17

As we hear the message of the gospel—the good news of salvation through Christ alone—faith comes to our hearts. As we respond in faith, we can receive the gift of salvation and forgiveness for our sins. Then, we need to share the good news of salvation with others. The importance of personal witness for believers cannot be overstated. There are many people who have not come to faith in God because they have not yet heard the gospel. Scripture clearly teaches that faith comes by hearing and hearing by the Word of God (Rom. 10:17). That is the reason for the Great Commission that Jesus gave to His disciples:

> Go therefore and make disciples of all the nations, baptizing them in the name of the Father and of the Son and of the Holy Spirit, teaching them to observe all things that I have commanded you.
>
> —Matthew 28:19–20

Faith in...

Contrary to prevalent philosophies of the day, it is important what you believe and in whom you believe. Scripture testifies to the truth that faith in the Son of God is the only way to eternal life:

> Nor is there salvation in any other, for there is no other name under heaven given among men by which we must be saved.
>
> —Acts 4:12

In order to experience faith in Jesus Christ, repentance is necessary. Repentance and faith are distinct but inseparable realities. Repentance involves turning from our unbelief in the testimony of God to accept His way of salvation. When Peter preached his great sermon on the Day of Pentecost, the people were convicted and asked what they needed to do to be saved. Peter responded, "Repent, and let every one of you be baptized in the name of Jesus Christ for the remission of sins" (Acts 2:38).

Through repentance and faith we turn from our sin to God; He bestows on us the forgiveness of sin and opens our eyes to spiritual realities we could not otherwise know. Scripture declares: "For you are all sons of God through faith in Christ Jesus" (Gal. 3:26). Receiving saving faith for salvation makes us sons and daughters of God as we are born into the family of God (see Day 12). Repentance and faith are the biblical description of conversion (Acts 16:31; Luke 13:3). They mark the beginning of the new life with God for the believer.

Faith for...

When Peter and John were going to pray one day, they encountered a man, lame from birth, who sat daily at the gate called Beautiful, begging for alms. Peter addressed the man, declaring, "Silver and gold I do not have, but what I do have I give you: In the name of Jesus Christ of Nazareth, rise up and walk" (Acts 3:6). The man was instantly healed, which caused no small stir among the people who were witnessing this miracle of healing. So Peter explained to them what happened. He spoke of faith in Christ as the source of supernatural power:

> And His name, through faith in His name, has made this man strong, whom you see and know. Yes, the faith which comes through Him [Christ] has given him this perfect soundness in the presence of you all.
>
> —ACTS 3:16

As we surrender our lives to Christ, not only do we receive faith for salvation, through which we have the hope of eternal life, but we also enter into faith to receive the promises of God. In this regard, we recognize that faith is more than giving mental assent to a religious creed. Faith becomes an obedience to the Word of God. In John's first epistle, he explains this obedience:

> And this is His commandment: that we should believe on the name of His Son Jesus Christ and love one another, as He gave us commandment.
>
> —1 JOHN 3:23

Through the obedience of faith, we learn to believe God for His wonderful provision, His healing power, His delivering power, and all the promises that are found in the Word of God. Jesus Himself taught that our loving heavenly Father wants to provide all of our needs:

> So why do you worry about clothing? Consider the lilies of the field, how they grow: they neither toil nor spin; and yet I say to you that even Solomon in all his glory was not arrayed like one of these.

Now if God so clothes the grass of the field, which today is, and tomorrow is thrown into the oven, will He not much more clothe you, O you of little faith?...For your heavenly Father knows that you need all these things. But seek first the kingdom of God and His righteousness, and all these things shall be added to you.

—Matthew 6:28–30, 32–33

Enemies of…

The apostle Paul's counsel to the young man, Timothy, was to "fight the good fight of faith, lay hold on eternal life, to which you were also called" (1 Tim. 6:12). He was acknowledging the fact that there are enemies to our faith that would love to defeat us in life. One of the most insidious enemies of faith is the one that lurks in every heart—*unbelief.*

Unbelief

Jesus Himself came to His own country and, according to Scripture, "could do no mighty work there" (Mark 6:6). The people knew Jesus as the young carpenter, the son of Mary, and were offended at Him. And Scripture says that Jesus marveled at their unbelief (Mark 6:6). The divine Son of God left his friends and neighbors in unbelief and would not perform miracles among them. It is dangerous to dishonor the Son of God through unbelief!

The solution to our unbelief is to fill our hearts and minds with the Word of God, which, as we have mentioned, is the source of faith: "Faith comes by hearing, and hearing by the word of God" (Rom. 10:17). While saving faith is initially a gift of God to those who seek it, believers must continually seek to know Him through His Word and through communion in prayer so that our faith will grow. Only in that way can we hope to displace unbelief more and more in our lives.

On one occasion, Jesus' disciples asked Him why they could not cast out a demon. They must have winced at His response:

> So Jesus said to them, "Because of your unbelief; for assuredly,
> I say to you, if you have faith as a mustard seed, you will say to
> this mountain, 'Move from here to there,' and it will move; and
> nothing will be impossible for you. However, this kind does not
> go out except by prayer and fasting."
>
> —Matthew 17:20–21

As our appreciation for God increases, we will find our faith increased to help us win the battle against unbelief. The importance of strengthening our faith cannot be overemphasized, for without it, we cannot please God:

> But without faith it is impossible to please Him, for he who
> comes to God must believe that He is, and that He is a rewarder
> of those who diligently seek Him.
>
> —Hebrews 11:6

The apostle James also instructs us to ask for wisdom from God in faith that He will give it to us:

> If any of you lacks wisdom, let him ask of God, who gives to all
> liberally and without reproach, and it will be given to him. But
> let him ask in faith, with no doubting, for he who doubts is like
> a wave of the sea driven and tossed by the wind.
>
> —James 1:5–6

"Common" sense

Perhaps an even more subtle enemy to faith is what we call plain "common" sense. We use this phrase to refer to a situation where you do not ignore the obvious realities "staring you in the face." Considering natural circumstances and making decisions accordingly seems to our minds the practical way to live life. That may be true for the natural person, but it does not work in the realm of spiritual realities.

When we have spiritual sight, there is a spiritual "common sense" that does not forget God's promise, God's Word, and God's work. Remember the biblical definition of faith: "Now faith is the substance of things hoped for, the evidence of things not seen" (Heb. 11:1). Faith has spiritual eyes to see what has not yet been manifested in natural circumstances as the will of God for our lives. It chooses to believe what God promises to do even before He does it. So we must ultimately consider spiritual sense versus natural sense. Oswald Chambers explains the fallacy of trusting common sense when faith is needed:

> Common sense is not faith, and faith is not common sense; they stand in the relation of the natural and the spiritual; of impulse and inspiration. Nothing Jesus Christ ever said is common sense, it is revelation sense, and it reaches the shores where common sense fails...Faith always works on the personal line, the whole purpose of God being to see that the ideal faith is made real in His children...To turn "head" faith into a personal possession is a fight always, not sometimes. God brings us into circumstances in order to educate our faith...Faith is the whole man rightly related to God by the power of the Spirit of Jesus Christ.[8]

The devil

There is another enemy to our faith who will never give up trying to defeat us—the devil. Scripture clearly teaches that the devil has come to kill, steal, and destroy (see John 10:10). Peter describes him as a "roaring lion, seeking whom he may devour" (1 Pet. 5:8). Yet the Word of God also teaches us that Satan was defeated at Calvary. It shows believers how to walk in victory over his attacks: "Submit to God. Resist the devil and he will flee from you" (James 4:7). The apostle Paul gives us a wonderful analogy of the spiritual weapons Christians must use against the devil:

Put on the whole armor of God, that you may be able to stand against the wiles of the devil...Stand therefore, having girded your waist with truth, having put on the breastplate of righteousness, and having shod your feet with the preparation of the gospel of peace; above all, taking the shield of faith with which you will be able to quench all the fiery darts of the wicked one. And take the helmet of salvation, and the sword of the Spirit, which is the word of God.

—Ephesians 6:11, 14–17

Growing in...

One of the most powerful prayers the apostle Paul prayed was for believers to grow in their faith in order to experience all God has for us:

For this reason I bow my knees to the Father of our Lord Jesus Christ, from whom the whole family in heaven and earth is named, that He would grant you, according to the riches of His glory, to be strengthened with might through His Spirit in the inner man, that Christ may dwell in your hearts through faith; that you, being rooted and grounded in love, may be able to comprehend with all the saints what is the width and length and depth and height—to know the love of Christ which passes knowledge; that you may be filled with all the fullness of God.

—Ephesians 3:14–19

I encourage you to read this prayer again and to meditate on the promises it offers the believer. As believers prayerfully seek to know Christ dwelling in our hearts through *faith*, we can come to know the love of Christ in a most profound way. And we can be filled with all the fullness of God. Growing in faith offers us the supernatural benefits of being strengthened by the Holy Spirit, experiencing the riches of His glory, and becoming rooted and grounded in the divine love of God. In this way, we will learn to walk in unity with our brothers and sisters within the body of Christ as well.

The ultimate end of your faith is to be revealed when you receive your eternal inheritance reserved for you in heaven. Until then, Peter concedes that you may have to suffer some trials in order that "the genuineness of your faith, being much more precious than gold that perishes, though it is tested by fire, may be found to praise, honor, and glory at the revelation of Jesus Christ" (1 Pet. 1:7). Trusting God in the midst of difficult circumstances is a test of your faith, proving its strength and genuineness.

As you walk in obedience, your faith will carry you through all the challenges of life. And you can join the hymn writer in expressing your dependence on Christ:

> My faith looks up to Thee,
> Thou Lamb of Calvary, Saviour divine!
> Now hear me while I pray, take all my guilt away,
> O let me from this day be wholly Thine!
>
> May Thy rich grace impart
> Strength to my fainting heart, my zeal inspire!
> As Thou hast died for me, O may my love to Thee,
> Pure warm, and changeless be, a living fire![9]

Then Jesus said to His disciples, "If anyone desires to come after

Me, let him deny himself, and take up his cross, and follow Me.

For whoever desires to save his life will lose it, but whoever loses

his life for My sake will find it. For what profit is it to a man if

he gains the whole world, and loses his own soul? Of what will

a man give in exchange for his soul?

—Matthew 16:24–26

Tracing the Hand of the Creator

Scientists estimate that the sense of smell in the human is about ten thousand times more sensitive than the sense of taste. When odor chemicals strike the hair cells, they trigger a cascade of reactions that convert to electrical signals in the nerve fibers. As little as a single molecule can trigger this reaction. The human nose can distinguish ten thousand different smells. Our sense of smell is closely related to our sense of taste. If we lose our sense of smell, most of our sense of taste will likewise disappear. Even though the sense of smell is exquisitely sensitive, it is also easily fatigued. This is why an odor can be highly noticeable at first but later is not sensed at all.[1]

THE CROSS

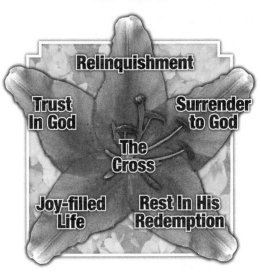

It is possible that the most important "tool" for cultivating our "spiritual garden" is taking up our cross to follow God. The theme of bearing the cross, though not a popular one, is a requisite for following Jesus. Jesus Himself declared: "If anyone desires to come after Me, let him deny himself, and take up his cross, and follow Me" (Matt. 16:24). It is not difficult to define this personal cross that we are commanded to bear. Wherever our ideas, thoughts, choices, or desires are in conflict with the will of God, in that "place" we encounter our personal "cross." Trouble or sorrow may also come into our lives, causing painful loss. It is there as well that we must surrender to bearing our cross.

A cross is a place of death—to personal plans and desires—to which we surrender in favor of choosing to fulfill the destiny of God over our lives. While bearing our cross is painful, demanding

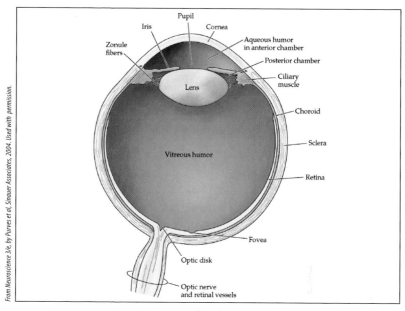

Anatomy of the human eye

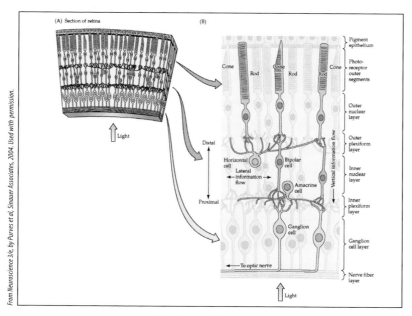

Structure of the retina
Left—overall arrangement of retinal layers
Right—diagram of the basic circuitry of the retina

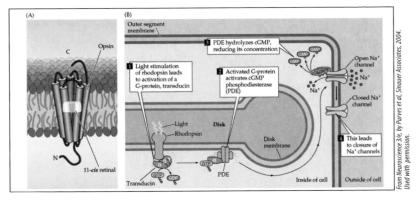

From Neuroscience 3/e, by Purves et al, Sinauer Associates, 2004. Used with permission.

Details of phototransduction in rod photoreceptors

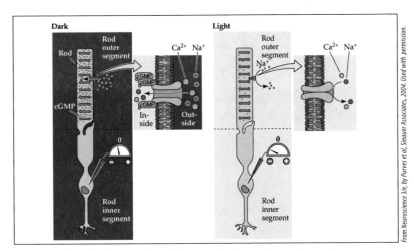

From Neuroscience 3/e, by Purves et al, Sinauer Associates, 2004. Used with permission.

Detailed intricacies of the rod, photoreceptor of the retina

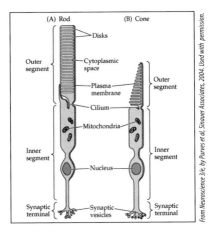

From Neuroscience 3/e, by Purves et al, Sinauer Associates, 2004. Used with permission.

Structural differences between rods and cones

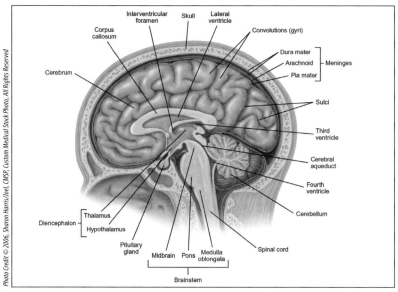

Brain—labeled cross section

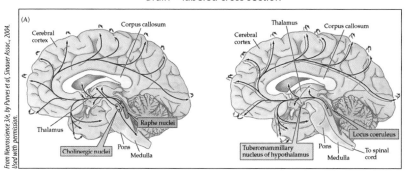

Important nuclei in the brain that regulate the sleep-wake cycle

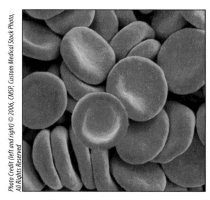

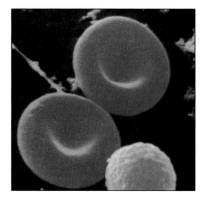

Normal human red blood cells

Human red blood cells and white blood cell

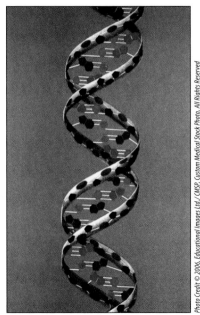

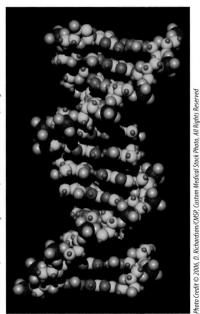

DNA—1953 model

DNA—computer model

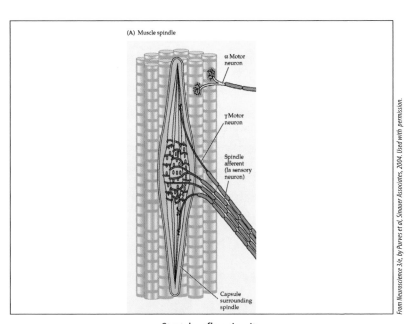

Stretch reflex circuitry
Diagram of muscle spindle, the sensory receptor that initiates
the stretch reflex

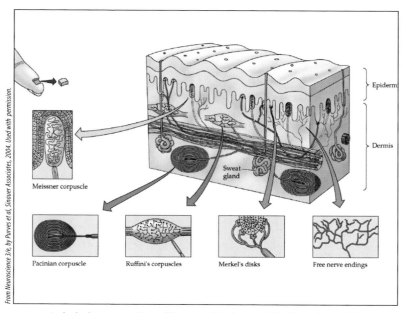

Labeled cross section of human skin (smooth, hairless fingertip)
The skin harbors a variety of morphologically distinct mechanoreceptors

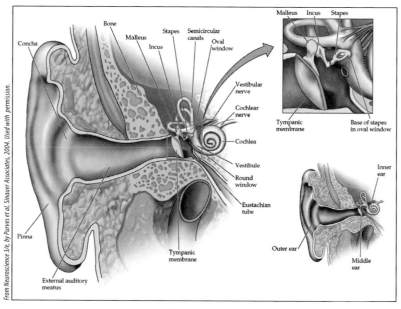

The human ear
Note the large surface of the tympanic membrane (eardrum)

Galaxy nebula side view

Earth viewed from space

Spiral galaxy in Cepheus

Saturn from Hubble Space Telescope

Moon viewed from space

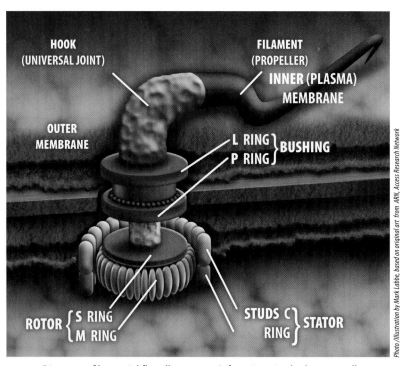

HOOK
(UNIVERSAL JOINT)

FILAMENT
(PROPELLER)

INNER (PLASMA)
MEMBRANE

OUTER
MEMBRANE

L RING
P RING } BUSHING

ROTOR { S RING
M RING

STUDS C
RING } STATOR

Diagram of bacterial flagellum motor's functions in the human cell

personal surrender to the will of God, it brings us to the wonder of experiencing resurrection life and power in the love of God.

Surrender to God

The definition of *surrender* is "to yield to the power, control, or possession of another upon compulsion or demand; to give up completely or agree to forgo in favor of another."[2] As we discussed in our *salvation* devotional (see Day 12), we are all called to surrender our lives to God, accepting Christ as our Savior (see Mark 8:34). Without the working of the Holy Spirit in our lives, even that surrender would not be possible. When we abandon ourselves to Him, our surrender becomes a sweet fragrance of love poured out to our Creator. Choosing to enter into relationship with God, by the power of the Holy Spirit, we receive new desires to be wholly united with and surrendered to our benevolent Creator.

God has a legitimate claim on our lives, as Creator and Savior, to require our surrender to Him. Yet, we need His grace in order to do so. A great part of maturity in a Christian's life is the discipline of choosing daily and heartily to surrender to God's will in every area of your life. There are expected rewards or consequences for decisions to "take up our cross daily." Jesus taught His disciples the principle of surrender to God:

> If anyone desires to be My disciple, let him deny himself [disregard, lose sight of, and forget himself and his own interests] and take up his cross and follow Me [cleave steadfastly to Me, conform wholly to My example in living and, if need be, in dying, also]. For whoever is bent on saving his [temporal] life [his comfort and security here] shall lose it [eternal life]; and whoever loses his life [his comfort and security here] for My sake shall find it [life everlasting].
>
> —Matthew 16:24–25, AMP

Relinquishment

Jesus challenged His disciples to relinquish—to leave behind—all that was important to them and to follow Him. In exchange, He would change their identity and their purpose in life, and fulfill their deepest desires with a revelation of eternal life. In simple abandon, they left their fishing nets, their homes, and their way of life to follow the Master. They had no idea how life-changing their surrender to Christ's call, "Follow Me," would become.

When we offer our lives to God through the redeeming work of Christ, we discover the sheer joy of *relinquishment*. As we focus our attentions on His majesty and bring all our thoughts and desires into alignment with His divine will for our lives, we become intoxicated with the lovely fragrance of the peace of relinquishment. There is nothing that makes our prayers so sweet as lying prostrate before the Lord, surrendering to His will alone, and asking for His divine help to get through a painful trial.

It is the suffering of life's trials that often brings us to a greater surrender to our Lord (see Day 20). When believers enter into intimate communion with God, making Him the essence of our lives, when we have lost "everything" that was of value to us—in that place of total surrender, we experience the unutterable sweetness of relinquishment. Then we realize that the things of the world were not important to our fulfillment. Our greatest joy is to honor God by surrendering to our Creator-Redeemer.

I experienced this pain and joy of deep relinquishment in a time of crisis. Engaging in a business endeavor, I decided to partner with a company that made lenses in order to be able to supply them to people in foreign countries who could not afford eyeglasses. Though my motive was to help the needy in this way, because of the business arrangements for the project, the federal government charged me with all kinds of wrongdoing. The financial issues raised were not even known to me; they were a result of actions of the workmen for the lens company. Yet, the government held me responsible for what they considered wrongdoing. Although no one was hurt in the final analysis, I suffered under their intimidation, while being wrongly accused.

During this painful trial, I learned a hard lesson—that you can try to be a humanitarian and yet get into trouble—just for wanting to do good to your fellow man. I also learned that it is more important to surrender to the will of God than to try to do good. As I agonized over the accusations and potential negative consequences of this situation, I lay before the Lord and relinquished my life and this "care" to Him. Through this painful "cross," He brought me into a deeper relationship with Himself that is profoundly satisfying. A more meaningful Jesus and a more meaningful life were the result of this trial, as I chose to relinquish it all to God.

Trusting in God

Imagine what would happen if one of the vital functions of your body refused to "surrender" to its assigned task. For example, an autoimmune disease occurs when the immune system loses its ability to recognize *self*, and the body begins to make antibodies and T cells that attack its own tissues. The results of this reversal can be devastating, leading to debilitating diseases such as rheumatoid arthritis, multiple sclerosis, juvenile diabetes, and psoriasis.

The ability of the immune system to respond to genuine threats in a balanced manner with appropriate toughness, is a major factor in healing and continuing health. This kind of "surrender" of the immune system to health and balance are necessary for our health, healing, and well-being overall. Similarly, when the pancreas cannot function properly to produce insulin needed to process sugar, the body develops diabetes. Every disease known to man is associated with a failure of some part of a healthy body to "surrender" to its duty.[3]

As in the natural, so in the spiritual; if we do not "surrender" to the redemptive plans and purposes of God, we may become so compromised in our pursuits that we begin to "attack" ourselves. Destructive attitudes, thoughts, words, and actions can devastate our lives. Following Christ wholeheartedly will result in the highest quality of life here on Earth, filled with purpose and meaning, love and divine blessing. Conversely, choosing to follow our own desires and "have it our way" will result in the misery that comes from living a selfish, self-centered life, which ultimately "attacks" itself, ending in self-destruction.

The good news is that God will enable you to surrender your life more and more to Him as you sincerely seek Him. It is a process as you build your relationship with God.[4] As a believer, you have the life of Christ, who lived a life of complete surrender to the Father, dwelling in you. He is living in your heart through the power of the Holy Spirit and He will draw you to surrender to the Father, energizing you with holy desires for God. It is God Himself who helps you to put your trust in Him and relinquish your life to His divine destiny for you.

If you determine not to trust in your own strength, but to fix your sights on God's majesty, you will enjoy a heart that is relinquished to God, trusting Him and depending on Him for all He has promised to give to those who trust Him.

Joy-filled life

Webster's dictionary defines *joy* as "the emotion evoked by well-being, success, or good fortune or by the prospect of possessing what one desires; delight; a state of happiness or felicity."[5] It comes by simple observation that most people seriously lack joy in their everyday lives. Yet, it was Jesus who promised to give His followers a life filled with joy:

> These things I have spoken to you, that My joy may remain in you, and that your joy may be full.
>
> —JOHN 15:11

Joy is a wonderful characteristic—"flower"—of the surrendered life. Indeed, it is difficult to imagine a joy-filled life without absolute surrender to God. Jesus clearly teaches the prerequisites for experiencing His joy. It is a result of cultivating relationship with Him: "If you keep My commandments" and "abide in My love" (John 15:10). That request is filled with promise of leading us into a life filled with joy—"well-being, success, delight, and a continual state of happiness." He is asking believers to live in complete surrender to God as He lived in total surrender to His Father.

Our Redeemer is the only source of true joy. When I let my mind be filled with imaginations of God, glorifying and worshiping Him, I find joy in my life every day. True joy depends on total abandonment to God and His sovereignty. Christ describes our relationship as joy being made full. We have a new spirit of joy, of love, of forgiveness, of peace, and of generosity. We have new imaginations that transform us internally and change the quality of our relationships with others. The fruit of the Spirit (Gal. 5:22–23) is God at work in us, producing the supernatural attributes of Christ in our lives. We cannot develop these qualities fully by ourselves, but only through our union with Christ. Our joy is a joy in Him.[6]

Resting in His redemption

Rest is a wonderful result of living a completely surrendered life to God (see Day 22). It is just a fact that in our nation people are purchasing more tranquilizers, sleep aids, and other over-the-counter drugs than ever before to try to find some rest. Yet, even if these medications produce the desired sleep, they cannot reach profoundly into the soul—mind, emotions, and volition—to produce quiet and restful peace. The promise for that profound rest of soul is found only in abandoning our lives to Jesus, choosing to receive the promises of His redemption. He will teach us how to think, how to respond, and will remove fear and other negative emotions from our minds and hearts.

As we learn to rest in His redemption, we will experience His joy and will leave worldly pursuits behind. As we focus on His sweet will for our lives, we will realize that what we own in life is not important. What owns us is very important. Does our desire for worldly success own us? Or have we truly surrendered ourselves to God. Taking on the mind-set of Jesus, surrendering to His will, transforms our priorities. We take on Jesus in our person; we see life differently.[7]

When you are filled with the joy of Christ, you experience rest for your soul. Then you can sing sincerely the beloved hymn:

All to Jesus, I surrender;
All to Him I freely give;
I will ever love and trust Him,
In His presence daily live.

Refrain

All to Jesus I surrender;
Humbly at His feet I bow,
Worldly pleasures all forsaken;
Take me, Jesus, take me now.

Refrain:

I surrender all, I surrender all,
All to Thee, my blessed Savior,
I surrender all.[8]

[Jesus said:] These things I have spoken to you, that in Me you may have peace. In the world you will have tribulation; but be of good cheer, I have overcome the world.

—JOHN 16:33

Tracing the Hand of the Creator

The discovery of the DNA code within our cells has dealt the theory of evolution a fatal blow. According to astute scientists, the reason for that is simple: "As regards to the origin of life, our uniform experience is that it takes an intelligent agent to generate information, codes, messages. As a result, it is reasonable to infer there was an intelligent cause of the original DNA code. DNA and written language both exhibit the property of specified complexity. Since we know an intelligent cause produces written language, it is legitimate to posit an intelligent cause as the source of DNA."[1] Thus, the defining of the DNA code as a *message* precludes the possibility of DNA arising by material forces; that would mean that information can arise by material forces, which is not possible.

The message of DNA transcends mere chemistry and physics. For example, whether we write a message with chalk, pencil, or pen, we can say the same ideas. There is no relationship at all between the *information* we write and the material used to transmit it. Instead, an outside source imposes information upon the pen (or chalk or pencil) using the elements of a particular linguistic symbol system. The information code within the genetic code is likewise entirely independent of the chemical makeup of the DNA molecule; it is the phenomenal data of the molecule that begs an intelligent source. These rather obvious facts are devastating to any theory that assumes life first arose by natural forces out of a "prebiotic soup."[2]

PEACE

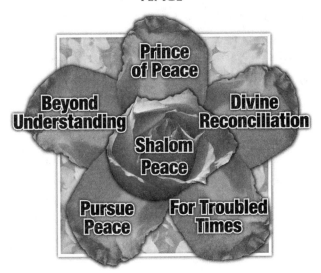

As a medical doctor and eye surgeon, I am often invited to speak to groups and organizations on various subjects. Often, in my presentation, I emphasize the topic of the devastating effects worry and anxiety—un-peace—have on our health. These negative forces can do far more damage to our body, mind, and spirit than any cancer and be less responsive to treatment.

There are so many different "reasons" for worry that, too often, we consider it a legitimate emotional response to life. For example, during the last few years I have worried about the rising problem of civil lawsuits. Physicians have to insure themselves against unrestrained litigation, increasing the costs of services to their patients. Our litigation society is wreaking havoc with physicians and other areas of business. And the cost of government keeps growing as well because of the complex accounting systems necessary to avoid loss from litigation. Yet, if we allow ourselves to worry even about these national economic issues, the peace of God in our hearts will be destroyed.

After enjoying athletic success as a marathon runner and competitor in the Ironman triathlon, I had the misfortune of breaking my leg in a skiing accident. For three and a half years I walked on crutches, then limped with a cane. It was during those years that I experienced the negative effects of worry over my health condition and my future. It was during that painful season of life that I also discovered the secret to conquering worry. I read in the Word of God the apostle Peter's blessing for believers:

> May grace (God's favor) and peace (which is perfect well-being, all necessary good, all spiritual prosperity, and freedom from fears and agitating passions and moral conflicts) be multiplied to you in [the full, personal, precise, and correct] knowledge of God and of Jesus our Lord.
>
> —2 PETER 1:2, AMP

Meditating on the wonderful promise of this and other verses filled me with the hope of experiencing "freedom from fears and agitating passions." This divine peace in the face of trouble is experienced by all those who enter into "the full, personal, precise, and correct knowledge of God." If we continually give in to anxiety and worry as part of our emotional "lifestyle," we can never know this wonderful peace God came to give us. But if we seek God, He will *multiply* His peace to us. Indeed, peace is one of the identifying characteristics of the kingdom of God:

> For the kingdom of God is not eating and drinking, but righteousness and peace and joy in the Holy Spirit.
>
> —ROMANS 14:17

Peace with God

Of course, there can be no true peace without first being reconciled to relationship with God. Scripture clearly teaches that we can only find true peace for our spirit, soul, and body in personal relationship with God:

> Therefore, having been justified by faith, we have peace with God through our Lord Jesus Christ.
>
> —Romans 5:1

> For He Himself is our peace...And He came and preached peace to you.
>
> —Ephesians 2:14, 17

According to Scripture, it is the will of God that you live in serenity of mind and heart, the harmony and tranquility that allows your body to function at optimum health. Peace is one of the greatest blessings of salvation. And it is perhaps one of the most longed for states of mind for millions of people who are looking for peace in all the wrong places.

It is a deception to think that financial security, relational happiness, fame, or the fulfillment of any other desire of the heart can, in itself, produce peace. Believing this painful deception has caused many to waste their lives seeking in vain for a peace of mind that only God can give. It is not coincidental that most of the New Testament writings begin with a similar salutation:

> Grace to you and peace from God the Father and our Lord Jesus Christ, who gave Himself for our sins, that He might deliver us from this present evil age, according to the will of our God and Father, to whom be glory forever and ever. Amen.
>
> —Galatians 1:3–5

Not only do these greetings to believers enforce the fact that God is the source of peace, they encourage us to appropriate that peace into our daily lives.

Shalom

Shalom (or shalowm), the Hebrew word for *peace*, has a broad and powerful meaning, as defined by *Brown-Driver-Brigg's Hebrew Lexicon*. Shalom inherently describes a state of completeness, soundness, welfare, and peace:

- Completeness (in number)

- Safety, soundness (in body)

- Welfare, health, prosperity

- Peace, quiet, tranquility, contentment

- Peace, friendship (used of human relationships and with God, especially in covenant relationship)

- Peace (from war)

The Greek word for peace, *eirene*, used most often in the New Testament, expresses the same quality of life as its Hebrew counterpart. It means "prosperity, quietness, rest, and being set at one again in harmony."[4] Scripture leaves no doubt as to the peaceful state of mind and heart God has promised to His children.

Peace is not a passive state of mind in which we sit back and allow life to go by. It is rather a positive perspective of life that allows us to be at our best in the situations where Christ has placed us to accomplish His work. I encourage you to take a moment to consider the rich promises of these biblical definitions of *peace*. Ask yourself how much real peace you enjoy in your life. Read again each quality of peace God promises you, and honestly evaluate the measure of rest and tranquility you enjoy.

Whether in my medical practice or outside of my vocation, as I work through tasks or projects which contain a certain amount of risk, I am sometimes tempted to worry that I will not succeed. I must admit that at times this anxiety overcomes me, and prevents the peace of God from settling into my heart and mind. Yet, even my desire to succeed must be submitted to the lordship of Christ, so that His peace can pervade my mind in the press of life.

For troubled times

Ever since the heinous attacks on our nation on September 11, 2001, our national peace has suffered a tremendous blow. Our lives have forever been altered. We have perhaps never needed as badly as we do now the divine peace that God offers us in this present evil age. Natural disasters are devastating this nation as well, affecting many families and entire cities with grief and loss. These troubled times demand a renewed effort to seek peace from a source other than natural circumstances. The secret for emerging from the thicket of anxiety and worry is to seek God's comfort. We need to follow the wisdom of God's Word:

> Be anxious for nothing, but in everything by prayer and supplication, with thanksgiving, let your requests be made known to God; and the peace of God, which surpasses all understanding, will guard your hearts and minds through Christ Jesus.
>
> —Philippians 4:6–7

The secret to finding peace in the midst of great trouble and sorrow is to call on God. Though it may seem difficult to be thankful in the midst of great loss, as believers, we can express our gratitude for the ability to look up to God and expect Him to help us. As we cultivate a thankful heart, we will be engulfed in the Lord's presence, which will bring His peace and comfort to our aching hearts. The simple act of thanksgiving brings us into the presence of God, who will give us hope and provision for our future.

Surpasses understanding

The apostle Paul declared that the peace of God surpasses all understanding (see Phil. 4:7). Even when we cannot make sense of life's circumstances, we can walk in the peace of God by faith, knowing that He loves us and will look out for our welfare. Jesus told His disciples that He was giving them His peace, which would remain even in face of the troubled world in which they lived:

> These things I have spoken to you, that in Me you may have peace. In the world you will have tribulation; but be of good cheer, I have overcome the world.
>
> —John 16:33

It is this transcending power of the peace of God that we so need in our troubled world today. As we accept this promise by faith, we learn to appropriate the peace of God to our personal circumstances. There is no situation so terrible that God's peace cannot permeate it. Scripture teaches that the peace of God guards our hearts (see Phil. 4:7). As we bow in worship and adoration to a loving God, He sets up a supernatural guard over our lives, which does not allow anxiety and worry to devastate us.

Christ is our peace.

At Christ's birth, the angelic hosts proclaimed to the shepherds: "Glory to God in the highest, And on earth peace, goodwill toward men!" (Luke 2:14). The coming of the Messiah offered peace to the whole world and harmony between the peoples of the Earth. This wonderful, divine gift of peace to the world was prophesied hundreds of years earlier by the Old Testament prophets:

> For unto us a Child is born, Unto us a Son is given; And the government will be upon His shoulder. And His name will be called Wonderful, Counselor, Mighty God, Everlasting Father, Prince of Peace. Of the increase of His government and peace [shalom] There will be no end.
>
> —Isaiah 9:6–7

We understand from Scripture that a day is coming when all wars will cease (Isa. 2:4). Yet, even Jesus prophesied that the world would be filled with wars and rumors of wars before His Second Coming (see Matthew 24). That is why He has given believers His peace that passes understanding to help us cope in this troubled world. We can learn from Old Testament saints who knew how to walk in that peace:

> Great peace have those who love Your law, And nothing causes them to stumble. LORD, I hope for Your salvation, And I do Your commandments.
>
> —PSALM 119:165–166

Our life of faith begins with reconciliation to God, by accepting Christ's sacrifice for our sin. Our experience of being born again gives us peace with God as we receive forgiveness for our sins. In deep gratitude for the newness of life and peace that we experience, we begin to learn what pleases God.

Pursue peace

Scripture also teaches that we must *pursue* peace if we are to enjoy its wonderful benefits:

> Pursue peace with all people, and holiness, without which no one will see the Lord.
>
> —HEBREWS 12:14

> He who would love life And see good days, Let him refrain his tongue from evil, And his lips from speaking deceit. Let him turn away from evil and do good; Let him seek peace and pursue it.
>
> —1 PETER 3:10–11

Our DNA code has been defined as a *message*, which is translatable in the same way our codes of language are. As we grasp the profound significance of our DNA, which gives us our unique identity, we understand that every facet of our lives issues from the information encoded there. I like to pray, for example, for my wife: *Lord, thank you for your DNA that gives her life and healing. May it be anointed by your Holy Spirit so that she learns to find her peace in You, and in nothing else.*

Our peace depends on entering into God's method of fulfilling His purposes in our lives so we can glorify Him. We learn to be in harmony with His conceptions, ideas, methods, ground plan, intentions, platform, projections, and notions. As we become one with His intention, we can pursue the things the Lord wants us to do. How to do that is not a mystery. The apostle Paul used the analogy of an umpire to describe the guarding power of peace:

And let the peace (soul harmony which comes) from Christ rule (act as umpire continually) in your hearts [deciding and settling with finality all questions that arise in your minds, in that peaceful state] to which as [members of Christ's] one body you were also called [to live]. And be thankful (appreciative), [giving praise to God always].

—COLOSSIANS 3:15, AMP

In the game of baseball, the umpire's word is the final authority. To live in peace, we must learn to let the peace of God determine our decisions. If a decision we are contemplating causes us "unpeace," we should not go forward with it until all questions have been settled by the Prince of peace. Surely, in our troubled world today, this divine gift of peace is a treasure worthy pursuing.

One of His disciples said to Him, "Lord, teach us to pray..." So He said to them, "When you pray, say: Our Father in heaven, Hallowed by Your name. Your kingdom come. Your will be done. On earth as it is in heaven. Give us day by day our daily bread. And forgive us our sins, For we also forgive everyone who is indebted to us. And do not lead us into temptation, But deliver us from the evil one."

—Luke 11:1–4

Be anxious for nothing, but in everything by prayer and supplication, with thanksgiving, let your requests be made known to God.

—Philippians 4:6

Tracing the Hand of the Creator

There have been many studies conducted recently to investigate the therapeutic effects of prayer. Formal studies have been conducted that demonstrate the positive influence of a religious faith on healing. This includes the positive effects of fellowship and worship attendance at church, of private religious activities, such as daily devotional prayer, and of intercessory prayer (individuals praying for the healing of other persons). So positive are these effects that health practitioners are finding faith difficult to ignore.[1]

The most widely cited study to date on the therapeutic effects of prayer was conducted by Dr. Randolph Byrd at the San Francisco Medical Center in 1988. Dr. Byrd studied a coronary care unit (CCU) population to determine if intercessory prayer to the Judeo-Christian God had any effect on the patient. In this study, 393 patients were assigned randomly to one of two groups. Group one had prayers made to God on their behalf by intercessors. Group two, the control group, received no prayers from anyone. The identities of the individuals in the first group, those being prayed for, were kept secret from the attending doctors, nurses, and from the patients themselves. All 393 patients received the same high-quality cardiac care at the hospital. Dr. Byrd recorded the positive results of his statistical study about the efficacy of remote intercessory prayer in this way:

> Analysis of events after entry into the study showed the prayer group had less congestive heart failure, required less diuretic and antibiotic therapy, had fewer episodes of pneumonia, had fewer cardiac arrests, and were less frequently intubated and ventilated.[2]

Dr. Byrd concluded that with intercessory prayer to God—from a distance and without the beneficiary's knowledge—"there seemed to be an effect, and that effect was presumed to be beneficial."[3]

PRAYER

Congruent with our analogy, portraying flowers as divine truths of God, we can consider our hearts as the "gardens" in which these lovely flowers grow. If we ask God to plant the flowers of truth, peace, and love in our heart—our spiritual garden—our lives will reflect the beauty and fragrance of these godly qualities. In fact, Scripture describes the people of God as a spiritual garden, filled with thanksgiving, joy, and gladness:

> For the LORD shall comfort Zion: he will comfort all her waste places; and he will make her wilderness like Eden, and her desert like the garden of the LORD; joy and gladness shall be found therein, thanksgiving, and the voice of melody.
>
> —ISAIAH 51:3, KJV

God has a special love for gardens, it seems, designing them especially so that they best suit His highest creation—mankind.

When He created Adam and Eve, He planted a garden for them to enjoy and to tend. And He came to commune with that first couple there in the cool of the day. In the New Testament, we read that Jesus retired often to pray in a garden place:

> When Jesus had spoken these words, He went out with His disciples over the Brook Kidron, where there was a garden, which He and His disciples entered. And Judas, who betrayed Him, also knew the place; for Jesus often met there with His disciples.
> —JOHN 18:1–2

Even in the place where Jesus was crucified, there was a garden, and the tomb where our Savior was laid was in that garden (see John 19:41). The beauty and tranquility of that garden place reflect the glorious benediction upon on that miraculous Resurrection day. It was in that garden that He allowed Mary to see Him; there He revealed the fact of His resurrection to the world.

As we cultivate the soil of our hearts, asking God to manifest His divine characteristics to flourish there, we prepare a beautiful garden for the Lord to come and commune with us, and we with Him. Filled with appreciation for our Creator, our lives yield the fragrance of thanksgiving, praise, and surrender to His will. Our hearts will then be characterized as a *garden of prayer*.

Worship

True worship is the highest expression of appreciation. Every expression of prayer, whether it is personal communion, petition with thanksgiving, or unselfish intercession, has its basis in worship. Worship is a much more profound relationship than we experience in any earthly relationship. When we acknowledge our Creator, we begin to see His power and glory and grace. We behold His countenance, and we are overwhelmed by His majesty. Our only creature response is to fall at His feet and worship.[4]

God is infinitely above any need that we may have of Him. He is above our reach, above our conceptions; we cannot comprehend Him. Yet when we surrender our lives to God and believe in His promises, we find our ultimate existence and purpose in Him. Once we are in God's presence, we cannot help but worship His majesty and praise Him. We also cannot help but find joy in God's grace and power. There is no other way to feel when we fall at the feet of the Master. We are in awe of the salvation and fellowship he bestows.[5]

We express our love and delight to God by worshiping Him. He wants us to adore and worship and exalt Him. When we do that, we cannot help but be filled with joy. John Piper, in his book, *Desiring God*, calls this joy and pleasure in God "Christian hedonism." We are satisfied with the excellence of God. We are overwhelmed with the joy of His fellowship. This is the feast of Christian hedonism, full of spiritual, godly pleasures.[6] Again, the psalmist describes this joyous state of the believer:

You will show me the path of life; In Your presence is fullness of joy; At Your right hand are pleasures forevermore.
—Psalm 16:11

Worship requires humility. We are not naturally humble. Yet God seeks humility in us. He declares: "I dwell on a high and holy place, And also with the contrite and lowly of spirit In order to revive the spirit of the lowly And to revive the heart of the contrite" (Isa. 57:15, nas). The divine Gardener cultivates the heart soil, breaking up the hard lumps of bad attitudes before we can ever begin to worship. A humble heart comes supernaturally when we let go of our own willfulness. Even Jesus humbled Himself. We have a hard time doing it, but He enables us to take on His thoughts and be broken before the Father. As we humble ourselves before God, we will in turn begin to see His greatness more and more. If we can but catch a tiny glimpse of our God as He truly is, our lives will gain eternal perspective.[7]

As you seek the humility required for worship, your life will begin to reflect the most profound expression of worship. Far more than simply an emotion or expression of love for God, however profound, your truest worship is to be lived out in your daily life. Scripture teaches:

> Therefore, I urge you, brothers, in view of God's mercy, to offer your bodies as living sacrifices, holy and pleasing to God—this is your spiritual act of worship.
>
> —ROMANS 12:1, NIV

When your heart is relinquished to Him, you hand over your desire to control your life; in that way you become a living sacrifice. This relinquished life is the most profound expression of worship in a believer's life.

Praise

Scripture is filled with commands for the people of God to praise Him:

> Make a joyful shout to the LORD, all you lands! Serve the LORD with gladness; Come before His presence with singing. Know that the LORD, He is God; It is He who has made us, and not we ourselves; We are His people and the sheep of His pasture. Enter into His gates with thanksgiving, And into His courts with praise. Be thankful to Him, and bless His name.
>
> —PSALM 100:1–4

I have experienced moments in which I become engaged in a "thanksgiving frenzy." At those times I am truly able to let all earthly concerns go. I am so filled with joy in God's presence that I can only express thanksgiving to Him for everything I can think of.

In this wonderful place of abandonment to God, I can gauge how close I am to Him, as I leave behind all other concerns.

As I think about the therapy for worry, I think of the best medicine—the thanksgiving frenzy to the Lord. This attitude of thanksgiving is more than something we do at meals, birthdays, and holidays. It's a mental attitude of continual thanks to God that permeates our thoughts and lives. It engulfs our relationship with God, our relationships with others and our relationship with our vocation. It's a daily necessity in the war against worry.[8]

When I express gratitude and praise, I feel closer to God than I do at other times. I just thank Him, knowing my lack and His greatness. He is from the beginning of time and all through eternity, and yet, He is at the center of my "little" life. These thanksgiving frenzies allow me to worship Him in a special way—I do not have to carry a tune or be a great theologian. I simply appreciate the Lord God almighty, who is everything to me.[9]

Petition

Jesus also gave us another means of liberation from worry—petition His divine provision:

> Be anxious for nothing, but in everything by prayer and supplication, with thanksgiving, let your requests be made known to God; and the peace of God, which surpasses all understanding, will guard your hearts and minds through Christ Jesus.
>
> —Philippians 4:6–7

Choosing to believe God's wonderful promises, we can learn to come to Him as our loving Father, Savior, and Friend. With thanksgiving for all He is and what He has already done for us, we can present our requests or petitions to Him. As we seek to rest in His redemption, we cease from worry and fretting, knowing that our loving God will respond to our requests and intervene in our lives with His good will. In preparation for His ascension, Jesus specifically told His disciples that they should ask God to supply their needs:

> And whatever you ask in My name, that I will do, that the Father may be glorified in the Son. If you ask anything in My name, I will do it.
>
> —John 14:13–14

Sometimes we fail to ask God for our needs because of a wrong sense of pride and self-sufficiency that thinks, "I can do it myself." However, it is in humble dependency on our loving Father that we will find an answer to our most troubling situations as we simply come to Him and "make our requests known."

Communion

Though the verb "commune" is used only a few times in Scripture, it is of great significance when describing God's relationship to His people. When God gave Moses the plan to build the ark of the covenant, He promised to commune with him there:

> And there I will meet with thee, and I will commune with thee from above the mercy seat, from between the two cherubims which are upon the ark of the testimony, of all things which I will give thee in commandment unto the children of Israel.
>
> —Exodus 25:22, kjv

The Hebrew word translated *commune* is *dabar*, which means "to speak, declare, teach, command, or arrange." Everyone who has ever opened their heart to God has done so because of God's drawing and prompting, speaking to their souls. This is God's delight and desire for all of mankind. It seems unthinkable that as finite creatures we could actually "hear" the voice of an infinite God, but Scripture is filled with examples of people just like us who did hear Him speak to them. Fuchsia T. Pickett describes the "communion mood" of the Holy Spirit in her book, *Presenting the Holy Spirit*:

Too often we think of prayer as simply our talking with God. We don't realize that God the Father, God the Son, and God the Holy Spirit want to talk to us in prayer. True prayer is two-way communication with God. When we look at communion in its deepest meaning, we will understand that it is the most intimate of all realms of prayer. It is that relationship ordained of God to completely satisfy our hearts as well as His own...In its purest essence...true communion with God is the result of a deeply personal love relationship with Him.[10]

It is difficult to comprehend that the infinite almighty God—the Creator of the universe—desires to come into our lives in a tangible way and commune with us. Yet, that reality has been experienced by many believers who dare to take God at His Word. Satisfaction comes through daily communion with God. He wants an intimate relationship of love with us. And Christ is the key to that intimacy. Our relationship with Christ is to be one of surrender, filled with desire to have intimate fellowship with Him until we are engulfed in, and intertwined with, His presence. Then we enter into the fullness of God![11]

In this quiet place of intimate communion, we can experience the deepest satisfaction for the "God-shaped vacuum" in our lives. And as we wait before Him, we will learn to hear His voice speaking His Word to us.

Intercession

Webster's dictionary defines the word *intercede*: "to intervene between parties with a view to reconciling differences; mediate, interpose."[12] In Scripture, Moses interceded for the rebellious people of Israel when God said He would destroy them for their sin. And the Book of Hebrews describes Jesus' position in heaven now as an intercessor:

Therefore He is also able to save to the uttermost those who
come to God through Him, since He always lives to make intercession for them.

—HEBREWS 7:25

While we must hate sin, as God does, we are called to love
the sinner, as He does as well. We are called to intercede for others—to pray fervently for each other. It is not always easy to be
a loving intercessor. There are times when others are difficult to
deal with. They may be filled with anger, worry, cynicism, or other
negative attitudes. But we need to be continually filled with the
Holy Spirit, praying even for those who "use" us, hate us, and act
against us.[13]

The Rev. Larry Jackson from North Carolina teaches that we
must pray from the position of the person for whom we are inter-
ceding. We use our imaginations to put ourselves in that person's
position. If that person is in a state of disarray, we must imagine
their anguish and pray for them. From that compassionate position, we often find ourselves awake to God, feeling the turmoil and
grief of the person as we pray for him or her.[14]

As we become more and more filled with the love of God, we
will feel His love for others who are hurting. In that way we learn
to become intercessors for them, rather than accusers. As we do,
we can fulfill the will of God revealed in Scripture: "Bear one
another's burdens, and so fulfill the law of Christ" (Gal. 6:2). Ask
God to give you a concern for another person and help you to *intercede* for their needs. And take time to quietly *commune* with God,
expecting to hear His response to your desire to feel His nearness.
Bow before Him in adoration and *worship* for who He is. Make
your *petitions* known to Him, for He delights in giving good gifts
to His children. The hymn writer found the place of prayer to be
filled with comfort:

Sweet hour of prayer! sweet hour of prayer!
That calls me from a world of care,
And bids me at my Father's throne
Make all my wants and wishes known.
In seasons of distress and grief,
My soul has often found relief
And oft escaped the tempter's snare
By thy return, sweet hour of prayer![15]

*Beloved, do not think it strange concerning the fiery trial which
is to try you, as though some strange thing happened to you; but
rejoice to the extent that you partake of Christ's sufferings, that
when His glory is revealed, you may also be glad with exceeding
joy...let those who suffer according to the will of God commit
their souls to Him in doing good, as to a faithful Creator.*

—1 Peter 4:12–13, 19

Tracing the Hand of the Creator

S ome of the wonders of the human body that scientists have discovered and measured seem almost amusing. Did you know that the average speed of a sneeze is sixty-eight miles per hour? Each sneeze can contain as many as five thousand droplets that can travel as far as twelve feet. The highest speed of sneeze-expelled droplets measured is 104 mph. And the longest sneezing fit ever recorded in the *Guinness Book of World Records* is 977 days.[1]

These fascinating wonders of the body are simply awe-inspiring. For example, just as the eye converts photons into electrical signals that can be "seen" by the brain, so the ear converts sound waves into electrical signals that can be "heard" by the brain—no less a miracle. In some ways the ear actually outperforms the eye. (See page 219.) It can hear over an even wider range of sound intensity (one trillion times) than the range of light intensity over which the eye can see (ten billion times). The eardrum, or tympanic membrane, has the same thickness as a piece of paper and is exquisitely sensitive to any vibration. Even sound waves that move the eardrum less than the diameter of a hydrogen molecule can be perceived by the brain as a sound. This sensitivity makes it possible to hear a cricket chirping one-half mile away on a still night. The ear is a microphone, an acoustical amplifier, and a frequency analyzer. It is a musical instrument of sorts: if a piano has eighty-eight keys, the organ of Corti has over twenty thousand keys. It can distinguish between two thousand different pitches.[2]

DIVINE TESTINGS

We sometimes are faced with trials of serious health issues, financial crises, and devastating relational or other problems. And we observe friends and family who are going through difficult experiences as well. These challenges present themselves at every stage of life. It is during these painful times, which the Bible refers to as *trials* or *tests*, that it is most important for us to engage in the grace of appreciation, adoration, and awe for our Creator. Recently, I wrote to encourage a friend in this regard who is facing a life and death situation through a recurrent metastasis:

> You have been on my mind quite a bit lately. I am currently writing a book about *appreciation*, because I feel my need to grow in this divine grace. I believe appreciation is the basis for worship and adoration of God. When we truly appreciate the Creator, meditating on the wonder of the DNA with which we are

made, we can have greater confidence in His capacity to heal us. But it is even more important that we adore the One who designed everything.

Adoration involves the grace of "standing in awe" of God. Psalm 119:161 says, "I stand in awe of your Word." When we stand in awe of God it is refreshing for our souls. In times of distress when we are overwhelmed or discouraged, one of the most invigorating things we can do is to stand in awe of God, our Creator-Redeemer. I have found this meditation on the greatness of God and His redeeming love to be the renewing strength that I need daily. My continued prayers are with you, my friend.

—Jim

God is with us

All of my life, I have been an avid athlete. I have enjoyed distance running and have competed in several major marathons, including the Boston marathon on two occasions. As an Ironman triathlon champion, perhaps one of the most significant competitive events that I participated in was a double Ironman event when I was fifty-six years old. The competition involved a five-mile swim, a 224-mile bike ride, and a fifty-two-mile run. To my surprise, I finished in second place, one minute behind a man who was half my age.

Because of my life-long involvement in and love for sports, I was planning to gradually reduce the time involvement in my medical practice so I could be involved in more sporting events as I reached my seventies. Unfortunately, when I was in my early sixties, I first had a wreck on my bike, which required several surgeries on my leg. It had to be lengthened three inches and strengthened. After that, I suffered a skiing accident, re-fracturing that leg. As a result, I lost about two inches in height, and suffered a severely limited athletic ability. My desire to increasingly enjoy the athletically trained body that had served me well was greatly disappointed.

These physical trials were very painful to me. Actually, they were life altering, especially as they limited my future in the sporting activities I loved. So I had to choose how to relieve my disappointment. As I sought God, He gave me a deeper appreciation for Him, for life, and for the health I still have. That growing appreciation for my Creator opened a larger capacity for intimacy with the Lord and helped me to find much greater satisfaction in life through my relationship with Him.

Instead of seeking satisfaction in athletic achievement, I have realized a new rest in God, which is of great benefit to every area of my life. In cultivating a positive attitude in the face of these physical trials, I have received great benefit from what otherwise could have remained a lifelong disappointment. As we choose to surrender to God in the face of painful situations of life, we will reap the eternal benefits of more intimate relationship with God in this life and beyond.

Trials, whether defined by illness, financial problems, relationship problems, a great emotional loss, or other painful situations, require us to rely more on God and not on worldly sources for strength and comfort. When I am tempted to be discouraged in the face of a trial, I love to read the promise of God found in Romans 8:28:

And we know that all things work together for good to those who love God, to those who are the called according to His purpose.

It is important to trust the loving heart of our God, who has promised never to leave us alone in our trouble. The writer to the Hebrews confirms the promise of God's continuing presence with all believers:

For He Himself has said, "I will never leave you nor forsake you."
So we may boldly say: "The LORD is my helper; I will not fear.
What can man do to me?"

—HEBREWS 13:5–6

Jesus promised those who followed Him: "Lo, I am with you always, even to the end of the age" (Matt. 28:20). It is our responsibility to enter into the relationship with our divine Creator offered to us through Jesus Christ. As we draw near to Him in adoration, standing in awe of His marvelous works, our hearts are comforted. To this end, many times it is our trials that motivate us to find relief through cultivating a deeper relationship with God.

Intimacy with God

If there is anything that can comfort the human heart in a time of difficulty and trial, it is enjoying the *intimacy* of a loving relationship with God. Learning to know our Creator through the wonders of His creation should evoke adoration from our hearts, which in turn will fill us with the healing presence of God. We have explained the human zygote as a wonder that should generate awe in our minds and hearts. Only a divine Creator could have engineered the complexity of the DNA molecule that creates a distinct identity for every individual ever born. Richard Swenson describes this wonder of our relationship with the Creator:

> Every human body is a miracle exceeding comprehension. The complexity and dimensions involved are staggering to the mind, straining our abilities to apprehend the grandeur...If we make the effort to reach for the meaning behind the biology...we will see anew the power and precision of God...[and] we will be increasingly aware of the intimacy with which He carries out His creative efforts. This is a hands-on God, both in the creating and sustaining phases...He watches over us more intimately than the human mind has the ability to perceive.[3]

Your unique individuality, planned by God Himself, is the basis of enjoying intimate relationship with God. As you seek to know God personally, you will discover that you can always live in God's presence. This divine perspective changes the dynamic of every trial you must face in life. God truly becomes a refuge for believers in our time of trouble.

Our comfort

It is a sad reality that it often takes a severe trial to draw us to God. Before we can become open and transparent before God, laying hold of the restoring "glue" of His grace, forgiveness, compassion, and comfort, often we have to suffer the pangs of personal trials. In our pain, we look up, and realize that God is waiting for us to call on Him for help. When we do, we experience a divine melding of our souls with God, through the cross and Christ's forgiveness, which fills us with His divine comfort. As believers, that divine love and grace permeates our being, then flows out to bless others we encounter as we live our lives.

Paradoxically, the pain that believers suffer through trials allows the wonderful grace and comfort of God to be revealed to us and through us in deeper ways. When the apostle Paul was buffeted by a "messenger of Satan," he pleaded with the Lord three times that it might depart from him. Yet, the Lord's loving response to him was: "My grace is sufficient for you, for My strength is made perfect in weakness" (2 Cor. 12:9).

It is simply a fact of human nature that when we feel strong, and have no need of help beyond ourselves, we do not seek the Lord. We usually have to be brought down by the pain of trials to become as children, crying out to God for help and comfort. In our pain, we are willing to forsake our busyness and activities that keep us from seeking God. We lay aside our pride and arrogance associated with our traditional religion. It is in our painful trials that we best learn to lean on God in total dependence.

In that place of humble abandonment to the will of God, we discover the wonderful secrets of His tender care. The apostle Peter explains this spiritual phenomenon:

> [You] are kept by the power of God through faith for salvation ready to be revealed in the last time. In this you greatly rejoice, though now for a little while, if need be, you have been grieved by various trials, that the genuineness of your faith, being much more precious than gold that perishes, though it is tested by fire, may be found to praise, honor, and glory at the revelation of Jesus Christ, whom having not seen you love.
>
> —1 Peter 1:5–8

Our attitude in these difficult times is to be one of rejoicing, putting our faith in the divine power of our God that will keep us from harm.

Cultivating humility

According to Scripture, these trials of our faith are "more precious than gold" (1 Pet. 1:5), giving opportunity for us to humble ourselves before God:

> Humble yourselves under the mighty hand of God, that He may exalt you in due time, casting all your care upon Him, for He cares for you...But may the God of all grace, who called us to His eternal glory by Christ Jesus, after you have suffered a while, perfect, establish, strengthen, and settle you.
>
> —1 Peter 5:6–7, 10

What a wonderful truth we can embrace, that we can cast all our care upon God, because He cares for us. Humility is required for us to give our troubles to God and ask for His help. Otherwise, we will strive to solve our problems in our own strength. Andrew Murray, in his classic volume, *Humility*, writes:

It is only by the indwelling of Christ in His divine humility that we become truly humble. We have our pride from another, from Adam; we must have our humility from another, too. Pride is ours, and rules in us with such terrible power, because it is ourself—our very nature. Humility must be ours in the same way; it must be our very self, our very nature. As natural and easy as it has been to be proud, it must be—it will be—to be humble.[4]

Our natural minds are "naturally" filled with pride. Only through Christ can we be set free from this terrible sin. The apostle Paul instructed believers:

> Let this mind be in you which was also in Christ Jesus, who, being in the form of God, did not consider it robbery to be equal with God, but made Himself of no reputation, taking the form of a bondservant, and coming in the likeness of men. And being found in appearance as a man, He humbled Himself and became obedient to the point of death, even the death of the cross.
>
> —Philippians 2:5–8

True humility is one of the most beautiful characteristics reflected in the Christian's life. And it is developed in us largely as a result of our proper response to tests and trials.

Eternal perspective

While Scripture does not promise immunity from trouble for the believer in Christ, it does give us a wonderful perspective in the face of trials. The apostle Paul, who suffered many things for Christ, declared:

> For our light affliction, which is but for a moment, is working for us a far more exceeding and eternal weight of glory, while we do not look at the things which are seen, but at the things which are

not seen. For the things which are seen are temporary, but the things which are not seen are eternal.

—2 Corinthians 4:17–18

As we turn to God in our trials, they will work in us an "eternal weight of glory." The glory of God is His divine presence, which He wants our lives to reflect. On another occasion, Paul declared that it is "Christ in you, the hope of glory" (Col. 1:27). Growing in our relationship with God through trials will reveal the presence and glory of God to us and through us. Our security in the love of God will deepen as we understand and embrace the promises of Scripture:

Yet in all these things we are more than conquerors through Him who loved us. For I am persuaded that neither death nor life, nor angels nor principalities nor powers, nor things present nor things to come, nor height nor depth, nor any other created thing, shall be able to separate us from the love of God which is in Christ Jesus our Lord.

—Romans 8:37–39

Bowing before God in adoration and worship, casting our care on Him, and seeking for His divine help, will cause us to grow in the grace of humility. Our minds will be transformed to become Christlike as we trust Him in the trials of our lives. And in that transformation, we will discover divine destiny—the purpose for which we were born.

For we are His workmanship, created in Christ Jesus for good works, which God prepared beforehand that we should walk in them.

—EPHESIANS 2:10

I therefore, the prisoner of the Lord, beseech you that ye walk worthy of the vocation wherewith ye are called, With all lowliness and meekness, with longsuffering, forbearing one another in love.

—EPHESIANS 4:1–2, KJV

Tracing the Hand of the Creator

Scientists can synthesize proteins suitable for life. Research chemists produce things like insulin for medical purposes in great quantities. The question is, *How do they do it?* Certainly not by simulating "chance and natural causes." Experiments formulated through specific choices, highly constrained at each step, continually adding *information*, make these syntheses possible. If we want to speculate on how the *first* informational molecules came into being, it is reasonable to conclude some form of intelligence had to be involved.

Scientists have observed that the structure of protein and of DNA has a high information content. We recognize its similarity to information (like poems and computer programs) generated by human intelligence. Therefore, we may scientifically infer that the source of information on the molecular level was likewise an intelligent being. In fact, we know of no other source of information. Efforts to produce information-bearing molecules by chance or natural forces have failed. While we have not seen the Creator, nor observed the act of creation, we do recognize the kind of order in all of creation that only comes from an intelligent being.[1]

PURPOSE: DIVINE DESTINY

Humankind has been elevated to a godlike status by the faulty philosophies of Darwinism and scientific materialism. They perceive the world and all of life as simply what our "natural senses" tell us. Embracing these godless philosophies denies us any genuine aspirations to transcend a world that can be perceived by our senses alone. Such philosophies would make us each accidental, incidental, and meaningless. Through accepting the philosophy of God's design, however, we become related, reliant, and replete with meaning. We celebrate the scientific evidence that says we are irreducibly complex, original, beautiful, and integrated. We are all one in design and in our purpose to care for others and let the love of God flow through us to those around.[2]

Some physicists describe the laws and principles of nature as *the essence of beauty*. Robin Collins declares of these laws: "They're beautiful, and they're also elegant in their simplicity. Surprisingly so. Scientists have found a world where fundamental simplicity gives rise to the enormous complexity needed for life. In physics, we see an uncanny degree of harmony, symmetry, and proportionality. And we see something that I call 'discoverability.' By that, I mean that the laws of nature seem to have been carefully arranged so that they can be discovered by beings with our level of intelligence. That not only fits the idea of design, but it also suggests a providential purpose for humankind—that is, to learn about our habitat and to develop science and technology."[3]

The sheer beauty of order in the physical universe has prompted leading scientists, not only to observe its intricate design, but to deduce a kind of purpose for mankind as a result. We witness the awesome design of God's presence in the bewildering details of the beauty, power, and precision of nature seen through our microscopes and telescopes. Yet, the true significance of the design and plan for each element in God's creation can only be apprehended as we discover purpose—the reason for which we were born. The vision that opens a future to us is not a matter of empirical evidence, but faith in the news of God's redemption through Christ's sacrifice. It is our abandonment to that faith that allows us to discover purpose on its deepest levels.[4]

Until we seek the source of truth—in our relationship with God, our Creator—we cannot hope to live with the wonderful sense of significance, meaning, and purpose that every soul longs to know. Rather than placing confidence in our own self-reliant, moral resolve, it is our honest search for truth that transforms us from self-centeredness to God-centeredness. Truth asks that the uncritical embrace of naturalism, with its attendant rootlessness, relativism, loneliness, and sense of futility, be replaced with the abundant life that Jesus promises (John 10:10). As we embrace God's truth, we learn to be motivated by love for the Designer and Savior, who promised that if we would seek Him with our whole heart we would find Him (Deut. 4:29).[5]

Christian Manifesto

God's plan for your life is what I call your "Christian mani-festo." As you surrender your life to the blessed Holy Spirit, He will teach you to develop the character and abilities you need to fulfill the divine purpose for which you were born. What you *do* can never define who you *are*. As believers, we become sons and daughters of God and find our significance and fulfillment in relationship with our Creator alone. He who made us unique individuals is also delighting in our fulfillment of personal destiny.

The Westminster Catechism describes the highest purpose for mankind, according to Scripture: "Man's chief end is to glorify God, and to enjoy him forever."[6] Part of glorifying God and enjoy-ing Him forever involves the satisfaction of what you do every day in the workplace. There you learn to appreciate your anointed purpose for life, accepting it as a blessed gift from God. It is in the daily duties of chosen employment or vocation where a sense of significance, valuable relationships, and the satisfaction of personal challenge can be realized.

For some, that workplace may be the home where you nurture and care for your family. For others, your workplace may be the farm, factory, corporate business, retail, education, hospital, emer-gency response team, athletics, military, research laboratory—or a myriad of other jobs and professions needed within our society. The important thing to consider in choosing your workplace is that you not simply look for a job. If you want to know true fulfillment in life, you must first seek personal relationship with God.

In cultivating that relationship, you will discover His hand guiding you into areas of purpose and destiny regarding your place of employment as well as in relationships and every other issue of life. That divine guidance that we can expect is taught plainly throughout Scripture. For example, the Book of Proverbs teaches: "Trust in the LORD with all your heart, And lean not on your own understanding; In all your ways acknowledge Him, And He shall direct your paths" (Prov. 3:5–6.)

Unfortunately, that is not the approach to life for many people. Armed with a naturalistic philosophy of self-reliance, these people are known only for what they do, not for who they are. As a result, they feel devalued, vexed by competition and their need to "fight" for success.

Only a personal relationship with God can restore lost dignity to a homemaker, schoolteacher, farmer, or laborer. Indeed, no matter the status given by society to a career, profession, or job, without meaningful relationship with God no vocation can give dignity or significance to life. Not even the "stardom" of Hollywood or athletic achievement can give a sense of fulfillment or destiny without knowing God.

Sometimes your Christian manifesto means simply being a servant, living without acclaim, and walking in satisfying relationship with God as you complete the tasks you are given each day. It is asking God to live out His life in you, whatever the nature of your vocation, profession, or work.

Work is a biblical injunction, which brings the blessing of God on your life. Scripture condemns laziness: "He who is slothful in his work Is a brother to him who is a great destroyer" (Prov. 18:9). Scripture also forbids greed and covetousness as a motivation or goal of our work. Jesus declared plainly: "For what profit is it to a man if he gains the whole world, and loses his own soul? Or what will a man give in exchange for his soul?" (Matt. 16:26). It is in cultivating relationship with your Creator that you will find the true meaning of life, not in the fortunes that you amass. He will reveal your unique purpose for life, which will guarantee personal fulfillment as a unique servant of God.

The law of sowing and reaping

Jesus taught the reality of the principle of sowing and reaping. In this agricultural analogy, He warns about the "poor soil" that does not produce a good harvest:

> The sower sows the word. And these are the ones by the wayside where the word is sown. When they hear, Satan comes immediately and takes away the word that was sown in their hearts. These likewise are the ones sown on stony ground who, when they hear the word, immediately receive it with gladness; and they have no root in themselves, and so endure only for a time. Afterward, when tribulation or persecution arises for the word's sake, immediately they stumble. Now these are the ones sown among thorns; they are the ones who hear the word, and the cares of this world, the deceitfulness of riches, and the desires for other things entering in choke the word, and it becomes unfruitful. But these are the ones sown on good ground, those who hear the word, accept it, and bear fruit: some thirtyfold, some sixty, and some a hundred.
>
> —Mark 4:14–20

In this parable, Jesus describes the folly of allowing the deceitfulness of riches, the worries and cares of this world, and persecution or tribulation to make you fail in life. The seed that is sown into each life is the same eternal, life-giving Word of God. There is a mystery involved in the different responses people have to God's Word. But we know from Scripture that personal failure in life is sometimes caused by the deceitfulness of riches or the thorns of tribulation. Surrendering your life to the Designer of your DNA is the only way to insure against deception and wrong desires for things that can result in personal failure.

Service

Surrendering your agenda and desires to God subsequently requires a willingness to serve others. If you desire the beauty of character of your Master and Savior, Jesus Christ, you will have to have the same attitude toward others He did as He walked the Earth. He taught His disciples:

> You know that the rulers of the Gentiles lord it over them, and those who are great exercise authority over them. Yet it shall not be so among you; but whoever desires to become great among you, let him be your servant. And whoever desires to be first among you, let him be your slave—just as the Son of Man did not come to be served, but to serve, and to give His life a ransom for many.
>
> —MATTHEW 20:25–28

Jesus, the Master, took a towel and a basin and washed His disciples' feet. We must cultivate that same humble attitude of servanthood in our lives, surrendering ourselves to become people who delight in caring for the most mundane needs of a human being. As a physician, it is a privilege for me to care for many people. I understand that service without love is a hollow, empty caricature of our Master's design. He wants me to be totally committed to a caring relationship with my patients, giving of myself to their needs in every way possible.

Fulfilling your Christian manifesto in the workplace means learning to appreciate your employers, coworkers, clients, and customers. You can even appreciate the difficulties of a seventy-hour workweek or other "negatives" you encounter as you determine to serve the Lord in love. The attitude of a servant is never hostile or lazy; it is conciliatory and selfless, intent on fulfilling the task at hand to the best of your ability. You must determine that your attitudes and actions toward others is ethical and, above all, kind. In that way you will fulfill the commandment of God in the workplace, which teaches you to love others as you love yourself.

Work is never 100 percent joy filled. I have experienced many seasons when my work has gone through what I call "dry spells." When I realized a lack of fulfillment in my work, I usually found that my attitude was at fault. Even if situations and people "grate" against my mind, I must be willing to put up with people and circumstances in order to enjoy the beauty of anointed purpose in my life.

God's grace is sufficient for all the negative challenges we face in the workplace He has designated for us. And Scripture teaches that we should not "grow weary while doing good, for in due season we shall reap if we do not lose heart. Therefore, as we have opportunity, let us do good to all, especially to those who are of the household of faith" (Gal. 6:9–10).

Encouragement

I knew a Christian businessman who assumed responsibility for a local restaurant that was in bankruptcy. Because of his caring management style, constantly encouraging his employees, creating a positive atmosphere, and giving them a sense of ownership, he succeeded in turning the business around. He was able to pay off all debt and make the restaurant a successful enterprise. He chose to demonstrate love in the workplace to his employees and customers, making a difference in the lives of those around him. In the process, he turned another's business failure into a wonderful success.

Barnabas was the apostle who took the newly converted Saul (who became the apostle Paul) under his wing and encouraged him when others still feared him because of his former murderous intent toward Christians. The name *Barnabas* means "son of encouragement." God used him to encourage Saul to fulfill his ministry for Christ. To truly enjoy success in the workplace, we must cultivate this Barnabas attitude of encouragement and respect for others. Encouraging others allows us to enjoy their successes as well.

It is also important to look in the mirror and encourage yourself. You don't have to live in fear, guilt, or remorse over past failures; you simply need to ask God for forgiveness. As you receive His cleansing through the blood of Christ, you will learn how to draw near to Him. You will know the fulfillment of living in dependence on Him for your life's vocation, relationships, and all activities.

One of the people closest to me has a beautiful personality with a lovely gift of analytical thinking. He can quite accurately understand not only what people do, but why they do it. Unfortunately, he has allowed this gifting to become a negative force in his life, forming critical and judgmental ideas of everyone with whom he relates. This kind of negative thinking not only affects personal relationships, it can also lead to physical ailments and mental depression as well. To enjoy health on all levels it is important to approve and affirm the people around you rather than be critical and demanding.

Divine provision

As you discover your Christian manifesto, you do not need to worry about financial provision. Of course, it is helpful to develop your skills and abilities to the highest level possible in the workplace. But there will always be factors beyond your control that affect your ability to earn a living. The economy, your health, and even politics in the workplace can sometimes hinder your success. However, as you learn to walk in dependence upon God, you will discover that He is your Jehovah-Jireh—your Provider. This is a wonderful promise to all who seek to know God.

Jesus taught His disciples plainly to "seek first the kingdom of God and His righteousness, and all these things shall be added to you" (Matt. 6:33). And Scripture teaches that God gives the power to get wealth (Deut. 8:18). As you place your faith in Christ, you also have this wonderful promise: "And my God shall supply all your need according to His riches in glory by Christ Jesus" (Phil. 4:19).

It is never too late, even if you have spent a "lifetime" being unhappy in your work, to begin to seek God. As you surrender your life to God, either He will open doors to another kind of employment, or He will empower you to change your attitude and become content and fulfilled where you are. True fulfillment, as we have discussed, comes from knowing God. Cultivating that divine relationship changes your perspective of all of life. Your desires and attitudes become so centered in loving Him and receiving His love that even the work and the workers you once despised can become pleasant to you, as you delight in God's purpose for your life.

Ultimately, your Christian manifesto can be fulfilled only as far as you surrender to become conformed to the image of our Lord Jesus Christ. As you yield your life continually to God, you can join with the hymn writer in expressing your desire to become like the Master:

O to be like Thee! blessed Redeemer,
This is my constant longing and prayer;
Gladly I'll forfeit all of earth's treasures,
Jesus, Thy perfect likeness to wear.

O to be like Thee! full of compassion,
Loving, forgiving, tender and kind,
Helping the helpless, cheering the fainting,
Seeking the wandering sinner to find.

O to be like Thee! Lord, I am coming
Now to receive th'anointing divine;
All that I am and have I am bringing,
Lord, from this moment all shall be Thine.

Refrain:

O to be like Thee! O to be like Thee,
Blessed Redeemer, pure as Thou art;
Come in Thy sweetness, come in Thy fullness;
Stamp Thine own image deep on my heart.[7]

Come to Me, all you who labor and are heavy laden, and I

will give you rest. Take My yoke upon you and learn from

Me, for I am gentle and lowly in heart, and you will find rest

for your souls.

—MATTHEW 11:28–29

TRACING THE HAND OF THE CREATOR

Humans are so much more than clumps of tissues and the results of their labor. We are not simply physical entities as codfish and fir trees are. We are physical, mental, emotional, and spiritual beings...Unification of all human components means balance and communication between body, mind, emotions, and spirit. Wholeness and balance at the mental and spiritual levels are proven to affect the capacity of your body to heal physically.[1]

Some illnesses heal under the energies of the body's systems. Some require medical intervention. Other illness can be attributed to one's mental and spiritual states. Errant emotions, fears, and anxieties can kill.[2] Yet, Christ promises to give rest and peace to all who come to Him and learn His ways.

DIVINE REST

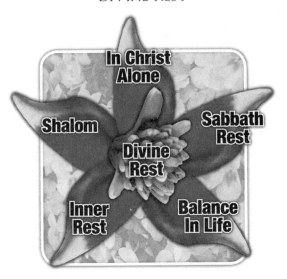

In Christ Alone

Shalom

Sabbath Rest

Divine Rest

Inner Rest

Balance In Life

A theistic scientists have gone on record reversing their philosophical position based on the empirical evidence of their scientific studies. For example, Patrick Glynn's atheism was dissolved by his understanding of the "anthropic principle," a term coined by Cambridge physicist, Brandon Carter. The principle says essentially that "all the seemingly arbitrary and unrelated constants in physics have one strange thing in common—these are precisely the values you need if you want to have a universe capable of producing life."[3]

Patrick Glynn concluded that "anthropic evidence does offer as strong an indication as reason and science alone could be expected to provide that God exists...Ironically, the picture of the universe bequeathed to us by the most advanced twentieth-century science is closer in spirit to the vision presented in the Book of Genesis than anything offered by science since Copernicus."[4] The kindness of God allows mankind to observe Him in the wonders of creation, so they might come to know their Creator. And in knowing their Creator, they can begin to experience the tranquility of rest He ordained for His creation.

In the biblical account of the beginnings, or "genesis," of life as we know it, God established a law and a pattern of rest for His creation. After He finished His work of creation, the Genesis account declares: "And on the seventh day God ended His work which He had done, and He rested on the seventh day from all His work which He had done" (Gen. 2:2). Was He fatigued? Did He need to sleep? No. It would be unthinkable for an omnipotent God to become weary. Hundreds of years later, the prophet Isaiah confirmed this fact:

> Have you not known? Have you not heard? The everlasting God, the LORD, The Creator of the ends of the earth, Neither faints nor is weary. His understanding is unsearchable. He gives power to the weak, And to those who have no might He increases strength.
>
> —ISAIAH 40:28–29

According to one theologian, "[God] did not rest, as one weary, but as one well-pleased with the instances of his own goodness and the manifestations of his own glory."[5] Yet, God built into all of creation an inherent need for rest, that is, for complete cessation from activity to allow for a time of "re-creation."

The Sabbath rest

The Hebrew word translated *rest* is *shabath*, from which we get the word *Sabbath*, meaning "to repose, desist from exertion, cease, and celebrate."[6] And in the Law of Moses, the fourth commandment declares:

> Remember the Sabbath day, to keep it holy. Six days you shall labor and do all your work, but the seventh day is the Sabbath of the LORD your God. In it you shall do no work...For in six days

the LORD made the heavens and the earth, the sea, and all that is in them, and rested the seventh day. Therefore the LORD blessed the Sabbath day and hallowed it.

—EXODUS 20:8–11

If we embrace the fact the God has blessed the Sabbath day and choose to abide by that "rest principle," we can be the beneficiaries of the blessing God intended the Sabbath to be for all creation. God's law regarding the Sabbath rest was not meant to be a burden to us, but a joy; it was given by a loving Creator, who understands the needs of His creation. He established a Sabbath rest to ensure our freedom from sickness and other ills.

The wisdom of the Creator addresses the need inherent in all of creation for re-creative rest. For example, God instructed His people to allow the land they cultivated to experience a Sabbath rest:

And the LORD spoke to Moses on Mount Sinai, saying...'Six years you shall sow your field, and six years you shall prune your vineyard, and gather its fruit; but in the seventh year there shall be a sabbath of solemn rest for the land, a Sabbath to the LORD. You shall neither sow your field nor prune your vineyard.

—LEVITICUS 25:1, 3–4

Agriculturalists now understand the terrible reality of depleting the soil by continually planting and harvesting it. It needs time to replenish the minerals and other elements required to produce healthy crops. Early in our nation's history, in the Virginia colony, the plantation owners failed to rest the land or rotate crops. As a result, the land became burned out and the best of the agricultural industry moved to other areas of the country to work "healthy" land.

We are like the land—our body as well as our psyche and spirit must have proper times of rest so that we don't "burn out."

Resting re-creates strength in life; it is necessary to every area of our health. Some studies have suggested that one third of the people don't get enough restful sleep every night. And science has correlated the amount of sleep one gets with your potential for longevity, as much as any other major factor. The importance of rest cannot be overstated as it relates to overall well-being.

As a competitive long-distance runner, I learned that when running a distance of over fifty miles, you can actually rest muscles by alternating between fast walking and running, and still maintain the same progress as if you ran all the way. For example, if you are doing a one hundred-mile run, you can run seven minutes and walk three minutes, which keeps the body from getting overly fatigued and causing damage to your health. Even in this strenuous sport, the ability to "rest" muscles from constant tension is one of the greatest benefits to performance over the "long haul."

In every area of life, we must consider the God-given need for rest of body, mind, and spirit. Whether in our work, our play, our relationships, or our generally busy lives, we will accomplish the most if we learn to live within the limitations designed by our Creator. While it is important to exercise, it is also important for general health that we get appropriate amounts of quality rest.

Shalom—Peace

From our infancy we have been made aware of the need for rest. Complete rest is a time for ceasing all physical, mental, even emotional involvement and simply "reposing." Usually that kind of rest implies hours of sleeping each night, but not always. Sometimes, to experience rest involves simply learning to release worries, cares, and conflicts of our daily lives, which can wreak havoc with our health on all levels.

As important as physical rest is to the body, so is peace vital to the rest of the soul. As we discussed in our devotional on *shalom*, this profound rest of spirit and soul implies completeness, safety, health, prosperity, and contentment (see Day 18). We also studied the promise of Jesus to give to us His peace, which transcends the troubles of this world (see John 16:33). According to Scripture there is a peace that "surpasses all understanding" (Phil 4:7). Christ taught clearly that He is the source of true quietness and rest for our souls:

> Come unto Me, all you who labor and are heavy laden, and I will give you rest. Take My yoke upon you and learn from Me, for I am gentle and lowly in heart, and you will find rest for your souls. For My yoke is easy and My burden is light.
> —Matthew 11:28–30

Here Jesus uses the analogy of a farming implement—the yoke— to give us a picture of a life that is surrendered to Him. The people He was speaking to were very familiar with Jesus' analogy of a yoke, which was used to bind two oxen together to walk side by side. One of the animals could not go or stop without the other, or change directions independently. An older oxen was typically yoked with a younger one to teach it how to yield to the yoke without rubbing against it and getting hurt. Jesus promised that if we would "yoke" up with Him, we could walk comfortably together with Him through life. He did not promise that we would not face problems. But, walking in harmony with the "older" ox, we will learn from Christ how to walk through every challenge of life. That dependency on our Savior will lead us into rest for our souls.

In Christ alone

Our state of mind is a key to being able to sleep well at night. As believers, we must follow the counsel of Scripture to bring all of our anxieties and fears and conflicts to God in prayer. As we learn to spend time quietly waiting in prayer before God, we will enter into the wonderful rest He promises. When we decide to try God's way, we can experience the healing power of His rest in our body, mind, and spirit.

To seek divine rest is a determined choice Christians have to make as we face the overwhelming conflicts of daily life. We must throw all of our care upon Him, because He cares for us (see 1 Pet. 5:7.) Choosing to rely on Christ alone in all of life's situations will teach us how to rely on Him especially in difficult situations with which we cannot cope. It is exhilarating to see the hand of God move into a situation and change it in ways we could never have done.

Inner rest

The most important aspect of rest is inner rest. More than simply an outward cessation from activity, the rest we need is spiritual. As we wait on God and fill our minds with His Word, we are enabled to trust His love with even the most devastating situations we face. Scripture promises:

> You will keep him in perfect peace, Whose mind is stayed on You, Because he trusts in You.
>
> —Isaiah 26:3

Inner rest may be the most important benefit we draw from Christ. We need a reasonable and peaceful state of mind in order to respond positively to the challenges of daily life. King Solomon understood the connection between inner wholeness and our physical health. He wrote: "A merry heart does good, like medicine, But a broken spirit dries the bones" (Prov. 17:22).

Intuitively, you may be aware that you are not a haphazard entity of divided portions—brain, body, and spirit. Each part of your DNA is intricately connected, part of a singularity, and therefore, each part influences the others. Science is just now testing out the details of the depth of those internal relationships. For example, recent research indicates that emotional pain excites the same parts of the brain as physical pain does. Numerous studies have now pointed out the weight of the mind-body connection. We are being increasingly informed about the role of depression, loneliness, unhappiness, fear, and anger in the development and prolongation of diseases such as cancer, heart disease, diabetes, and asthma.[7]

The need for physical rest and for freedom from the tensions of life in order to enjoy true rest for our physical bodies has long been established. On a deeper level, this inner rest is the state of mind in which we can be truly happy in Christ. Emotional and spiritual contentment depend on being at peace with God and with ourselves to such an extent that we need nothing else to stimulate our happiness. We cease to look for satisfaction in all the wrong places and discover complete fulfillment in our relationship with our Creator.

Balance in life

Scientifically, the primary characteristic of both cure and healing in all of life is understood to be *balance*. For example, the human body was designed to maintain balance and to make the necessary adjustments when natural balance is overturned. Take the relatively simple examples of heat and cold. When you become chilled, you start to shiver. By this mechanism, your body is trying to generate heat and reestablish appropriate body temperature. Likewise, sweating is the body's attempt to lower the temperature of the body when it is exposed to a hot environment. The evaporation of sweat off the skin is intended to rebalance the body's temperature to its preferred level.[8]

Balance is also required in order to experience rest for our souls. Surrender to our divine destiny in vocation and work will help to affect this balance. Taking time for rest and recreation will also create balance. Perhaps most important, however, is that we learn to rest in God—in His redemption. As we seek mental and emotional satisfaction through study of the Word of God, prayer, and communion with Him, we will discover His wonderful provision for all our needs. And we will not "suffer" a sense of lack, which seeks to be satisfied with apparent happiness from lesser sources.

We can truly appreciate the rest that Peter described, receiving from God His "perfect well-being, all necessary good, all spiritual prosperity, and freedom from fears and agitating passions and moral conflicts" (2 Pet. 1:2, AMP). I wish everyone could enjoy this divine promise for perfect balance and well-being. This profound, inner rest from mental, emotional, and relational conflicts promised in Scripture sounds almost too good to be true. But for one who dares to seek God, to wait on Him, and to fill his or her mind with the truth of God's Word, the divine rest of God will increasingly rule in every dimension of life. Pursuing a relationship with God will create a divine balance for all of life. And that balance will bring profound rest to your life.

Balance and recreation

While divine rest comes from seeking Christ primarily, that does not mean we cannot enjoy natural forms of recreation. I have a friend who says when he goes to a medical conference, he plans for half the time to be spent in work and half in pleasure. It is important that we make choices for our lives that allow for a certain amount of time devoted to meaningful employment, as well as time set aside to have fun. In these ways, also, we achieve balance, on which all of creation thrives.

My father loved investigating the English language. One of his favorite hobbies was reading good literature. More importantly, my father loved the truths of Scripture and delighted in searching out one or two biblical truths at a time and meditating on them. His studies enabled him to know the Lord in a deeply meaningful way. In contrast to my father's meditative mind, my mother loved to be outdoors and enjoy God's nature. She enjoyed spending time with friends on the golf course, participating in one of her greatest delights—the sport of golf. My parents enjoyed two very different, yet healthy, forms of "re-creation." People who are "mental" can get great pleasure from mental activities, while others find pleasure in doing something physical, such as playing golf or tennis.

In order to find balance in life and enjoy relief from constant work and other demanding activities, many people engage in a time of spiritual retreat. This retreat may take the form of a gathering of believers who study and pray together for several days in a beautiful resort area. It may simply be a time of open-hearted sharing with a friend, or it could be stealing away for a few private moments during your workday to engage in prayer and meditation. The time we take to recreate and meditate on the greatness and beauty of our God will work an inward change in our lives, making us true worshipers of God. It will also help us become a better example of Christlikeness to our neighbors.

John Piper has stated: "God is most glorified when we are satisfied with Him."[9] As we learn to rest in the redemption of Christ, we will become completely satisfied with God alone. And as we enjoy His divine rest in our mind and spirit, we will respond to life's most demanding situations in a positive way. The prophet Isaiah knew the power available to those who wait on God:

> Even youths shall faint and be weary, and [selected] young men shall feebly stumble and fall exhausted; But those who wait for the Lord [who expect, look for, and hope in Him] shall change and renew their strength and power; they shall lift their wings and mount up [close to God] as eagles [mount up to the sun]; they shall run and not be weary, they shall walk and not faint or become tired.
> —Isaiah 40:30–31, AMP

The people in whom I recognize the glow of God's Spirit, who are truly anointed to fulfill their divine destiny in life, are those who have found their rest in Christ. They learn from yielding their lives to the Holy Spirit how to find the balance in life that is so necessary. As they cultivate the habit of waiting on God, they are prepared to face any situation in life with a peaceful mind and restful spirit.

The Lord is my shepherd; I shall not want...I will fear no evil;

For You are with me; Your rod and Your staff, they comfort me.

—Psalm 23:1, 4

Now may our Lord Jesus Christ Himself, and our God and

Father, who has loved us and given us everlasting consolation

and good hope by grace, comfort your hearts and establish you

in every good word and work.

—2 Thessalonians 2:16–17

Tracing the Hand of the Creator

Although we may not think of it as such, the skin is the largest organ of the body. It weighs eight or nine pounds and has a surface area of over two square yards. The skin performs remarkable services. Our bodies are 60 percent water, and were it not for the skin we would quickly puddle the floor. The skin must keep almost all of the water in, while allowing some to escape, through sweating, for temperature control. In addition, it must be waterproof from the outside as well. About a pint of water is undetectably lost through the skin every day, called insensible perspiration. When the thermometer is blistering, however, it is possible to lose as much as two gallons a day through overt perspiration.[1]

We have nine thousand taste buds in our mouths and over four hundred touch cells per square inch of skin. Skin cells are continuously turning over—billions every day. The epidermis is replaced every couple of weeks. Over a lifetime we each shed forty pounds of dead skin. Though we often take it for granted, such a resilient organ should demand our deep appreciation.[2]

DIVINE COMFORT

Emotional loss, broken hearts, mental anguish—all are part of the human experience; no one is exempt. After suffering the painful loss of a loved one, we often hear the timeworn cliché, "Time heals all wounds." Unfortunately, the experience of many is that even if the passage of time dulls the ache, they never really "get over" their loss; they just learn to manage their pain. Some look for "escapes" into alcohol or tranquilizers, activities, or other relationships. Sadly, they have never appreciated the wonderful promise and power of divine comfort offered to us in Scripture and realized by many believers who testify of its healing power.

By definition, comfort is "consolation in time of trouble or worry, a feeling of relief or encouragement; solace; contented well-being; a satisfying or enjoyable experience."[3] *Solace*, a synonym for *comfort*, means "alleviation of grief or anxiety; a source of relief or consolation."[4] As we learn to receive the tangible comfort of God offered in Scripture, our hearts will be filled with joy and contentment, even in the face of life's painful realities and losses.

Our Shepherd

The twenty-third psalm, one of the most beloved of all the psalms, paints a beautiful picture of our Lord as a Shepherd, full of comfort and all that is needed to satisfy His sheep. Countless people of every nation on Earth have found this endearing analogy of our Lord to be a healing balm, a real comfort, in their time of sorrow and pain. I am convinced that if you take a moment to declare reverently: "The Lord is *my* Shepherd," you will experience the comfort of God.

W. Phillip Keller, author of the bestselling book, *A Shepherd Looks at Psalm 23*, gives us wonderful insight into the pastoral aspects of shepherding, which make the promises of this psalm more meaningful. Regarding the statement: "He makes me to lie down in green pastures," he writes:

> The strange thing about sheep is that because of their very make-up it is almost impossible for them to be made to lie down unless four requirements are met. Owing to their timidity they refuse to lie down unless they are free of all fear. Because of the social behavior within a flock, sheep will not lie down unless they are free from friction with others of their kind. If tormented by flies or parasites, sheep will not lie down. Only when free of these pests can they relax. Lastly, sheep will not lie down as long as they feel in need of finding food. They must be free from hunger...to be at rest there must be a definite sense of freedom from fear, tension, aggravations, and hunger...it is only the shepherd himself who can provide release from these anxieties.[5]

Jesus referred to Himself as the Good Shepherd (see John 10:14), and to His followers as sheep. And He promised that He would provide all that His followers need to experience freedom from the anxieties of life that would keep us from "lying down in green pastures." In a personal relationship with Christ, we have everything we need for true satisfaction. He continually offers those who love Him the blessings of *provision, protection, peace,* and *joy,* and most of all, His divine *presence* to guide and comfort us. Here are just a few of those precious promises that offer profound comfort for all who will receive it:

Presence

Jesus answered and said to him, "If anyone loves me, he will keep My word; and my Father will love him, and We will come to him and make Our home with him.

—JOHN 14:23

Provision

Therefore do not worry, saying, "What shall we eat?" or "What shall we drink?"…For your heavenly Father knows that you need all these things. But seek first the kingdom of God and His righteousness, and all these things shall be added to you.

—MATTHEW 6:31–33

Protection

Holy Father, keep through Your name those whom You have given Me, that they may be one as We are…I do not pray for these alone, but also for those who will believe in Me through their word.

—JOHN 17:11, 20

Peace

Peace I leave with you, My peace I give to you; not as the world gives do I give to you. Let not your heart be troubled, neither let it be afraid.

—JOHN 14:27

Joy

These things I have spoken to you, that My joy may remain in you, and that your joy may be full.

—John 15:11

Divine Comforter

Jesus understood that we would have problems in this life, that we would suffer grief and loss. He told His disciples: "These things I have spoken to you, that in Me you may have peace. In the world you will have tribulation; but be of good cheer, I have overcome the world" (John 16:33). When the disciples were filled with grief because Jesus told them He would be going away, He gave them this wonderful promise:

> And I will pray the Father, and he shall give you another Comforter, that he may abide with you for ever; Even the Spirit of truth, whom the world cannot receive, because it seeth him not, neither knoweth him: but ye know him; for he dwelleth with you, and shall be in you…But the Comforter, which is the Holy Ghost, whom the Father will send in my name, he shall teach you all things.
>
> —John 14:16–17, 26, kjv

It is awesome to think that the Holy Spirit, God Himself, is given to us that we might receive the divine comfort we so desperately need in life's most painful circumstances. God's divine power to give relief from grief and anxiety offers true healing that time alone cannot give. As we receive Christ as Savior and trust the Holy Spirit to do His precious work in our lives, God's presence in our lives heals our minds and hearts and give us supernatural peace and joy. This is what the apostle Paul referred to when he declared: "For the kingdom of God is not eating and drinking, but righteousness and peace and joy in the Holy Spirit" (Rom. 14:17).

Comfort in affliction and tribulation

Pain. That dreaded word is well-known to every human being. From the tiniest child who scrapes his knee on the sidewalk, to the elderly who has suffered numerous kinds of physical, emotional, relational, and psychological pain, the word itself brings a cry for cure—for comfort.

Regarding physical pain, our skin is both our shield from pain and an important method of sensing pain that comes from our external world. Because of its contact with the external world, skin is inevitably prone to suffer lacerations, abrasions, burns, punctures, and exposure to irritants. Scabs, blisters, rashes, and inflammation are the painful testaments of skin's tireless self-curing processes at work. They are not the injury—rather they are evidence of the body healing itself.

Consider the genius of our divine Creator in the complex processes of the *skin* to protect and "comfort" your body. (See page 219.) On occasion of an injury to your skin—such as a cut—a highly complex series of reactions is immediately initiated, requiring involvement by many kinds of specialized cells. It also requires the production of, and appropriate use of, specialized proteins for rebuilding as well as communication and coordination through signaling pathways. No link in the chain will engage in the absence of other links.

The immediate healing response in the skin is a nervous constriction (narrowing) of the blood vessels. Then, within the first five minutes after trauma, vasodilation (opening the vessels) allows a flood of platelets borne by blood plasma into the area from the capillaries. Strands of fibrinogen, a protein synthesized by the liver, weave together to form substantial portions of a blood clot, which will stanch the blood flow. Within one to six hours after injury, white blood cells (polymorphonuclear leukocytes) are mobilized and attracted to the site by chemicals in the blood plasma to fight bacteria and remove debris such as dead cells. Macrophages (Greek for "big eaters") respond within twenty-four to forty-eight hours to remove clotted blood and damaged tissue.[6]

Just as God designed complex mechanisms of the skin for our physical healing, so He has given believers the necessary healing processes for every painful circumstance of life. Even Old Testament saints understood that God offers relief from distress and emotional and mental pain. The psalmist declared: "This is my comfort in my affliction, For Your word has given me life" (Ps. 119:50). The prophet Isaiah proclaimed: "'Comfort, yes, comfort My people!' Says your God. 'Speak comfort to Jerusalem, and cry out to her, That her warfare is ended, That her iniquity is pardoned'" (Isa. 40:1–2). Pardon from sin brings the comfort of God and peace to our hearts and fills us with His joy.

The kindness of God is so great, that even if the cause of our suffering is our own wrongdoing, He will hear our cry and forgive us, giving us His divine comfort. Who can fathom the mercy of God—the God of all comfort—who loves His children so much that He will find a way to alleviate our pain and misery with His divine comfort? (See 2 Cor. 1:7.)

When mankind chose to live independently from God, all manner of evil and sorrow resulted from that tragic decision. It is this fallen state of mankind, with all of its inherent misery, from which Jesus came to redeem us. And God is continually offering us His love and redemption, which includes His peace and joy—and divine comfort. It is in coming to Christ (see Matt. 11:28) that we enter into relationship with God. In that relationship, He gives to us the comfort we need for the pain we experience in our fallen world. Ellen Vaughn comments:

> In the beginning, human beings were lovingly made by our Creator, crafted with clear purpose and clean lines. But sin dents, nicks, burns, stains. We ended up far from Home, in the garbage, on the curb, sitting in the dark display window of some dusty pawn shop. God found us, wherever we were. At great price, He redeemed us. We are twice His: He made us, and He bought us back.[7]

God's divine comfort is not only healing; it is redemptive. His divine comfort changes our hearts and motivates us to walk in His ways.

Consoling others

In a uniquely mysterious way, trouble and sorrow can open our hearts to receive the healing compassion and comfort of God. In turn, our capacity to comfort others who are hurting is enlarged. The relief we find from our sorrow and pain serves as a catalyst that will serve to alleviate the suffering of others as well. The apostle Paul explains this divine phenomenon:

> Blessed be the God and Father of our Lord Jesus Christ, the Father of mercies and God of all comfort, who comforts us in all our tribulation, that we may be able to comfort those who are in any trouble, with the comfort with which we ourselves are comforted by God.
>
> —2 Corinthians 1:3–4

God's purpose for the comfort we receive in our troubles is not only to heal our hearts; it is to empower us to comfort others as well. In the body of Christ, we are to live in such a way that "if one member suffers, all the members suffer with it; or if one member is honored, all the members rejoice with it" (1 Cor. 12:26). We should try to comfort a fellow believer who is suffering any kind of trouble or sorrow. Sometimes comfort is expressed simply by "being there," and letting the person know you care. The apostle Paul wrote to the Philippian church encouraging them to comfort one another:

> Therefore if there is any consolation in Christ, if any comfort of love, if any fellowship of the Spirit, if any affection and mercy, fulfill my joy by being like-minded, having the same love, being of one accord, of one mind…Let this mind be in you which was also in Christ Jesus.
>
> —Philippians 2:1–2, 5

It is clear from Scripture that divine comfort is to be a prominent characteristic of believers. First, we are to receive God's divine comfort and then we are to comfort others. Scripture teaches us especially to comfort the poor and needy. Jesus told a parable about the rich man and the beggar, Lazarus. The rich man had shown no mercy to the beggar during his lifetime. While Lazarus was comforted after his death, the rich man was in torment. When he saw Abraham at a distance, he begged for mercy. "But Abraham said, 'Son, remember that in your lifetime you received your good things, and likewise Lazarus evil things; but now he is comforted and you are tormented'" (Luke 16:25).

And in Jesus' parable about the sheep entering into eternal life and the goats failing to do so, He commends the sheep for ministering to the poor and needy:

> "For I was hungry and you gave Me food; I was thirsty and you gave Me drink; I was a stranger and you took Me in; I was naked and you clothed Me; I was sick and you visited Me; I was in prison and you came to Me." Then the righteous will answer Him, saying, "Lord, when did we see You hungry and feed You, or thirsty and give You drink?"...And the King will answer and say to them, "Assuredly, I say to you, inasmuch as you did it to one of the least of these My brethren, you did it to Me."
>
> —Matthew 25:35–37, 40

As we learn to appreciate God's wonderful gift of comfort and receive it for the healing of our own hearts, we will be empowered to give the comfort to others that they so desperately need. In this way, we can influence other lives as we share the comfort of the love of God.

By humility and the fear of the LORD Are riches and honor and life.

—PROVERBS 22:4

Tracing the Hand of the Creator

These simple facts about your body can help you appreciate the awesome design our Maker created in giving us the gift of life:

- The human body is composed of ten thousand trillion trillion atoms—a number greater than the stars of the universe. In each person, more than a trillion of these atoms are replaced every one-millionth of a second.

- We tear down and rebuild over a trillion cells every day. Each cell is a remarkable miniaturized world, with electric fields, protein factories, and hundreds of ATP energy motors two hundred thousand times smaller than a pinhead.

- We each manufacture over two million red blood cells every second. Laid side by side, our red blood cells would stretch one hundred thousand miles.[1]

MARGIN

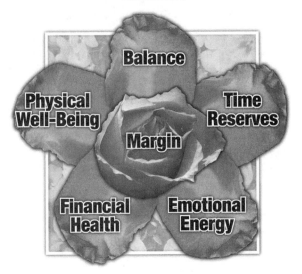

Have you ever admired the beauty of a flowering bush or a species of flowers that you did not recognize and made a comment like, "How beautiful! What is it?" Though you are unfamiliar with the plant, you are attracted to it because of its exquisite beauty. You may respond similarly to the "flower" we are calling *margin*. Its "petals" are beautiful, attractive, and attention-getting. Consider their design—emotional energy, physical energy, financial health, time reserves, and balance. Perhaps it has been a long while since you enjoyed these qualities of life personally. It is even possible that some have never experienced the wonderful freedom they represent.

Remember, by definition, that to truly *appreciate* something or someone we have to have an accurate understanding of their quality of worth. It follows, that to truly appreciate *margin* and give it proper place in our lives, we must understand its meaning and purpose. In Dr. Richard Swenson's book, *Margin, Restoring Emotional, Physical, Financial, and Time Reserves to Overloaded Lives,* he declares that margin is easy to define because the math involved is straightforward. He uses this simple equation to help us define the term:

DEFINING MARGIN

Power minus Load = Margin.

Power is made up of factors such as skills, time, emotional strength, physical strength, spiritual vitality, finances, social supports, and education.

Load combines internal factors (such as personal expectations and emotional disabilities) and external factors (such as work, relational problems and responsibilities, financial obligations, and civic involvement).[2]

The *power* we have to function in life is different for every person. And it changes for each person during different stages of life, as does the *load* we carry in life. What does *not* change is this basic principle relating to margin: "If *load* becomes greater than *power* at any given time, we enter into negative margin status—we are *overloaded.*" According to Swenson, negative margin for an extended period of time is another name for *burnout.* It is easy to conclude that to increase margin we need only to increase power or decrease load—or both.

While the definition of margin may be simple, finding and implementing the solution for overloaded lives is not. Swenson suggests that is because the pain caused by overload is not as visible as, for example, a physical injury. Emotional, psychological, social, relational, and spiritual pains are not as visible as a skin abrasion. Yet, they can be exquisitely more painful.

Living without margin in any area can cause a deep-seated subjective ache, a heaviness and pain that is difficult to describe. There are four major areas of life that need to be diligently managed in order to create the balance in life that is necessary for health:

- Emotional

- Physical

- Financial

- Time management

Of these four aspects of life, Dr. Swenson cites *emotional energy* to be paramount in importance.[3]

Emotional energy

It is vitally important to be emotionally resilient in order to confront our problems with a sense of hope and power. Dr. Swenson concludes that emotional overload saps our strength, paralyzes our resolve, and maximizes our vulnerability, leaving the door open for even further margin erosion. As we seek for necessary energies to properly address relationships, work situations, traffic jams, financial issues, and other "stresses" of our modern world, we must acknowledge our finiteness. We only have a certain amount of emotional reserves—that zest and vitality that enjoys life and enables us to initiate positive responses to people and situations. Some have more than others, but all of us can become depleted when we are required to discharge too much emotional energy at a time.[4]

We need to learn the difference between those influences that drain our emotional batteries and those that recharge them. For example, when we are sad or angry, frustrated or depressed, our emotional reserves are being spent at a rapid rate. Conversely, if we receive encouragement from significant others or enjoy the satisfaction of completing meaningful activities, our emotional reserves are being replenished.[5]

Among the solutions for restoring margin to emotional energy reserves, these are most important: Learning to cultivate social support of family, friends, community, and church, reconciling relationships, and volunteering to help others. Of course, the simple realities of enjoying rest and relaxation, learning to laugh, and allowing ourselves to cry are also extremely helpful. "Laughter lifts; crying cleanses. Both are partners in the process of emotional restoration."[6]

Expressing appreciation for the good things in life, giving of thanks, and above all, giving love, are powerful weapons in fighting against the enemies to emotional margin. Dr. Swenson states succinctly the power of giving love:

> Love is the only medicine I know of which, when used according to directions, heals completely yet takes one's life away. It is dangerous; it is uncontrollable; it is "self-expenditure"; and it can never be taken on any terms but its own. Yet as a healer of the emotions, it has no equal.[7]

Physical well-being

One of the marvels of God's creation is that He built margins into our bodies within which we can enjoy optimal health. For example, normally we use only about 20 percent of the oxygen that is present at any given moment in the blood. However, our normal heart rate of between sixty to seventy beats per minute can immediately race up to one hundred ninety to cope with an emergency. If we need to fight off a predator or run to the rescue of our child, the body provides the means needed to respond. In those few moments, we can utilize almost all of the oxygen in the bloodstream, which is available for just such emergencies.

Our body is built so that it can repair and rejuvenate when we do our part to provide it the margins of rest it needs to do so. During physical activity the human body utilizes a lot of our glycogen and other resources for energy and metabolism function. During rest periods, these vital resources can be replaced. Lack of rest caused by sleep deprivation is one of the three main factors that deplete the margin of physical energy. The other two factors are *poor conditioning* (lack of exercise) and *obesity*. According to Dr. Swenson, these three factors "constitute a physical energy desert where no margin can grow."[8]

Doctors today are dealing more with "diseases of lifestyle" than with historical infectious plagues, which are largely under control. Our civilization has created ailments that come as a result of our bad habits and poor health practices. Doctors must address patients who are victimizing themselves as a result of stress-induced illnesses, lack of sexual restraint, illicit drug use, cigarette-related disease, alcohol and drug abuse, as well as the increasing pollution-related diseases.[9]

According to Martin Shaffer, author of *Life After Stress*, "maximum bodily strength and efficiency depend upon three factors: sleep, exercise, and nutrition. Only a body that is well rested, properly exercised, and correctly fed will be able to maintain its energy reserves in the face of serious stress."[10] It is a fact that more people die in America of too much food than of too little. And most Americans do not get enough physical exercise.

Restoring margin for a healthy level of physical energy requires taking personal responsibility for your health. You have to address your needs for emotional margin, which is paramount. Then you need to change poor habits of nutrition, poor exercise patterns, and poor sleep hygiene. Simple steps to creating physical energy reserves involve eating a balanced diet, avoiding overeating, drinking a lot of water, and exercising for the heart (aerobic). It is also important to realize that you must determine to *maintain* this healthy lifestyle until you don't need it anymore. You can't store up energy or exercise benefit for the future—it has to become a part of a healthy, enjoyable lifestyle.[11]

Time reserves

With all the emphasis we hear about recreation, vacations, and holiday privileges, you may be surprised to know the average American workweek has actually increased from under forty-one hours to nearly forty-seven hours since 1973. According to a study by the National Sleep Foundation, the average employed American works a forty-six-hour workweek; 38 percent of the respondents in their study worked more than fifty hours per week.[12] This does not represent the "workaholic," who is so driven to work that they are miserable if they have a day off. Their addiction to work does not allow them to notice the lack of time for balance in their lives.

Employers are so conscious of time that they have developed skills for "time-compression techniques." They make sure that work efforts are time-intensive, creating a sense of time urgency, which results in time pressure and time stress. All these efforts create crisis time. While work time is important, so is discretionary time—margin. It is important to take time for leisure, play, free time, and time off. Time to think, time for solitude, and personal time should be a part of our lives. And, ideally, we should consider all of our time to be God's time, given to us to be used for His purposes.

Accepting personal responsibility for the twenty-four hours a day God gives us and for which we are accountable to Him is the first step in restoring the margin necessary to avoid burnout in our lives and relationships. Noted family researcher, Dolores Curran, has listed the top ten family stressors, and notes that four of them have to do with a lack of time: insufficient couple time, insufficient "me" time, insufficient family playtime, and overscheduled family calendars.[13]

According to family psychologist Dr. James Dobson, " The inevitable loser from this life in the fast lane is the little guy who is leaning against the wall with his hands in the pockets of his blue jeans. Crowded lives produce fatigue—and fatigue produces irritability—and irritability produces indifference—and indifference can be interpreted by the child as a lack of genuine affection and personal esteem."[14] Everyone needs personal time, family time, sharing time, and God time.

To restore balance to time margin, you must first become aware of the problem and the consequences it brings. Some practical suggestions for resolving the problem include: Learn to say no, turn off the television, prune back your activity calendar, practice simplicity and contentment, create buffer zones, and plan for free time.[15]

Financial health

The average credit card debt for the American family stands at eight thousand five hundred dollars. Personal bankruptcies are on the rise according to current financial news sources. And as a culture, we have become enamored with "plastic." We consider only whether we can afford the monthly credit card payment, not what the consumer debt will actually cost us, after calculating the exorbitant interest rates. We think that to have a financial margin we simply need to earn more money. The fact is that money *is not* margin. According to Dr. Swenson, establishing financial margin involves breaking the power money holds on us and learning to use it instead of being used by it.[16]

Most of us would agree that money is powerful. Jesus taught that it rivals God's place in our lives:

> No one can serve two masters; for either he will hate the one and love the other, or he will stand by and be devoted to the one and despise and be against the other. You cannot serve God and mammon (deceitful riches, money, possessions, or whatever is trusted in).
>
> —Matthew 6:24, amp

The prescription for establishing financial margin first of all involves settling this primary issue of lordship. "We are not talking about restoring financial margin for the purposes of pride, of wealth, or of meeting our security needs in a way that bypasses the Father. Instead, we are talking about the kind of financial margin that honors Him." One powerful way to break the power of money over our lives is to give it away.[17]

As we learn to walk in appreciation for our Creator, and for His many gifts to us, we must allow our financial situation to come under His lordship as well. Laws of biblical finance are clearly taught in Scripture, promising blessing and security to all who will obey them. In our book, *A Biblical Economics Manifesto*, Dr. Nash and I outline many of these biblical principles for living within financial margin, which can help sincere Christians apply biblical truth to serious economic questions.[18]

Balance

The Creator gave the body a defense system that is truly remarkable. Red blood cells are equipped to fight any inflammation of damaged tissues, and the entire immune system goes into action when there is an injury to the eye or other organ. In fact, the diseased state has been defined as *the body's reaction to injury*. When we become ill or injured, it is vitally important that the body respond to the crisis in a balanced way.

Regarding our physical well-being, if people live in a "hothouse" environment where their immune systems have not been challenged by various bacteria and viruses, they are frequently more susceptible to these disease-causing agents because their immunities have not been built up against them. Vaccines are simply "weak" challenges that present bacterial exposure to various diseases, allowing the body to build up immunity to these viral protein structures. They allow the body to give a balanced reaction instead of overreacting to full exposure of dangerous bacteria. Too great a reaction can create a crisis in the body; too little reaction can do the same. Balance is the key to recovery.

So it is in all areas of life—balanced response is key to recovery. Whether you are addressing psychological injuries of life, emotional hurts, spiritual maladies, or financial woes, you need to find the balanced response that will allow for full recovery. Consider, for example, some of the major areas of life in which you want to succeed—personal health, employment, financial security, civic duties, and relationships—with God, family, friends, and self. It is clear that you need to strike a balance of priorities in order to succeed. There are those who throw aside any thought of balance, and pursue one goal, such as athletic success, career, or even spiritual pursuits, at the peril of health, financial security, and relationships. They are certain to fail in many areas of life, sacrificing them to their primary goal.[19]

There will always be more opportunities, activities, requests, and demands placed on your time than you can advisedly accept if you are to maintain, or restore healthy balance to your frenzied life. Of course, as you learn to appreciate your Creator, taking time to wait on Him and seeking His direction for your life, you will become sensitive to what pleases Him. In that place of intimate communion with God, as you bow in adoration and worship of Him, you can expect to receive His wisdom that is promised to those who seek Him (Prov. 3:21–24). Even before our modern "fast lane" living, the hymn writer discovered the solution to living within healthy margin:

> Take time to be holy; speak oft with thy Lord;
> Abide in Him always, and feed on His Word.
> Make friends with God's children, help those who are weak,
> Forgetting in nothing His blessing to seek.
>
> Take time to be holy, the world rushes on;
> Spend much time in secret, with Jesus alone.
> By looking to Jesus, like Him thou shalt be;

Thy friends in thy conduct His likeness shall see.

Take time to be holy, let Him by thy Guide;
And run not before Him, whatever betide.
In joy or in sorrow, still follow thy Lord,
And, looking to Jesus, still trust in His Word.[20]

Waiting on the Lord, meditating on Scripture and giving ourselves to prayer will bring to us the supernatural wisdom we need to pursue balance in the exacting challenges of life. There can be no true success in life without giving God His rightful place at the center of all we are and all we do. He teaches us how to live life successfully in every area of life by maintaining a healthy margin.

God anointed Jesus of Nazareth with the Holy Spirit and with power, who went about doing good and healing all who were oppressed by the devil, for God was with Him.

—Acts 10:38

Tracing the Hand of the Creator

In terms of sickness and healing, all of life can be conceived of as a reaction to injury that is both appropriate and balanced. This is true for trauma, or disease, or a lost and confused spirit. The grandeur of the design—*your* design—is evident in every cell and its particular task. Each one of those cells developed from the zygote.

The zygote is the "computer chip" that contains all of the Creator's design stored in the "memory banks" of its DNA molecule. The awesome programming of this biological computer chip determines all of your growth and functions of life—from eyelids that blink, to stomach acids that digest food, to sneezes that expel irritants. They all have purpose, and they all develop from the intricate instructions of the zygote.[1]

The healing in a simple cut finger is a remarkably potent manifestation of a Creator's design for your healing. The capacity for inner healing is also determined by our design, by the nature with which we were created.[2]

HEALING

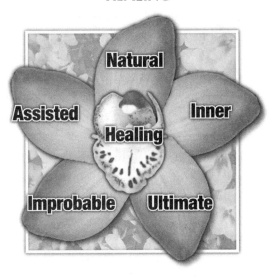

When the Creator designed your DNA, He programmed it with vast amounts of information to make you the unique individual you are. He placed those microscopic strands of DNA into the first man He created, who then perpetuated their awesome design as he proceeded to populate the world. The design of that DNA molecule was passed down from the first man to his children and through them to every generation since the beginning of time. You and I are a product of that DNA design, and you will pass it along to your children. These self-perpetuating identity strands are all a little different, resulting in the uniqueness of personality and race. But there is very little substantive difference between the two.

What is important is not the superficiality of external appearance, but our recognition of the awesome wonder of our Creator's design for mankind. Unfortunately, though every person is a product of the same genius-designed DNA, many refuse to look deeper than the superficialities of outward appearance of the design. They ignore the wonder of the design that conclusively leads to considering the nature of the Designer. The key to enjoying the ultimate potential of our inherited DNA is to appreciate and adore God, our Creator.

I have a friend who is obese. He is an angry man as well. His basic DNA is very similar to yours and mine. Yet, he has abused his body and allowed his mind and emotions to become poisoned through his negative reactions to life. His physical health, as well as his emotional and relational well-being, suffer as a result. Another colleague has a "smiling" personality. He is always pleasant and helpful, and one of the most polite gentlemen I have ever met. His personal lifestyle is one of personal conditioning—physically, mentally, and spiritually. His grateful attitude manifests these positive traits, strengthened by enhancing the basic DNA he has been given.

In his book, *Captured by Grace*, David Jeremiah quotes 2003 research that concluded: "Grateful people receive a wide range of benefits simply because of their perspective on life. They sleep better and enjoy better physical health. Their social relationships are enhanced. They have a deeper and rewarding sense of spirituality. Gratitude is one heaping helping of wellness—something more beneficial than ten thousand vitamins or ten years of workouts at the gym."[3]

Our health—our physical, mental, and spiritual well-being—is directly related to our relationship with the Creator. If we seek God to receive His anointing on our lives, to live in relationship with Him, and to rest in His redemption, we will enjoy the health He has ordained for us to experience. Our relationship with Christ will fill us with His love and motivate us to care for the gift of life He has given us on every level.

God placed within the body a remarkable *natural* "healing mechanism," which springs into action at the first sign of trauma or injury. Along with this phenomenal, innate healing power of the body, He has given wisdom and knowledge to doctors to *assist* the body in its healing processes. When we need *inner* healing of our minds and emotions, our Creator has made provision for that need as well through prayer, forgiveness, and other means of grace. And doctors and scientists are now attesting to the wonderful healing power of prayer when a supernatural intervention is needed for an *improbable* healing. Of course, eternity with God will provide for us the *ultimate* healing of our entire being, when we are fully satisfied, resting in His loving arms forever. In this devotional, we will present the basic concept involved in each of these provisions for healing that our Creator has given to us as His gifts.[4]

Natural healing

Your body was created with an intricate design for health that requires *balance*. It is so efficient, that even when balance is disturbed, the body can make adjustments to help maintain its necessary balance. By simple definition, the basis of all disease is a response to injury. In order to cure disease, the body must provide a balanced physical response, using a combination of its many inborn healing mechanisms.

Scientists still cannot explain all of these healing mechanisms observed in the body's natural defense system. Every tissue in the body displays an almost inexplicable complexity in its rejuvenating and renewing capacities. These healing, restorative functions are innate to the body's fabulous design, originating in the essence of the human zygote at conception (consisting of forty-six chromosomes—twenty-three from the mother and twenty-three from the father). While scientists do not understand how it works, they have observed that the human body is the most intricate, extravagant, and misunderstood *engineering feat* in the universe.

We mentioned that when we cut a finger there is an immensely complex response for repair in each cell in the area of the injury. Through an elaborate cascade of reactions, protein messages are sent and received. Vessels are narrowed accordingly, protective scabs are constructed, and cell duplication for the regeneration of new flesh begins. This all involves thousands and thousands of individual reactions amongst the trillions of atoms that make up the cells around the wound site. It is a process of unfathomable complexity, mystery, and mastery.

Indeed, if the skin were not able to "heal itself," no type of surgery could be performed on the human body. When a wound occurs to the skin, the healing of that wound requires the emergency involvement of many kinds of specialized cells, which spring into action spontaneously upon "knowledge" of the situation. Physical healing also requires the formation of specialized proteins for rebuilding the tissues involved. There are intense communications and coordination of the innate healing processes involved that occur through signaling pathways. If one link in the healing chain were to malfunction, no other link would engage in its task relating to the healing process. The repair process of the skin demonstrates a level of specificity and interconnectedness much more elaborate than the inner workings of a Swiss clock.

There simply is no explanation, outside of the existence of an *innate design for healing* created by a caring Designer, for the incredibly complex and ordered process of skin healing. This propensity for life through the innate healing ability of the body could be demonstrated in every system of the organism; it is built into the intricate design of the DNA of every human being. This phenomenon alone should cause us to bow in adoration of our Creator.

Assisted healing

There are times when the body is not able to effectively use its innate healing properties without the intervention of a knowledgeable physician's assistance. Because of severe injury or catastrophic events such as heart attacks and strokes, the body would not survive without medical assistance. Only as we understand that all knowledge comes from the Creator, will we properly assess the wonders of medical science and its learned ability to assist the body in its healing processes.

The essence of medical science is the observation of, appreciation for, and careful intervention in the natural design when it is needed. In medicine, at least, our practice is bound as tightly to our scientific understanding of the manifestations of the Creator's knowledge as fruit is to the tree. When you are sick or injured, you turn for healing to those men and women who must do their job within their understanding of our created design. They employ techniques and apply scientific knowledge to reestablish the integrity of a body whose natural ability to defend or develop is enfeebled, broken down, or nonexistent. They apply the techniques in line with principles of nature, of the divine design of the body.[5]

As an eye surgeon, I am very familiar with the need for and meaning of "aligning" medical practice with the intricate details of the Creator's design. Cataracts, which are a clouding of the lenses in the eyes, are usually a natural result of aging, although other factors sometimes contribute to the formation. The intervention of a physician is needed to correct the impairment of vision caused by a cataract. Cataract surgery is an excellent example of the physician's role in assisting the body's God-given abilities to heal by entering where natural processes are limited or absent.

Physicians and surgeons are not the only "assistants" to the healing of your body. Without researchers, we would not be able to apply their invaluable knowledge of the body's "engineering systems" to our healing techniques. Because the DNA provides such detailed instructions for the construction of the whole human body, understanding its intricate function helps researchers to pinpoint damaged genes and to analyze the body's remedy for them.

They can then apply this knowledge to potential cures for genetic disease.

We cannot end our discussion of assisted healing without at least defining the terms differentiating *disease* and *illness*. Because as human beings we are more than a body, when our body does not function properly it affects our entire human experience. If we describe *disease* as a process that causes biological malfunction, then *illness* is the lived experience of this discomfort. Illness involves the entire human experience, including feelings and moods, fears, a sense of helplessness, powerlessness, and vulnerability. For this reason, we must differentiate between the terms *cure* and *healing*. *Cure* can proceed by simply advancing scientific techniques; *healing* may not proceed if fear and a sense of loss cannot be addressed appropriately.[6]

Real healing by doctors must constitute the caring restoration of balance and wholeness to the person. There should be an element of awe, humility, and respect in the physician for the sheer magnificence of design and function in the human body. The physician who wants to truly heal must comprehend pain and suffering and recognize them in a fellow human who is "just like me."

Inner healing

Scripture integrally links our spiritual well-being with our physical health:

> Beloved, I pray that you may prosper in all things and be in health, just as your soul prospers.
>
> —3 JOHN 2

Wholeness and balance at the mental and spiritual levels are scientifically proven to affect the capacity of your body to heal physically. How is this inner healing accomplished? In what ways do we need to be "aligned" to achieve the balance of mental, emotional, and spiritual well-being? God's Word tells us that we need to be transformed through receiving and resting on Christ as our Savior in order to be the recipient of all that He is. Full surrender to His lordship is required to engage this integration of the Godhead into all that we are: body, soul, and spirit. We must be willing to declare: "Not My will, but Yours, be done" (Luke 22:42). This denial of self presents us to God as a holy, pleasing, and available recipient of all He is.

Mentally we must have the "mind of Christ" (1 Cor. 2:16), remain positive and hopeful, and constantly rejoice with great feelings of thankfulness. Spiritually, we must submit to God's Holy Spirit to reign in every part of our being. And by focusing on eternal life rather than temporal existence, we seek to align ourselves with God and His eternal purposes.

Learning to adore your Creator and walk in intimate relationship with Him is based on the fact that all of the promises of God are "Yes, and in Him Amen" in Christ to you! (2 Cor. 1:20). Scripture is clear concerning His desire for you to experience love, peace, hope, and joy in your daily life. In fact, God so desires your health in every area of your life that the Bible says His eyes run to and fro throughout the whole Earth to show Himself strong on behalf of those whose hearts are turned toward Him (see 2 Chron. 16:9). This includes His intervening supernaturally in answer to your prayers.

Improbable healing

We are defining the term "improbable" healing as documented healings that modern medicine and science cannot explain or account for, nor could they have predicted them. Hospital files across the country contain records of modern day improbable healings, which cannot be explained or refuted by medical science. Numerous scientific studies initiated by universities and other medical groups show convincingly that patients who received prayer had better recovery rates than those who did not. Some studies indicate that even when the patients did not know they were receiving prayer, they fared better than the others who received no prayer. And the number of studies is growing, which indicate positive healing results of prayer, regardless of denomination or proximity to the patient.[7]

Of course, in the New Testament we read of Jesus, the great Physician, who performed many miracles of healing. The Gospels are filled with accounts of these improbable healings, which the physicians of the day could not have accomplished. In Jesus' ministry, there are accounts of the blind seeing, the lame walking, the deaf hearing, and even of the dead being raised.

As we learn to appreciate our Creator and Lord, we will be open to receive His mercy. And our hearts, minds, and bodies will be receptive to the possibilities of improbable healing. I believe there are at least four things we should do to seek healing that seems unlikely or even impossible:

- Search Scripture for promises to hear our prayer, which will build our faith.

- Align yourself with God's design for healing, following His principles for diet, exercise, and emotional and spiritual well-being. This involves living in gratitude, without bitterness, and offering forgiveness to those who have offended us.

- Honor God by seeking counsel. Wisdom may indicate seeking physician-assisted healing. Only God can heal. A wise physician assists the body's immune system and seeks to remove hindrances to the normal healing processes God has made.

- Live in a constant attitude of rejoicing as you wage a battle for your healing. Be grateful that God designed you for healing, and call upon Him to manifest His power in your body, mind, and soul through prayer with thanksgiving.[8]

As we bow in deep appreciation and adoration before God, our improbable healing rests in God's hands, but many can testify and document that God delighted to surprise them with healing that no one could have predicted. As we have discussed, health must ultimately be defined in terms of our relationship with our Creator. As we surrender our lives to our benevolent Redeemer, we can trust His eternal will for our lives, which is to bring us into His presence—forever.

Ultimate healing

As believers, we have the most beautiful part of life to look forward to when life as we know it on Earth ends. Ultimate healing is somewhat like graduation day for us—the day God brings a beloved child home to be with Him forever in absolute joy and bliss. Scripture describes our eternal state in heaven:

> And God will wipe away every tear from their eyes; there shall be no more death, nor sorrow, nor crying. There shall be no more pain, for the former things have passed away.
> —REVELATION 21:4

While we live our lives on this side of eternity, it is wonderful to meditate on the blessed life that awaits us. As believers, we can look forward to complete satisfaction as we enjoy the intimacy of a bride adorned for her husband (see Rev. 21:2), living forever in the presence of our blessed Savior. Our longing to know His presence will finally be fulfilled as we experience the complete fulfillment and joy of being with Him continually. It is incomprehensible to anticipate the glories of heaven from our earthbound perspective. Old Testament prophets had a glimpse of the glory that believers enjoy:

The ransomed of the LORD shall return, And come to Zion with singing, With everlasting joy on their heads. They shall obtain joy and gladness, And sorrow and sighing shall flee away.

—ISAIAH 35:10

Of course, for this eternal bliss to be a future reality for us, we must seek to remove our alienation from God and return to alignment with God's design for us in this life. It is necessary to receive forgiveness and to surrender our lives to the Lord Jesus Christ, our great Physician. Our eternal reconciliation with God must begin now if it is to be fulfilled after this life is completed.

Living a life of adoring appreciation of our Lord is a result of the Holy Spirit's work in our hearts, anointing us to enjoy eternal life, both now and in heaven. Jesus defined eternal life as a "quality" of life, not just a place: "And this is eternal life, that they may know You, the only true God, and Jesus Christ whom You have sent" (John 17:3). Cultivating intimate relationship with Christ as we live on Earth prepares us for blissful relationship, without any hindrance of sin, sickness, or tribulation, which we will enjoy for eternity in heaven.

These things I have spoken to you, that in Me you may have

peace. In the world you will have tribulation; but be of good

cheer, I have overcome the world.

—John 16:33

Tracing the Hand of the Creator

Scientists recently cracked open the genetic library of the humble creature we call *yeast* and read it from beginning to end. What they found on yeast's DNA bookshelves shocked the scientists. The results seem to throw yet another monkey wrench into Darwin's theory of evolution. Scientists "read" the complete library of DNA found in each cell of baker's yeast—a genetic micro-library they call the *genome*.[1]

Each yeast cell has about six thousand three hundred genes. Each gene is a unique segment, or string, of DNA that has several hundred chemical letters arranged in linear fashion. One of the most shocking features of the yeast genome is the huge number of these genes—about three thousand—that are of unknown function and have no genetic parallels among the other kinds of living things. These "orphan" genes could be compared to rare and exotic "books" in the DNA library. For our evolutionary friends, these unique genes, in such large numbers, spell trouble since there is no known source they could possibly have evolved from.[2]

THE HUMAN STRUGGLE

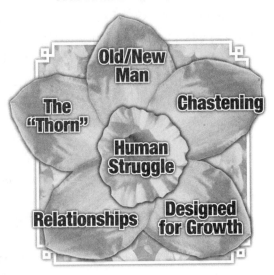

In spite of the wonders of the Creator's design of life we have described, it is a paradox that without the very real element of *struggle*, all is not intended to function optimally. Nor is this struggle, apparent on many levels of existence and in all spheres of creation, primarily a result of the Fall of mankind. Sin, resulting in the alienation from God of all mankind, does account for much of the tragedy and death we experience. Yet, the elements of struggle to which I refer are "built into the systems of creation" as a *positive* catalyst for growth and life.

Designed for growth

Whether we are considering the wonders of plant life, animal life, or human life, we cannot underestimate the necessity and power of the struggle that is innate to the healthy development of every form of life. For example, without monumental struggle, butterflies would not emerge from their deathtrap cocoons, fragile plants would not push their way up through crusted Earth, and babies would not develop into healthy adults. The changes required for a child to mature, learning to take responsibility for his or her actions, train for a vocation, and enter into adult relationships of marriage and parenting simply cannot be accomplished without struggle and conflict.

As a physician, I have applied an analogy of the way our muscles develop and strengthen in our bodies to explain these larger elements of human struggle. Within God's wondrous design of the human body there are two hundred types of tissues with sixty trillion cells that are aligned in perfect order. Muscle tissue contains hundreds to thousands of myofibrils, slender threads stacked lengthwise in muscle fiber, running the entire length of the fiber. They are actually bundles of tiny contractile protein filaments. The function of the myofibrils illustrates the effect of various stresses, a kind of physical conflict, which these fibers must endure in order to develop properly. (See illustration of human muscle spindle on page 218.)

Skeletal muscle is made up of thousands of cylindrical muscle fibers bound together by connective tissue, through which run blood vessels and nerves. The number of fibers is probably fixed early in life, and each is designed for growth. Myofibrils are set within a muscle for the purpose of stretching the muscle as the person grows. With usage, these myofibrils become stronger, but without exercise, they will atrophy.

When excess weight and pressure is put on a myofibril, it will expand, causing edema or swelling. However, although some portions will break down, there will be a rebuilding process wherein new strength is gained. Knowing just how much exertion to place on a muscle results in the greatest degree of strengthening. So it is the stretching movement and exercise that creates muscle tension, placing pressure on the muscular system, which is imperative for healthy growth and development. Without this physical "struggle," muscles would atrophy and normal movement of the body would not be possible.

In this same way, the larger struggles of life become positive means of growth and strengthening of character, without which we would continually weaken and "atrophy" in the face of life's challenges.

The "Thorn"

R. T. Kendall's book, *The Thorn in the Flesh*, portrays the fact that we all struggle with conditions in life that we may perceive as impossible to overcome. His title refers specifically to the thorn in the flesh the apostle Paul experienced, which he asked God to remove. Paul explains:

> And lest I should be exalted above measure by the abundance of the revelations, a thorn in the flesh was given to me, a messenger of Satan to buffet me, lest I be exalted above measure. Concerning this thing I pleaded with the Lord three times that it might depart from me. And He said to me, "My grace is sufficient for you, for My strength is made perfect in weakness."
> —2 Corinthians 12:7–9

God allowed a thorn in the flesh to "buffet" or oppose the apostle Paul in order that the grace of God and His divine strength could be perfected in Paul's weakness. The apostle Paul admitted to the possibility of his becoming conceited and proud because of the great revelations of God he had experienced. He knew that God had sent an undesirable "thorn in the flesh" to keep that from happening.

According to R. T. Kendall, the reference to Paul's *flesh* may have been referring to a physical problem, but not necessarily. The Greek word translated "flesh" is *sarx*, which can also refer to the fallen human nature—the unregenerate part of the soul. Our mind, will, and emotions, which comprise the soul, will sometimes suffer a "thorn" experience in life. We are called to respond in such a way that our pain serves to strengthen our godly character.[3]

While it is not clear from Scripture what this "thorn" was literally in Paul's life, the divine principle it teaches is that we must seek for the grace of God to be perfected in our lives through difficult situations. It is always right to call on God in the difficulties we encounter in life. Scripture clearly teaches that God hears our cry, He cares and delights to deliver us from our troubles:

> He sent His word and healed them, And delivered them from their destructions. Oh, that men would give thanks to the Lord for His goodness, And for His wonderful works to the children of men!
>
> —Psalm 107:20–21

Yet, the reality of human struggle is also expressed clearly in Scripture, relating to those difficulties that are necessary to strengthen our faith and stimulate our growth in Christ:

> [You] are kept by the power of God through faith for salvation ready to be revealed in the last time. In this you greatly rejoice, though now for a little while, if need be, you have been grieved by various trials, that the genuineness of your faith, being much more precious than gold that perishes, though it is tested by fire, may be found to praise, honor, and glory at the revelation of Jesus Christ, whom having not seen you love.
>
> —1 Peter 1:5–8

According to Dr. Kendall, our "thorn" is not simply general trials and tribulations (the tests) that every Christian encounters. Rather, it refers to a "crushing blow so definite and lasting that one knows that the term, 'thorn in the flesh,' is the best explanation of it. It is not the same for every person…For some it is a handicap or disability. It could be unhappy employment or even lack of employment. It could be an enemy who despises you. It could be loneliness. It could be coping with unhappy living conditions. It could be a sexual misgiving. It could be an unhappy marriage. It could be chronic illness. It could be a personality problem...the list is endless. The thorn may be recognizable to you but unseen by others."[4] Dr. Kendall explains that a "thorn" is a trial that we are "locked into." It will not go away soon, if ever. It will stay with us as long as we need it, with the purpose of keeping us humble and allowing the grace of God to be perfected in our lives.[5]

We can always expect to live in peace as we surrender our lives to the redemption of Christ, knowing that He has overcome every potentially destructive force we will ever face in life. And it is right to call on God in time of trouble to receive His deliverance. Paradoxically, we must also accept the reality that we will suffer in our human struggle on many levels. Yet, if we choose to seek God, we will find the grace of God to be sufficient for us, helping us to grow in faith and in godly character.

Applying the analogy of the muscle myofibrils again, we understand that the benefits of repeated movement under tension are necessary for their physical development. As this relates to our human struggle, when challenged by pressures that are unbearable in our own strength ("thorns"), we are reminded that the Lord uses these very circumstances to draw us to Himself. It is His life in us that is essential to turning these challenges into triumphs that glorify God.

The alternative to being "stretched" mentally, physically, and spiritually, is to become a "couch potato" in all three dimensions of life. In the physical body, muscles that are not used become soft and prone to atrophy. So in our spiritual life, if we do not properly address the challenges of life, we will be weakened in our faith. Bitterness, unforgiveness, anger, and other negative responses will diminish the health of our souls, supplanting the positive graces of the peace, love, and joy of our Savior.

Those who struggle with mental challenges or physical impairments understand that conflict is a constant part of life. And millions who suffer the effects of poverty or the perils of living in war zones would perhaps consider the whole of life nothing but a painful struggle. Whether our life struggles come from physical difficulties, circumstances that cause extreme pressure, or relationships that create discomfort, we can triumph in life in the face these "thorns" with the all-sufficient grace of God. If we seek Him and receive His divine help, our "thorns" will make us better people.

Relationships: advocate or accuser?

Relational conflicts will cause us to make a choice between being *advocates* or *accusers*. Being disposed to intercede in prayer for an adversary will stretch our faith in the God who desires to grow us up into the likeness of Christ. I am reminded of a personal situation in which a lengthy lawsuit arose over a land rights dispute. In the end, my prayerful intercession for my opposition in the case resulted in differing reactions from the two attorneys representing the person who had come against me. Though this "thorn" had affected each of us in differing ways, each was responsible for his own response. Would we choose to grow in the Lord or would we suffer "atrophy" in our souls through rejecting Him?

How blessed are those who rest in Christ's redemption, which results in our growth by design, as a result of these challenges that He causes to work for our eternal good. His purpose to make us Christlike will be accomplished as we in faith give the proper response in our struggle and the "thorns" we face in any area of our lives. The promises of Scripture are clear in this regard:

> And we know that all things work together for good to those who love God, to those who are the called according to His purpose. For whom He foreknew, He also predestined to be

conformed to the image of His Son, that He might be the first-born among many brethren.

—Romans 8:28–29

We must accept the truth that "all things" means "all"—not just what is pleasant, but what is troublesome as well. While it is obvious that "all things" are not good, and that bad things do happen to good people, Scripture declares plainly that all things will *work for our ultimate good*. The suffering of Christ portrayed in Scripture shows us the value of obedience to God in spite of the pain endured. It is the determination of Christ to have "many brethren" who are just like Him, filled with the love of God, empowered by the Spirit of God, and living in obedience to the will of God. Christ is even now making intercession for those who do not yet know Him, who by their very lives are rejecting Him:

Therefore He is also able to save to the uttermost those who come to God through Him, since He always lives to make intercession for them.

—Hebrews 7:25

Our responsibility to those who oppose us is the same as our Savior's—to intercede for them rather than to become accusers. In the face of painful accusations, we must allow these "thorns" to work for our good, strengthening our faith and teaching us to trust our souls to God. As we choose to commit our lives to the will of a loving God, He will allow even these painful relationships to work for our good, strengthening our spiritual "muscles" as we seek to become more like Christ. Scripture teaches:

When a man's ways please the Lord, He makes even his enemies to be at peace with him.

—Proverbs 16:7

The solution to the kind of struggle that presents itself through people who oppose us is to do as Christ did—intercede for them. In that way we will please the Lord and can expect to see miracles on our behalf, making all things to work for our good.

Chastening of God

In our modern culture, where acceptable discipline of our children involves "time-outs" and loss of privileges through "grounding," terms like *chastening* and *punishment* are fast becoming obsolete. However, Scripture is relevant for today's culture as it has been for thousands of years for our ancestors. It clearly references the term *chastening* as it applies to our human struggle and our relationship to our heavenly Father. For example, in the Book of Job, we read:

> Behold, happy is the man whom God corrects; Therefore do
> not despise the chastening of the Almighty. For He bruises, but
> He binds up; He wounds, but His hands make whole. He shall
> deliver you in six troubles, Yes, in seven no evil shall touch you.
> —Job 5:17–19

The Hebrew word translated *chastening* comes from a root that means "to chastise literally with blows or figuratively with words, hence, to instruct or reform." It also means to reprove, warn, correct, discipline, and restrain. We are instructed, corrected, and reformed through the chastening that God allows in our lives to teach us His ways. In His wisdom, He keeps us from self-destructing by teaching us to change our destructive patterns of thoughts and actions. Again, the writer of the Proverbs shows us our need for this divine chastening, as well as its redemptive power:

> My son, do not despise the chastening [*muwcar*] of the Lord,
> Nor detest His correction; For whom the Lord loves He corrects, Just as a father the son in whom he delights. Happy is the
> man who finds wisdom, And the man who gains understanding.
> —Proverbs 3:11–13

In a very real sense, our happiness depends on our correct response to God's correction. In accepting the correction of God, we are acknowledging His love to us as a Father. The New Testament declares this spiritual reality:

> If you endure chastening, God deals with you as with sons; for what son is there whom a father does not chasten? But if you are without chastening, of which all have become partakers, then you are illegitimate and not sons...Now no chastening seems to be joyful for the present, but painful; nevertheless, afterward it yields the peaceable fruit of righteousness to those who have been trained by it.
>
> —Hebrews 12:7–8, 11

The New Testament word translated *chastening* is quite similar to the Old Testament rendering. The Greek word *paideia* literally means "tutorage, i.e. education or training, and by implication, disciplinary correction." The writer of the Book of Hebrews insists that we must subject our lives to the training processes of our heavenly Father, whose goal is that we become holy and Christlike. This element of human struggle must be accepted in humility of heart as we submit our lives to a loving heavenly Father. Only in this way can we expect to become like Him.

Old man-new man

Our human struggle must also include the concept of the "old man—new man" taught in Scripture by the apostle Paul. Understanding this true nature of our salvation will help us to grow in our faith and become Christlike in our character. Paul teaches clearly that growth in the Christian life involves a process of learning to deny the sinful desires of the "old man," which have been crucified with Christ (see Rom. 6:6). Paul strongly exhorted believers to "Reckon yourselves to be dead indeed to sin, but alive to God in Christ Jesus our Lord" (Rom. 6:11).

This does not mean we have to struggle against the power of sin in our own strength; we could not win that battle. It means that because Christ destroyed the power of sin through His death on the cross, we can now enter into relationship with Him and trust Him to set us free from the power of sin in our lives. As we discussed in the devotional for Day 14, Christ *imputes* righteousness to believers and has placed us into a new kingdom; we must reckon it to be so and then walk in it. Yet, that reality does not preclude a struggle to enter into that freedom. The apostle Paul honestly describes the tenacious struggle between the desires of the born-again, redeemed "inner man" and the law of sin that works in his "outward" members. He explains:

> For the good that I will to do, I do not do; but the evil I will not to do, that I practice. Now if I do what I will not to do, it is no longer I who do it, but sin that dwells in me…O wretched man that I am! Who will deliver me from this body of death? I thank God—through Jesus Christ our Lord! So then, with the mind I myself serve the law of God, but with the flesh the law of sin.
> —ROMANS 7:19, 24–25

Paul gives thanks to God that Christ is greater than the sin principle working in our members, and that He will help us to serve the law of God. Yet, he warns us that we must choose to be "spiritually minded" in order to enjoy life and peace (see Rom. 8:6). Those who do not, are carnally minded, which results in death, "because the carnal mind is enmity [an enemy] against God; for it is not subject to the law of God, nor indeed can be" (Rom. 8:7).

No one can save himself from the power of the sin principle that still resides in the believer. Yet, it remains for us to seek God so that our minds will be "renewed in knowledge according to the image of Him who created him" (Col. 3:10). It is this inevitable human struggle to cooperate with the divine work of the Holy Spirit within us that many misunderstand. They bow in despair at the recurrence of sinful passions or angry responses. We need not be defeated because of the struggle. If we bring our sinful behavior to Christ, and bow in worship before Him, we will receive the forgiveness for which we ask. And we will receive the cleansing power to live more and more free from sin as we grow in His grace.

A key element in my own spiritual journey to become an authentic Christian has been the issue of *inward disposition*. As I go through my days, I make an effort to measure whether or not I am depending on Christ's godly affections at work in me to permeate my inner disposition. Am I caring for others, including my patients, as Christ would? As I experience new depths of the love of Jesus Christ in my life, I become aware of positive changes in my inner disposition. Madame Jeanne Guyon, a saint of the seventeenth century, wrote:

> If your outward actions are a result (a by-product) of something that has taken place deep within you, then those outward actions do receive spiritual value and they do possess real goodness. But outward activities have only as much spiritual value as they receive from their source.
> —MADAME JEANNE GUYON, 1685[6]

We have to assume that Paul had learned the great help there is in the battle against the sin principle through the power of the Holy Spirit, or he would not have admonished believers to live in the same manner as they saw him living. He experienced the peace of God and taught others they could also. And he was continually growing in His relationship with Christ through correct response to the pressures of life. As believers, we live with the human struggle of continually "pressing" toward our destiny in Christ Jesus. Yet, in the process, we must pursue the intimate delights, the peace, joy, and grace of God being revealed to us—and through us—for we have been designed to grow in Him.

*But those who wait on the L*ORD *Shall renew their strength;*

They shall mount up with wings like eagles, They shall run

and not be weary, They shall walk and not faint.

—ISAIAH 40:31

Tracing the Hand of the Creator

Our pets have the same DNA as we do, although it differs in structure and type. These phenomenal variations in nature allow us to see the intricate planning involved in God's creation. For example, every dog since creation has had the same DNA as your dog's puppies will have. While geneticists have been able to "create" adaptations in certain breeds of dogs, for example, there has never been a comprehensive change from the "basic kind" of animal (or plant).

More than in any other era, the truth is now made clear. Advances in biochemistry, molecular biology, and medicine have shown that the complexity of our own design is quite beyond complete comprehension and entirely beyond imitation. It is unconditionally beyond an impersonal process of evolution...The observations of human science all point to the Designer, Creator, and Father, and they remind us of our need to appreciate Him.[1]

WAITING ON THE LORD

Too often, we simply do not appreciate the great generosity and unfathomable works of our Creator. It is awesome to consider the significance of every minute detail needed for the creation to function so superbly and to maintain every form of life simultaneously. Even the "nano-particles" scientists have discovered in our cells, which live only a fraction of a second and whose significance we have not yet discovered, serve some unknown purpose initiated by the Creator. Perhaps in the days ahead we will learn other clues about the intricacies of the DNA, and discover even more of the marvels of creation's microscopic molecules that make us who we are. But the more important goal is to get to know who God is and give Him the adoration He deserves.

Believers enjoy a mutual relationship with God, but we still have much to learn in order to interact with our Creator-Redeemer as we should. We are "ignorant" of God's ways, unable to understand the depths of God's thoughts, words, and actions. The truth is that from eternity, God created our DNA with a "template" or program that must function in "time." Yet, there is a part of us that intuitively knows we will live on—forever. It is that eternal sense that motivates us to want to know God.

Scripture is filled with instruction regarding our need to wait on the Lord, to "be still, and know that I am God" (Ps. 46:10). Scripture promises that if we seek God we will find Him (see Matt. 7:7) and that if we draw near to Him He will draw near to us (see James 4:8).

It is our "forever" relationship with our Creator that fills us with hope for the present as well as for the never-ending future. As we wait on God, we must prepare our hearts to commune with Him.

Preparing our hearts

As a good traveler, if you were planning to take a long road trip, you would probably prepare for the trip by consulting an online mapping service, which can tell you every turn to make from your home to your destination. You would pack what you need for the trip, and get your car checked for mechanical soundness. Then, you would make sure it was filled with gas and make any other preparations for the care of your pets and home that are needed in your absence.

In the same way, as Christians, we need to prepare our minds and hearts to seek God. It is important that we clear away any distractions as we prepare to wait on the Lord. The psalmist exhorted us to "rest in the Lord, and wait patiently for Him" (Ps. 37:7). Our focus must be on God as we set aside special times during our day to seek Him in prayer. A time of solitude allows us to bring our whole being to the Lord, to quiet ourselves mentally, and to seek only Him.

As we seek the quietness of solitude, we open our spiritual ears to be in tune with God's voice. Noise is to the ear what excessively bright lights are to the eyes. Richard Swenson writes: "Noise is not only toxic to the sensitive hair cells of the ear, but it is also damaging to the cardiovascular and nervous systems, as well as to our relationships with God and others."[2] Dietrich Bonhoeffer declared: "Regular times of quiet are absolutely necessary. After a time of quiet we meet others in a different and a fresh way. Silence is the simple stillness of the individual under the Word of God."[3]

Another important aspect of preparation for waiting on the Lord is the study of God's Word. Scripture is our "road map." It teaches us through instruction and by example of the lives of godly men and women recorded within how to wait on the Lord. And they are filled with wonderful promises of hope for those who seek to know God. Scripture also reveals the grandeur of God and helps us understand our finiteness.

As we humble ourselves before God, we will in turn begin to see His greatness more and more. And as we see His greatness, we are humbled more. These two separate acts merge into one profound expression of worship. If we can but catch a tiny glimpse of our God as he truly is, our lives will gain eternal perspective. King David expresses both humility and awe in the psalms:

> O Lord, our Lord, How majestic is Your name in all the earth, Who have displayed Your splendor above the heavens!...When I consider Your heavens, the work of Your fingers, The moon and the stars, which You have ordained; What is man that You take thought of him? And the son of man, that You care for him?
> —Psalm 8:1, 3–4, nas

In prayer

There are entire volumes written on prayer, which give good instruction for our successful pursuit of communion with God. For our purposes, we can only highlight a few keys to effective prayer as we learn to wait on the Lord. One of these keys is to let our thoughts be conformed to the Word of God. The apostle Paul instructed believers:

> Whatever is true, whatever is noble, whatever is right, whatever is pure, whatever is lovely, whatever is admirable—if anything is excellent or praiseworthy—think about such things.
>
> —PHILIPPIANS 4:8, NIV

As we approach God in prayer, we must also surrender to Him our agendas and express our needs and concerns, "casting our care on Him," so that these issues don't clutter our minds. It is helpful to fill our minds with the Word of God in order to know how to pray. Then we need to consider our motives in prayer. If we are coming to God to ask selfishly for things that will gratify us only, we have wrong motives. We must first of all desire to be surrendered to God's will for our lives.

The apostle James addressed this important issue: "When you ask, you do not receive, because you ask with wrong motives, that you may spend what you get on your pleasures" (James 4:3, NIV). One of the primary reasons we pray is to receive from God. He wants to provide for us, but it must be according to His will for our lives. As we adjust our thinking and correct our motives for effective prayer, we must also be honest about any sin lurking in our hearts.

Psalm 66:18–19 says, "If I had cherished sin in my heart, the Lord would not have listened; but God has surely listened and heard my voice in prayer" (NIV). And the prophet Isaiah declared: "Your sins have hidden his face from you, so that he will not hear" (Isa. 59:2, NIV). We must come to prayer prepared to ask, and receive, God's forgiveness for our sins.

Prayer is the primary way we grow closer to our Creator, Savior, and Lord. Yet, no matter how much we desire that relationship and want to show our love for Him, we're never free from obstacles. We must successfully battle our own egos, the agendas of our families and peers, and what the world tells us about success, in order to stay in a relationship of prayer with our Lord. Watchful prayer helps us be victorious over those temptations, because as we spend time with our Lord, we receive the guidance and direction that keep us focused on God's will. Then we base our decisions on His will, not our own.

In hope

Hope is birthed in an attitude of gratitude that causes you to expect joyously even if you have to wait awhile for the answer. You are assured of the character of God. You can develop a habit of thankfulness toward God and others. It puts you in a frame of mind to expect to receive and enjoy in the future.

My friend Dr. James Avery works with hospice patients, those who are dying and are without hope of recovery. He believes that not only is hope a real possibility in one's last days, it is also a necessity. True, the hopes of those facing imminent death differ greatly from those of us who are healthy. They include hope for a peaceful death, hope for loved ones left, and hope for an improbable healing. But the important thing is that hope flowers in every heart. Our Creator endowed us with the inner capacity for hope; it is part of His design for healing; we must nurture it in ourselves and in each other.[4]

Hope is actually an antidote for illness. To pass words of hope to an emotionally drowning soul is to drag them into the "life raft" by hand. You can't hold back a man or woman whose hope is in the Lord. To that person, God is always bigger than the giants of the promised land. The truths in God's Word bring hope. Saturating your soul in His Word enables you to rise above despair. It isn't human nature to "hope against hope." In fact, such a response seems contrary to human sanity. But according to Scripture, an irrepressible trust in God is always rewarded (see Rom. 4:13–25).

It should be mentioned that faith gives substance to hope

(Heb. 11:1). While hope is very important, it lacks substance until it is rooted in faith. I like to use this acronym for F.A.I.T.H.— Fully Assured I Trust Him! Hope is faith talking aloud, drowning out voices of defeat. Whatever situations we face in life, we can be filled with hope as we learn to wait on God. Joyous faith founded in hope cannot be explained, but it is steadfastly based on Scripture: "the substance of things hoped for, the evidence of things not [yet] seen" (Heb. 11:1; see also 1 Pet. 1:7–8). Hope breaks out of the net of reasoning and moves forward in faith and confidence in God and His Word. Hope renews our minds.[5]

In joy

Scripture is filled with promises of joy for those who seek to know God, their Creator and Redeemer. As we acknowledge God as our Creator, Redeemer, and Friend, we cannot help but adore Him. Our adoration of God is our greatest source of joy. It is in worship and adoration that we find the greatest fulfillment, joy, and delight in being a person. Worship gives us the highest expression of our unique DNA as an anointed individual. That joy should permeate our work and our relationships with our spouse, family, and others—our entire life for our entire lifetime.[6]

French theologian and reformer John Calvin said that we can never thank God enough for His grace and His salvation, but we can praise Him for it. The psalms are full of prayers of praise and rejoicing in the Lord. Contemplation of the psalms can help put us in the posture of praise and thanksgiving. In my own life, praising the Lord and affirming His works fills me with hope and joy; it gives me the grace to move beyond the concerns of this world.[7]

As our personal lives of prayer progress "from glory to glory" (2 Cor. 3:18), we will discover what it really means to be aligned with God. And the Holy Spirit will bring forth His fruit in our character—love, joy, peace, patience, kindness, goodness, faithfulness, gentleness, and self-control (see Gal. 5:22–23). Our spirit will radiate the joy of salvation in all that we think and do, and we won't get tired of doing God's will. As Nehemiah 8:10 says, "For the joy of the LORD is your strength." As such joy grows in us, cultivated by our relationship of prayer with our Redeemer, we experience new freedom. No longer do the anxieties and fears of this world bind us. No longer do we struggle to satisfy our own desires or impress others.[8]

In prayer we have the freedom to give our fears, our worries, and our problems to God. And we then abide in Him, knowing by faith that He will provide for us because He loves us. Our relationship with God through prayer offers a limitless supply of peace and joy that will fill our lives continually—throughout eternity.

In sorrow

We have discussed the reality of tests and trials as well as the innate human struggle that challenges each of us in our daily lives. It is especially important that in difficult times of pain and sorrow we learn the strength available to us as we wait on God. The psalmist knew the powerful results of crying out to God in trouble:

> The righteous cry out, and the LORD hears, And delivers them out of all their troubles. The LORD is near to those who have a broken heart, And saves such as have a contrite spirit. Many are the afflictions of the righteous, But the LORD delivers him out of them all.
>
> —PSALM 34:17–19

While it is not possible to live in this world without suffering sorrows of many kinds, as believers we have the promise of God to heal our broken hearts (Luke 4:18). He also promises us the comfort of the Holy Spirit (John 14:26), as well as the comfort of our brothers and sisters in the body of Christ (1 Thess. 5:11). And we have the wonderful hope for our future—eternal life with our Savior, where there is no more sorrow or suffering.

It is one of the great joys on this side of eternity to pause and meditate on the blessedness that awaits us. One of the best ways to engage in this refreshing anticipation as we wait on the Lord is to take a walk through Revelation 21 and 22, the last two chapters of the Bible. The apostle John described what lies ahead for Christians.

Though we tend to live in denial regarding death, it is "hopeful" to consider the wonder of what I call our "ultimate healing," when we will rest in the arms of our Redeemer forever. When the great Physician puts on His surgery clothes for His last operation, He will come out of the operating room with "new heavens and a new earth in which righteousness dwells" (2 Pet. 3:13). No pediatrician has ever held forth such a perfect newborn to the wondering eyes of all around as God will on that day. The new creation of God's glorious kingdom will be the ultimate and final healing work of *Jehovah Rapha*. The healing of the inner man as well as the healing of the outer man will be complete on that day. Believers, formerly assaulted by fears, will be healed from their fears when they see the lost cast away but hear the Lamb say to them: "Come, you blessed of My Father, inherit the kingdom prepared for you from the foundation of the world" (Matt. 25:34).[9]

As a believer, you will receive your ultimate healing in the context of being prepared as a bride adorned for her husband (see Rev. 21:2). You will be fully satisfied with the greatest intimacy with your blessed Savior that is possible—but it will still be incomprehensible. Your joy will be complete. You will no longer be homesick for Him. You will no longer pine away in your sense of distance from Him. You will be with Him forever. And you will say good-bye forever to trouble and sorrow. In one verse of Scripture, this ultimate healing in glory is described in six ways (Rev. 21:4):

God will wipe away every tear from their eyes; there shall be no more death, nor sorrow, nor crying. There shall be no more pain, for the former things have passed away.

Waiting on the Lord not only offers us temporal benefits of the divine presence of God in our everyday lives, but eternal rewards as well. Not only do we receive the peace and joy and comfort of the Holy Ghost for our earthly lives, we enter into a relationship of profound intimacy with our Creator, which will continually deepen as we live throughout eternity with Him.

A new commandment I give to you, that you love one another;

as I have loved you, that you also love one another.

—John 13:34

We, being many, are one body in Christ, and individually

members of one another.

—Romans 12:5

Tracing the Hand of the Creator

Your complex immune system is working even before birth. Immunologists refer to our innate (nonspecific) immunity, and our adaptive (specific) immune system. Our innate immune system refers to our skin, tears, stomach acid, and other innate protectors against invaders. Our adaptive immune system consists of two arms: First, *humoral* immunity is mediated by soluble protein molecules known as *antibodies*. The primary function of an antibody is to bind the antigen and mount a direct neutralizing effect. Our immune system can produce more than a hundred million different types of antibody.

Second, *cellular* immunity is mediated by a variety of specifically sensitized white blood cells, lymphocytes, which attack the contagion in "hand-to-hand" combat. It refers to the T cells, which were not discovered until the 1960s. One important T cell, the *helper T cell*, is the conductor of immunity. It releases chemical messages to identify specific invaders. The *killer T cell* is a very advanced hunter, seeking out its quarry, whose particular identifying markers it has learned, and destroying the pathogen hiding in cells by destroying the cells that have been invaded. It initiates a self-destruct code already programmed into every cell, helping the cell to "commit suicide" once it has been invaded by a pathogen that poses a danger to the body as a whole. The *suppressor T cells* have the special role of maintaining the balance of immune responses, which is very important to avoid autoimmune responses. After the various T cells have waged their immunological war on a particular invader, more macrophages are called in to clean up the "debris." The superb design of your immune system is far beyond the probability of the realm of "chance." There is no way to look at it and not glimpse the Creator's wisdom within.[1]

Day 28

RELATIONSHIPS

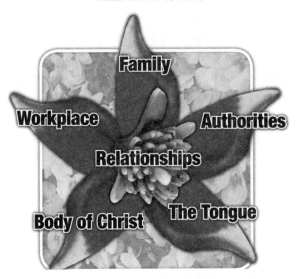

Psychologists at McGill University took a group of heart attack survivors who were being discharged from the hospital and divided them up into two groups. Both groups received the same excellent heart care from the cardiologists and their own family physicians. However, one group also received a monthly phone call from some of the research team. If the researcher making the phone contact sensed any psychosocial problem, a specially trained nurse was scheduled to visit the patient in the home. Just the little personal contact that was made resulted in a 50 percent reduction in the patients' death rate after one year in the group who were cared for by occasional phone calls and visits.[2]

Stanford researchers randomly assigned women with metastatic breast cancer to receive usual medical care plus a weekly support group designed to help them manage the stress of their illness. The support group patients lived twice as long as those who were not in the program. At UCLA, patients with malignant melanoma who participated in only six ninety-minute sessions with a support group that also provided relationship training had a 50 percent reduction in patient death and recurrence of symptoms when compared with the usual care patients receive. Over the six years of this study, more than three times as many patients in the nonintervention group died as compared to the group that received support.[3]

Healthy relationships are important. Loneliness kills—we should avoid it like the plague. All of us need interaction with others. It causes us to forget about ourselves when we focus on others. God made us to need one another. We need listening ears and caring hearts. And it must be a two-way street in order for a family, a community, or a church to be made up of healthy, emotionally fulfilled people.

The body of Christ

The New Testament teaches that when we are born again, accepting Christ as our Savior, we are baptized into the body of Christ. The apostle Paul teaches, "For as the body is one and has many members, but all the members of that one body, being many, are one body, so also is Christ. For by one Spirit we were all baptized into one body" (1 Cor. 12:12–13). He continues: "Now you are the body of Christ, and members individually" (v. 27). And Paul teaches throughout his letters to the churches how we should treat other members of the body of Christ, as well as those who are not yet born again:

> Let love be without hypocrisy...Be kindly affectionate to one another with brotherly love, in honor giving preference to one another; not lagging in diligence, fervent in spirit, serving the Lord...distributing to the needs of the saints, given to hospitality. Bless those who persecute you; bless and do not curse. Rejoice with those who rejoice, and weep with those who weep. Be of the same mind toward one another.
>
> —ROMANS 12:9–11; 13–16

Richard Swenson offers this interesting perspective of the body of Christ:

> One reason God chose to call the church a body is because it is such a perfect metaphor. But it goes beyond that. Is it possible that somehow, in a spiritually organic way, we indeed are all connected, networked together by a Spirit who has no trouble with such complexity? Is it possible that when one prays, everyone in the body benefits? That when one loves, everyone in the body is mysteriously lifted? That when one sins, everyone in the body takes the hit and feels the wound? I rather suspect so. God always creates with several levels of meaning. He uses words precisely, with profound intentionality. Why did He put each of us in a body, and then put that body within a Body? There is something here for us, and it has to do with connectedness, dependence, order, and the common goal of life within Life.[4]

Connectedness and *dependence* are paradoxical terms especially for Americans, at once denying the independence that is so dear to us, and yet offering comfort and refuge from loneliness and unhealthy solitude. We must learn to cultivate healthy relationships in every arena of life if we are to escape the destructive elements of our own soul.

Family

We discussed the dynamic of cultivating loving relationships in our devotional on love (see Day 11). We outlined there the characteristics of four kinds of love presented by C. S. Lewis: storge, eros, phileo, and agape or charity, which is divine love. As we consider briefly here the marriage relationship, which I believe is the most dominant relationship in life, we must understand that love between a man and a woman should be centered in Christ's love for them. How blessed is the couple who have surrendered their hearts to Christ! This concept of love is foreign to many people.

Respect, godly character, friendship, affection, and enjoyment are the basis of a good marriage. Two people who marry should endeavor to understand each other, love each other, and care for each other. In marriage, as in all relationships, we can be truly happy if we are thankful and have an appreciative heart for one another.

When I wake up every morning, I ask Jesus to be revealed in every area of my wife's life. I ask God to bless Heather each day, letting her enjoy the presence of Jesus in her mind and her eyes and her heart, so that she thinks and sees and loves as Jesus does.

Do you look at your spouse as God's gift to you? The role you give Jesus in your marriage relationship says much about the role He has in the rest of your relationships, indeed, in the rest of your life.[5]

The tongue

Communication in relationships is a primary way we share love. Whether in friendship, or as parents, husbands and wives, employees, or authorities, it is largely our words that cause us to relate positively or negatively. And the Bible places great importance on our words. It declares that the power of life and death are in the tongue (see Prov. 18:21). And the New Testament teaches that if we do not control our tongues, while confessing that we are religious, we are deceived, and our religion is useless (see James 1:26).

Did you know that that when a child enters school, he or she has a vocabulary of between three thousand to four thousand words? During school years, the acquisition of vocabulary continues to climb, with the average adult gaining an *active* or *use* vocabulary of ten thousand words, and a *passive* or *recognition* vocabulary of thirty thousand to forty thousand words. For comparison, *Webster's New International Dictionary* defines four hundred thousand words, and the English language contains about one million words, though there is no exact number. This astonishing gift of language is not shared by any other species of creation—it is reserved for humans. Surely, God's purpose for giving us vocal chords, hearing, and a capacity for communicating through language was largely for developing relationships.[6]

Expressing encouragement and caring has been scientifically proven to enhance health in the individual receiving the affirming words. Conversely, expressing worry and anxiety can destroy relationships. Sometimes two people want to become very close, yet one person is always worrying. That worrying prevents real intimacy because the other person can get only so close without getting caught up in that unhealthy worry mentality. In marriage, for example, it is difficult to maintain a healthy mental attitude and still cultivate intimacy with a "worrying" spouse.[7]

Another destructive habit of the tongue is reflected in a critical spirit. The habit of finding fault with everything and everyone devastates relationships. It can also hinder our worship. A faultfinding spirit runs contrary to the attitudes and actions of Jesus. He is set upon delivering us from our sinful ways, rather than simply criticizing and condemning us. When we criticize rather than encourage a brother or family member, we condemn not only him, but also ourselves. When we cultivate a habit of pointing out another's weaknesses, we are less likely to focus on our own sin, not allowing God to cleanse us.[8]

It is vital to relationships of all kinds that we learn to control our tongue. Jesus declared that out of the heart the mouth speaks (see Matt. 12:34). So if you are continually speaking negatively about those around you, it would be good to check your own heart. Consider David's prayer, "Create in me a clean heart, O God" (Ps. 51:10). I often pray as David did: "Set a guard, O LORD, over my mouth; Keep watch over the door of my lips" (Ps. 141:3).

We can also learn from the psalmist the highest purpose for our words: "I will bless the LORD at all times; His praise shall continually be in my mouth" (Ps. 34:1). As we use our tongue to bless the Lord and to bless the people in our lives, supernatural blessing will return to our own hearts as well.

Workplace

For me, the workplace is an outpatient clinic where I primarily perform eye surgeries to help restore improved vision to my patients. Of course, that brings me in close proximity as well with other doctors and valued staff members who work with us in a team effort to help our patients. It is extremely important that we maintain a positive atmosphere among ourselves because it helps to promote the healing process in our patients. Understanding this reality, we strive, not only to serve our patients well, but to serve other members of the staff also.

What do you expect out of your relationships? Is it better to get as much as you can? Or do you try to serve the other person? C. S. Lewis says there is a parallel between creation and redemption. God didn't need to create us. He did it for His own enjoyment, to have a relationship with us. The same is true of redemption. He didn't need to give us Jesus as a Savior. He did it because He wanted to restore the relationship with His people. God's free and giving heart made Him first create us and then later redeem us. It is simply the nature of God to give and love.[9]

When our mind finds satisfaction in God's promises, we find His free and giving heart reflected in our own attitude. We are less concerned with what we receive and with having our own needs met, and we give to others freely. We know that God will satisfy us and always provide for us, according to the measure that we give. Dr. Elizabeth Vaughn of Dallas says, "Before I go into surgery, I always pause and humble myself before God and ask Him to make these patients see extremely well again."[10] "I have learned to value the power of prayer and its significance in bringing the patient and family, the nurses, the students and the physician closer together and closer to our Lord Jesus Christ," says Dr. Juan Batlle.[11]

Learning to share the love of God in the workplace can transform your situation as well as your own attitude toward your work and toward those with whom you work. In reality, that is what Jesus did when He walked on the Earth, demonstrating the power of the Holy Spirit—the life-giving power—to change everyone He touched with the love of God.

Authorities

The independent mind-set of the average American makes it difficult to relate in a godly manner to those in authority, whether it be a teacher, employer, or civil authority. We are often guilty of "doing what is right in our own eyes." Yet, Scripture is very clear about our responsibility to the authorities in our lives:

> Therefore I exhort first of all that supplications, prayers, intercessions, and giving of thanks be made for all men, for kings and all who are in authority, that we may lead a quiet and peaceable life in all godliness and reverence. For this is good and acceptable in the sight of God our Savior, who desires all men to be saved and to come to the knowledge of the truth.
>
> —1 Timothy 2:1–4

In the church, there is also delegated authority, to which God expects us to submit our lives:

> Remember those who rule over you, who have spoken the word of God to you, whose faith follow, considering the outcome of their conduct...Obey those who rule over you, and be submissive, for they watch out for your souls, as those who must give account. Let them do so with joy and not with grief, for that would be unprofitable for you.
>
> —Hebrews 13:7, 17

As individuals we are to walk with one another in a submissive attitude. Scripture teaches the importance of wives submitting to their husbands (Eph. 5:22), and husbands loving their wives and giving themselves for her as Christ did for the church (v. 25). It also teaches that we are to submit to one another in the body of Christ in the fear of God (v. 21). This attitude of humble submission to godly authorities will strengthen our relationships in every sphere of our lives.

Proper attitudes in relationships are cultivated most effectively when we bow in adoration to our God, spending time with Him. In His presence we gain His divine perspective of our human relationships.

You have made known to me the path of life; you will fill me with joy in your presence, with eternal pleasures at your right hand.

—Psalm 16:11, NIV

These things I have spoken to you, that My joy may remain in you, and that your joy may be full.

—John 15:11

Tracing the Hand of the Creator

A terrestrial planet must have a certain minimum mass to retain an atmosphere. You need an atmosphere for the free exchange of the chemicals of life and to protect inhabitants from cosmic radiation. You need an oxygen-rich atmosphere to support big-brained creatures like humans. Earth's atmosphere is 20 percent oxygen—just right, it turns out. The planet also has to be a minimum size to keep the heat from its interior from being lost too quickly. It's the heat from its radioactive decaying interior that drives the critically important mantle convection inside the Earth. Also, the Earth has a lot of water in its crust. The only reason we're not a water world right now—which is a dead world—is because we have continents and mountains to rise above it. Life on Earth is also possible because we have the energy-rich sunlit surface of the oceans, which is teeming with mineral nutrients. Tides and weathering wash the nutrients from the continents into the oceans, where they feed organisms.[1] These are only a few of the "fine-tuning" factors involved in making the Earth perhaps the only known inhabitable planet in the universe.

JOY

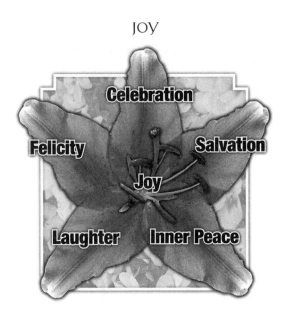

For many, joy is a foreign word, one whose significance cannot be appreciated without clear definition. What do you think of when you hear the word *joy?* Perhaps a child who is carefree and secure in parents' love, giggling in delight? Or a quiet romantic dinner with candlelight flickering on the face of the one you love?

C. H. Spurgeon, the great nineteenth century preacher, described joy as "peace that is dancing."[2] As we have discussed, that inner peace is a result of turning our lives over to God and being reconciled to our Creator, allowing Him to anoint the dance of our DNA. C. S. Lewis writes that we discover true joy only when we are looking for something else—which is God. He describes joy as the response or result of the felt sense of God's love in our soul.[3] According to Scripture, God promises a joy-filled life for all who will trust Him. Jesus told His disciples: "These things I have spoken to you, that My joy may remain in you, and that your joy may be full" (John 15:11). He wants us to "en-*joy*" life rather than endure it.

Salvation

Joy is a journey we begin when we surrender our lives to God. As we willingly submit our past, present, and future to God, every worry, concern, and aspect of our lives is yielded to Him. And we begin to care only about living in God's presence and believing His promises.

I believe there are three critical steps in this journey to a joy-filled life: *grace, relinquishment, and faith.* Sometimes we are reluctant to talk about joy in the context of our relationship with God. We tend to associate joy only with personal comfort, ease, and luxury. But joy is a much deeper and richer experience than that. It is the natural outpouring of our hearts in every relationship and situation of life as God's presence becomes the central pillar of our lives. When we have a personal relationship with Him, we cannot help but be filled with infinite, glorious joy. Our desire to worship and adore God increases as His presence in our lives increases, which is the source of ultimate joy.[4]

One of the greatest hindrances to living a joy-filled life is looking for joy in all the wrong places. Sometimes we mistake a life full of activities for a life of fulfillment. Others believe that if they search hard enough for that "special someone," they will find the joy they seek in the encounter. Unfortunately, they do not understand that unless they become the "right" person themselves, they will continually be disappointed in relationships. The list of choices is endless for those who pursue their goal of a joy-filled life apart from its only true realization—in God alone.

Until we realize, early or late, that what we seek is not within ourselves, we will not have the joy God intends to give us. Our own pursuits will inevitably lead to despair, frustration, anger, anxiety, and loneliness. I have described joy as a heart that is changed by knowing

God. It takes our breath away. It is an infinite host of angels singing glory to God. It is the greatest music or words we can ever imagine, and still more. This great joy puts everything else out of our heads and our hearts. In turning from earthly things we find God. And by putting our faith in Him, we are filled with abundant joy.[5]

Inner peace

While knowing God is the prerequisite for living a joy-filled life, it is sadly true that many Christians still lack joy because their minds and hearts are filled with worry and anxiety. As I discussed earlier, I believe that worry is the greatest sickness of mankind. Many illnesses are caused by a broken heart, loneliness, fear, and worry. For example, it has been determined that personality is an important factor in the emergence of and healing of cancer. People who suppress toxic emotions such as anger become "cancer-susceptible" personalities. They are people who also tend to suffer their burdens in life alone rather than seek comfort from others. It is difficult for them to cope with stress, which is known to suppress the immune system.[6]

Scripture declares, "the joy of the LORD is your strength" (Neh. 8:10). When I let my mind be filled with imaginations of God, glorifying and worshiping Him, I find joy in my life every day. True joy depends on total abandonment to God and His sovereignty. As we choose to exercise faith in God, to forgive those who hurt us, and to fill our thoughts with the Word of God, the fruit of the Spirit of God works in us. He produces in our lives His supernatural attributes of "love, joy, peace, longsuffering, kindness, goodness, faithfulness, gentleness, self-control" (Gal. 5:22–23).[7]

When Christ is fixed in our thoughts, we become recipients of His supernatural joy. We walk with Him in everyday life, at work, and in relationships. He abides in us and we in Him, and we receive His strength, His love, His peace, and His joy.

Felicity

Felicity was a servant saint who lived around the year 200 AD. She was executed because she refused to renounce her faith in God. Even when she was put into an arena with a wild bull, she did not deny Christ, but died praising Him. Hers is a story of a girl who desired God above all things. Felicity's life teaches us that it is possible to have God's ultimate joy in the face of certain death when we abandon our whole lives to Him. That attitude of total trust can be called felicity—God's tranquility personified. Felicity, the martyred saint, had that profound tranquility within her. Her faith in God and love for Him set a shining example for us today. When we relinquish ourselves to God, we rest in the peace that He will be Jehovah-Jireh—the great Provider of all (see Gen. 22:14). This attitude of felicity, which brings ultimate satisfaction, peace, and joy, is also evidence that we are in right standing with God.[8]

For years I have been involved in the Department of Ophthalmology at the University of South Florida in Tampa. I am a clinical professor there, and serve on the board that selected the head of the department. I chose Dr. James Rowsey to come from Oklahoma City to serve in that capacity. Jim is an outstanding man. He is brilliant, pleasant, and delightful. As much as anyone I know, he exhibits the joy of God. He has also gotten into trouble because of his faith. He has been sued because he prays for patients. He has also been sued by employees because they thought he was partial to employees who are Christians.

While Jim has had to face difficulties because of his Christian commitment, his joy in knowing Jesus helps him to overcome the problems. What did he accomplish in his position at the University of South Florida? He was able to revive a department that was dying. His strength and ability he attributes to one source—the joy of the Lord. Jim's joy is sincere and genuine as it shines through the beauty of his meek and humble character.[9]

Laughter

Joy is the natural outpouring of our hearts as God's presence becomes the central pillar of our lives. Psalm 16:11 says, "You will fill me with joy in your presence" (NIV). I once had the opportunity to fish in Alaska with Chuck Swindoll. When we were there, the one thing I did in addition to fish was listen to Chuck laugh. And I do not remember a half-hour going by in which Chuck was not laughing. I have never met a person who laughs as much as Chuck Swindoll. And it is genuine joy—he is enjoying himself. He has holy joy! He lives Philippians 4:4: "Rejoice in the Lord always. I will say it again: Rejoice!"[10]

As we focus on the Person of Jesus, we will live lives of spontaneous emotion—of joy, of love, and of caring. The laughter of joy releases all the stress and anxiety within us. Psychotherapists have developed laughter therapy as an effective tool in their therapeutic kit. The medical world is using the therapeutic effects of laughter to bring healing to their patients, confirming the truth of the Word of God: "A merry heart does good, like medicine" (Prov. 17:22). God placed within us a valuable, healing emotion expressed through laughter.

Mainstream publications are explaining the healing power of laughter. One of the first to describe profound healing he experienced through laughter was author/editor Norman Cousins. Diagnosed with a degenerative disease—ankylosing spondylitis— and almost completely paralyzed, he was given only a few months to live by the doctors. Cousins checked himself out of the hospital, checked into a hotel, consumed high doses of vitamin C, and immersed himself in humor. He details in his book, *Anatomy of an Illness*, his astounding rejuvenation through the use of humor. Cousins describes how he "laughed himself back to health." He read funny stories and watched old comedies by Keaton, Chaplin, and the Marx Brothers. Norman Cousins eventually recovered and lived another twenty years of a healthy, productive life.[11]

Celebration

Too often we use the word *celebrate* for a temporal, trivial event in which we enjoy momentary happiness. A much deeper significance of true celebration is reflected in our worship of God, our Creator and Savior. We understand celebration as we seek to discover "the chief goal of mankind," which, according to The Westminster Catechism, is to "glorify God, and to enjoy him forever."[12] When I first read that statement years ago, it seemed like an easy thing to do. Since then, I have come to understand that God does not want just words of praise.

He wants us to celebrate His love and His gift of salvation by committing our lives to worshiping Him. In our deepest worship we learn to relinquish all to Him. The apostle Paul exhorted believers: "I beseech you therefore, brethren, by the mercies of God, that you present your bodies a living sacrifice, holy, acceptable to God, which is your reasonable service. And do not be conformed to this world, but be transformed by the renewing of your mind, that you may prove what is that good and acceptable and perfect will of God" (Rom. 12:1–2).

It is in living a relinquished life that we worship Him most profoundly. And when we praise and worship Him in that place of total surrender, we experience true joy and celebration. We no longer desire to do anything more than to worship His majesty and stand in awe of His creation. This is the wonderful celebration of God that I call a "thanksgiving frenzy." It is a spontaneous, exuberant, praise and adoration for our Creator.

Living a joy-filled life is based on exalting and worshiping God. Enjoying Him fills us with joy. Praise, love, and enjoyment of God produce in us an everlasting felicity and bliss as we struggle in a world that is mean and contemptible. Humility is essential for the happiness and joy that comes with godly felicity. Scripture promises that those who humble themselves in worship of their God will be filled with joy:

But may all who seek you rejoice and be glad in you; may those who love your salvation always say, "The Lord be exalted!"
—Psalm 40:16, niv

And He said, "My Presence will go with you, and I will give

you rest."

—Exodus 33:14

For He Himself has said, "I will never leave you nor

forsake you."

—Hebrews 13:5

Tracing the Hand of the Creator

S cientific research continues in the exciting field of gene therapy to find ways to treat our deadliest diseases. For example, genetic engineers are removing the immune cell known as the tumor-infiltrating lymphocyte, or tumor cells themselves, inserting a gene that boosts the cells' ability to make quantities of a natural anticancer product, and then growing the restructured cells in quantity in the laboratory. When the altered cells are returned to the patient, they seek out the tumor and deliver large doses of the anticancer chemical. They also appear to mobilize, in some unknown way, additional anti-tumor defenses.[1]

Such complexity of design and function in the human body continually points to a Designer. Without an intelligent Creator, we would not have the intelligence to understand, even to the extent we do, the unending marvels of our magnificent DNA, which enables scientists to do such promising research for the healing of genetic disease.

PRESENCE OF GOD

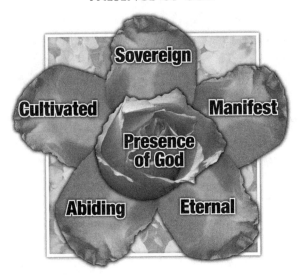

My epiphany in medical school led me to understand that although we could look at cells and study them, we could neither create them nor fully comprehend them. Nobel Prize-winning biologist Alfred Gilman admitted, "I could draw you a map of all the components of a cell and put in all the proper arrows connecting them...but...I or anyone else would look at the map and have absolutely no ability to predict anything."[2] Even with the amazing advances in understanding the wonders of creation, the unfathomable mystery of life still causes us to bow in humility before the Creator and declare, "You are sovereign Lord of all."

In our physical body, the individual cell is a universe of activity in itself. Yet, its life and health depend on its ability to relate, in a most sophisticated fashion, to the cells surrounding it. And the life of the whole depends on the "companionship" of entire systems of cells, working together in intricate complexity far beyond even what our imagination can conceive.

Similarly, though each individual is a "universe" within itself, in order to nurture a healthy psyche and enjoy spiritual health, we must seek to relate to God. Cultivating companionship with our Lord, Jesus Christ, assures the optimum, intricate workings of our spirit, soul, and body. Scripture teaches that the Son of God sustains all things by His powerful Word (see Heb. 1:3, NIV). We are among those "things" that He sustains in life. Without heeding His Word for our lives, we must surely become victim to many destructive forces, both from within and without.

Sovereign presence

Unless we recognize the sovereign power of God, the Creator, we will never know His personal presence in our lives. Only by giving Him His rightful place as absolute sovereign Deity, can we hope to find our purpose in His creation, in His kingdom. *Sovereignty* simply means God ruling over all as an all-wise King—benevolent, gracious, majestic, and powerful. Scripture clearly teaches the absolute power of a sovereign God: "But our God is in heaven; He does whatever He pleases" (Ps. 115:3). Of course, because God is love, it "pleases" Him to do good to His creation. God's wisdom, power, love, and holiness are implemented by His sovereignty. The psalmist also acknowledged our sovereign God's goodness:

> For the LORD Most High is awesome; He is a great King over all the earth. He will subdue the peoples under us, And the nations under our feet. He will choose our inheritance for us...Sing praises to our King, sing praises! For God is the King of all the earth.
>
> —PSALM 47:2–4, 6–7

And the prophet, Isaiah, records this declaration made by God Himself:

Remember the former things of old, For I am God, and there is no other; I am God, and there is none like Me, Declaring the end from the beginning, And from ancient times things that are not yet done, Saying, "My counsel shall stand, And I will do all My pleasure."

—Isaiah 46:9–10

It is the existence of this sovereign God that Darwin and all evolutionists deny. In my book, *Darwinism Under the Microscope*, I explain the consequence of this godless worldview:

With the encouragement of, and under the pedagogy of, the scientific community, the primacy of God has been superceded by a belief in the near omnipotence of science and of human knowledge. Stretching our hands toward the "tree of life," seeking, in some manner, not only to displace the Creator but to *become* creator is more than just reckless...We must realize His redemption, His omniscience, and remain vigilant that we do not lose sight of the greater, deeper truth. This truth is that life was created by God. We may be its stewards...but we can never create life...The essential attitude to life should be one of awe, appreciation, and respect while devoid of pride and a desire to transcend or manipulate without discipline.[3]

The providence of God—His divine guidance and care—reveals His sovereignty. His sustaining guidance of human destiny, taught clearly in Scripture, is also testified to by many throughout modern history. Unexplainable deliverances of soldiers during wartime, divine intervention in the lives of children, miraculous cures and protection from life-threatening forces—all these and many other circumstances, played out in the lives of people from every century, testify to the goodness of God working for His people.

We understand God's sovereignty when we recognize that He made us and we see His wisdom in all of creation; when we know that God has placed us where we are in life and see His goodness in it; when we realize that God is working through our lives to use us for His glory and we thank Him for it. Even in our trials, we are thankful for God's sovereignty, teaching us our most valuable lessons and gently forming Christlikeness in our character.

We need to integrate the concept of God's sovereignty into our lives. When we do, His grace is manifest, His future grace becomes our contemplation, and we find our rightful place with Him. He truly becomes our Father, our Provider, the eternal One. All things exist because of the power of God. We should stand in amazement and bow in wonder at the awesome display of the power of the sovereign God in all of creation.

Cultivated presence

Once we accept the reality of the sovereign power of God in the Earth, we can begin to cultivate appreciation of His presence in our lives. We have discussed the importance of submitting our lives to the lordship of Christ, and learning to abide in Him, as Jesus taught (see John 15). We cannot overemphasize the importance of spending time in prayer and reading the Word, fellowshiping with other believers, and continually submitting our lives to obedience to Christ. As we bow before God in deep thankfulness and worship for who He is and for the gift of life He has given us, we will become more and more aware of His presence in our lives. In cultivating the presence of God, we allow His thoughts to become ours and His attitudes to shape our lives. His presence influences all our relationships, activities, and words...and there is more!

I like to think of at least nine different ways of cultivating the presence of God in our lives. They help us to develop our love for Him. As I have stated, I believe our biggest failure in life is the lack of appreciation. Consider these nine ways we can overcome this failure and learn to appreciate God.[4]

Appreciating nature

The stars are the majesty of this privileged planet. God's glory is seen in the waters, their tides, and the mathematical intricacies that make nature as gorgeous and as beautiful as it is. The DNA and the intricacy of the single cell is evidence of the overwhelming vastness of nature. We can simply look at nature's wonders around us and bow our hearts in worship as we appreciate the beauty of God's creation. Because knowledge enhances appreciation (you can't appreciate what you don't know), I encourage you to read and study an aspect of the creation that interests you. You will be amazed at the new level of appreciation you have for your Creator.

The senses

Scientists understand that the greatest activator of the Reticular Activating System, the brain's attention center, is *sound*. Because the beauty of music excites and thrills our minds and hearts, worship music is especially effective in helping people to experience God. Through the arts or other means that cause a sensory response, we may cultivate an appreciation of God and His presence. Enjoy the fragrances of plant-life; gaze upon the brilliant night sky or the snow-covered mountains. Taste the delicious flavors of your favorite fruits. Feel the cool softness of the grass on your bare feet—and appreciate your Creator.

Tradition

Many people have come to know God simply through their religious tradition. Symbolic meaning in religious expressions can cause us to think of the majesty of God and worship Him. However, religious formalities are not always helpful in bringing an intense presence of God into a person's life. This overwhelming presence of God, called the manifest presence of God, can be cultivated in other ways, which we will discuss.

Meditation of God's Word

Scripture teaches that the Word of God is food for our spiritual life, helping us to cultivate appreciation for God and all of life. The more we study the Word of God and meditate on it, allowing it to fill our minds and hearts, the more we will believe its promises and discover their life-giving power. And as we heed its warnings, we will be spared the consequences of violating the commandments of God.

Develop a purpose or project for Christ

To work with prisoners, to help people recover from homosexuality, drug addiction, domestic abuse, or other problems of society, to help inner-city children, or adopt any other project for helping others will cause you to grow in your appreciation of God. We grow in our love of God and others as we find ways to give to them. Sometimes we call people like Jim Kennedy and Chuck Colson "Do-Gooders," but they are much more than that. They demonstrate the power of a godly life that is passionate about giving to others.

Caregivers

Many physicians are wonderful caregivers. They implement their love of God with their caregiving and make it something that is special. I have physician friends who pray for two or three hours a day before beginning to care for their patients; these doctors have become unbelievably godly people. Sharing God's love with their patients is one of the most wonderful ways they have to enjoy God's presence and live a fulfilled life. In other words, God's presence is felt where there is love shared.

Enthusiasm

The root meaning of *enthusiasm* is "inspired," which originates from *en-theos*—in God. Living a life inspired by God gives one a new purpose for life. Our enthusiasm for life should overwhelm every other difficulty in life, making it of less importance. For believers who rest in God's redemption, our enthusiasm for life should be greater than other people's excitement for lesser pursuits. Our satisfaction that results from resting in God's redemptive purpose for our lives should result in great enthusiasm for all of life. In this way, God will be most glorified in our lives.

Study of theology

In depth study of the words of God from a theological perspective is important for all of life. It teaches us how to intermingle the Word of God totally in every area of our life. Being a theologian is one of the most important pursuits for Christians. It enables us to truly understand why we are here, for what purpose we live, and how to find the meaning for life. For example, when we study the Book of Romans, which has been called the "Constitution of Christianity," we are able to formulate our Christian worldview of life. To study the Book of Revelation and try to understand the future in God enlarges our eternal perspective of life. These kinds of theological studies help us prioritize the mundane activities of the day and to focus on the presence of God in our lives.

Study the mind of God

According to Scripture, the mind of God is revealed in every aspect of His magnificent creation (see Rom. 1:20). Studying the mind of God is overwhelmingly beautiful when you begin to understand, through creation, all that He did so that we could enjoy the gift of life. If we study God's mind, we will truly appreciate what it means to be with Him and to love Him.

Each of these nine avenues for appreciating God will result in our having the presence of God in our lives, changing our lives for the better. They will help us understand that, amazingly, our Christian walk is not a religious tradition but a *relationship of appreciation* with a Person, Christ Jesus, who died for us to forgive our sins against Him. In our journey toward appreciation of God, it is paramount that we understand we are sinners and need God's redemption for our sin. As we learn to walk with Christ continually in deepening appreciation, that divine relationship will bring an end to our rebellion and indifference.

As I subject myself to the reality of the wonderful design of my person, revealed from the mind of God, I realize how far short I fall in coming to Him completely with gratitude for my life. Worshiping the mind of God is one of the truly great ways to enjoy the cultivated presence of God. And as we worship, we will experience more and more the manifest presence of God in our lives.

Manifest presence

The Old Testament hero, Enoch, knew God in such a way that He walked in His presence daily. Such was the reality of God's presence in Enoch's life, that one day God simply "took him" home to be with God forever (see Gen. 5:24). Scripture gives many examples of God's manifest presence, where God presented Himself in a tangible form: in the burning bush of Moses' desert, in the Ark of the Covenant between the cherubim, as a pillar of fire and cloud protecting the Israelites in the wilderness, as a still, small voice to Elijah, and as the angel of the Lord visiting with Abraham. There are occasions when God still chooses to presence Himself in a demonstrative way in the life of a believer, a church, or a nation.

No one is ever the same after such an encounter with the Creator of the universe. An eternal God appears in temporal situations and finite human lives to affect an eternal work in them. It is an awesome thing just to read of such encounters in Scripture. The prophet, Isaiah, was overwhelmed in his encounter with God:

> In the year that King Uzziah died, I saw the Lord sitting on a throne, high and lifted up, and the train of His robe filled the temple. Above it stood seraphim; each one had six wings: with two he covered his face, with two he covered his feet, and with two he flew. And one cried to another and said: "Holy, holy, holy

is the LORD of hosts; The whole earth is full of His glory!" And the posts of the door were shaken by the voice of him who cried out, and the house was filled with smoke. So I said: "Woe is me, for I am undone! Because I am a man of unclean lips, And I dwell in the midst of a people of unclean lips; For my eyes have seen the King, The LORD of hosts."

—ISAIAH 6:1–5

Isaiah also reveals the purpose of his divine encounter. After a seraph touched his mouth with a live coal from the altar and purged his iniquity (vv. 6–7), Isaiah heard the voice of the Lord asking, "Whom shall I send, And who will go for Us?" (v. 8). Then Isaiah embraced this call and new commission from God, though it proved to be a difficult one (vv. 8–9). His personal encounter with God had opened up the future of his personal destiny.

Of course, Jesus Christ is the New Testament revelation of God to mankind, walking the Earth as the Son of God. In the Book of Hebrews we read: "God, who at various times and in various ways spoke in time past to the fathers by the prophets, has in these last days spoken to us by His Son, whom He has appointed heir of all things, through whom also He made the worlds" (Heb. 1:1–2). And though Christ ascended on high, returning to the right hand of the Father after His crucifixion and resurrection from the dead, He continued to manifest His presence in the Earth through the power of the Holy Spirit.

Christ appeared to Saul, in his conversion experience, transforming him into the apostle Paul (see Acts 9). There are many other biblical examples of God's manifest presence. The result of a personal encounter with God's manifest presence is always life changing. Jesus promised: "And he who loves Me will be loved by My Father, and I will love him and manifest Myself to him" (John 14:21).

Those who have experienced this transforming encounter reflect the love of Christ in their lives. The anointing of His Holy Spirit permeates their attitudes, words, and actions. Yet, it is the abiding presence of Christ in our lives that is designed to satisfy our hearts on a daily basis, giving us the companionship and divine love that we crave.

Abiding presence

Jesus taught His disciples clearly how to cultivate His abiding presence in their lives. In John 15, we read His instructions to allow His words to abide in them. In this way, they would cultivate His presence and enjoy a healthy relationship to Him, the vine. As believers, we are branches that derive our lives from Christ, the vine. Branches abiding in the vine is a picture of our total dependence on Christ, as well as the total protection and provision for our lives resulting from our relationship with Him.

This relationship is analogous to the relationship of a beloved spouse, who so completely consumes our thoughts and affections that we desire nothing in life except to be with the beloved and to please them. When we abide in Christ, we have no goals, no aspirations, no motivation outside of living in constant communion and fellowship with our Lord. We covet His companionship above any human relationship. We seek to spend time in worship and prayer and praise, filled with and expressing gratitude for the altogether satisfying relationship we enjoy with Him.

Scripture is filled with analogies and instructions regarding the intimate relationship we are to enjoy with our Lord. For example, the Song of Solomon is a picture of the exquisite delights of marital love, which is a type of our enjoyment and companionship with Christ. Without cultivating this abiding presence of God in our lives, we will not gain an eternal perspective of life; and we will not walk in the fulfillment of personal destiny. Likewise, we will not be preparing for a life lived in His presence for all eternity.

Eternal presence

Have you noticed that whenever Scripture pulls back the curtain of eternity and gives us a glimpse of heaven, what we witness is the worship of those who are there? Isaiah saw the seraph worshiping and crying out, "Holy, holy, holy is the LORD of hosts" (Isa. 6:3). And when John the revelator was given wondrous visions of the eternal realm, he saw four living creatures who do not rest day or night, saying: "Holy, holy, holy, Lord God Almighty, Who was and is and is to come!" (Rev. 4:8). He also saw twenty-four elders "fall down before Him who sits on the throne and worship Him who lives forever and ever, and cast their crowns before the throne, saying: 'You are worthy, O Lord, to receive glory and honor and power; For You created all things, And by Your will they exist and were created'" (Rev. 4:10–11).

Through Jesus, death is swallowed up forever! Death is conquered eternally. Death is no longer a barrier between God and us, but is a doorway to Him. When we step into heaven, we will say, "This is my God! I've waited for Him. I rejoice in Him." Eternity is where we put all our hopes, our goals, our cares, and our concerns. Where there is Christ, there is hope. Where there is Christ, there is joy. What a promise! We belong to the Lord! We have eternity with Him! This eternal perspective becomes the focus for our life, the foundation for our life. We now live in anticipation of His eternal presence. We make all of our decisions based on that premise. We see that our life on Earth is short and soon passes away. But we are with the eternal God forever![5]

This eternal perspective of unending bliss in the presence of God is the key to everything we have discussed. We were created by an eternal Creator, whose sole desire is to live in communion with His creation—eternally. As we realize the wonders of God's love and the intricacies of our own DNA, along with the wonders of all of creation around us, we cannot help but bow in humble adoration for the genius Designer and be filled with radical gratitude for the gift of life.

This adoring gratitude leads us ever deeper into the heart of God, our Creator, our loving Father, and our Redeemer. There we find the ultimate satisfaction our soul craves in intimate relationship with our God. There we discover personal destiny—the divine purpose for which we were born. There we are empowered to face and conquer every difficulty of life. And there we learn to love others as we love ourselves.

You open Your hand And satisfy the desire of every living thing.

—PSALM 145:16

For He satisfies the longing soul, And fills the hungry soul with goodness.

—PSALM 107:9

Tracing the Hand of the Creator

For Darwinian scientists, the naturalistic evolution of life from prebiotic chemicals, and its subsequent naturalistic evolution into complexity and humanity, is *assumed* as a matter of first principle in Darwin's theory of evolution. For them, the only question open to investigation is *how* this naturalistic process occurred.

However, more recent empirical evidence gives no reason for confidence that natural selection has the creative power, regardless of the amount of time available, to build up complex organs from scratch or to change one body plan into another. Darwin's hypothesis requires the existence of an immense quantity of transitional forms that became extinct as they were gradually replaced by better-adapted descendants. To date there is no evidence of these transitional forms in the fossil record or otherwise.

The refusal (or inability) of the scientific establishment to acknowledge that Darwinism is in serious evidential difficulties, and probably false as a general theory, is due to the influence of scientific materialist philosophy and certain arbitrary modes of thought that have become associated with the scientific method. For them, a paradigm, to be acceptable, must conform to the philosophical tenets of "scientific materialism." For example, the hypothesis that biological complexity is the product of some preexisting creative intelligence or vital force is not acceptable to scientific materialists. They do not, in fairness, consider this hypothesis and then potentially reject it as contrary to the evidence; rather they disregard it as inherently ineligible for consideration. Because the escape from Darwinism seems to lead nowhere, Darwinism for scientific materialists is inescapable.[1]

SATISFACTION

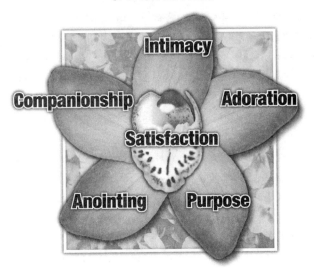

Surrender, submission, selflessness—all lead to ultimate satisfaction found only in complete abandonment to our Creator. It is a theological and experiential reality that when we bow in subservient worship to God, we are filled with joy. When we get rid of our egos and independence, we find ourselves filled with glorious, abundant peace. We are at peace with ourselves because we have found peace in God. Then we are full of joy because we love God and depend on Him, not ourselves. We must never forget that it is receiving the love of God by believing His promises which is the fountain of our inner life toward God.[2]

Adoration

One of the main goals of this devotional has been to evoke wonder and awe in your soul through observing the wonders of your Creator, especially as witnessed in your DNA. Knowledge of the magnificent complexities of creation leads inevitably to appreciation for the Creator, who became our Savior. It is humbling to consider the intricacies of life created and maintained by a loving God. Our spontaneous response to such divine love is first of all, gratitude, which we express in our daily lives in a thousand ways. Our next response becomes deep adoration, a giving of worship and honor to the Creator of all.

Worship involves giving something back to God. In a spirit of thankfulness, we present Him a gift for who He is and what He has done, because "The LORD has done great things for us...we are glad" (Ps. 126:3). Yet, all we have to give to God, who has given to us the gift of life itself, is our desire for relationship, fulfillment, and satisfaction. As we yield our lives to Him, which is His gift to us, we begin to realize the purpose for which we were born—to walk in intimate relationship with God. Because that is our ultimate purpose, we cannot hope to find true satisfaction in any other pursuit.

In *Dynamics of Worship*, I described the power of worship to transform our lives:

> Worship! *Momentous*—significant...decisive...pivotal. *Urgent*—compelling...imperative...crucial. *Glorious*—superb...transcendent...sublime. And the superlative of all these adjectives describes worship...Worship lifts the spirit to soar heavenward...It keeps the fires of the heart burning brightly, regardless of situations in which we find ourselves. Passionate, fiery worship, when balanced with a well-founded knowledge and steadfast covenant with the Lord, makes the following promise a reality: "But in all these things we overwhelmingly conquer through Him who loved us" (Rom. 8:37).[3]

We discussed worship earlier (see Day 19) as an aspect of our prayer life. We must also understand that it is through bowing before our Redeemer in humble adoration that we find true satisfaction for our souls. It is a part of our complex design that our deepest desires can only be fulfilled in an adoring relationship with our Creator. That inward "God-shaped vacuum" aches for His presence to fill it. When we choose to seek Him, His anointing on our DNA truly makes us dance—expressing the joy of life with God!

Anointed purpose

We discussed earlier the beauty of your anointed DNA as it relates to discovering purpose and destiny. *Anointing* is also a strong theme relating to personal satisfaction. The inner healing found through the new life—the life of God in one's soul—is ultimately expressed in an anointed purpose. To effectively live the anointed life requires asking God to anoint everything you do, rather than attempting to live by your own strength.

The anointed life is, in essence, being a real Christian rather than superficially practicing a religious tradition. The added significance, meaning, and love in living an anointed life is only found when you ask for and receive greater influences of the Spirit of God in your life. Then life has real purpose. There is the deepest richness associated with an anointed purpose in your life, because it has an impact now and for eternity.[4] Scripture confirms that what we do in this life will not go unrewarded:

> But without faith it is impossible to please Him, for he who comes to God must believe that He is, and that He is a rewarder of those who diligently seek Him.
>
> —HEBREWS 11:6

> And behold, I am coming quickly, and My reward is with Me, to give to every one according to his work.
>
> —REVELATION 22:12

The anointed purpose of life in Christ gives meaning to it now and for eternity. Everything you do in life will be judged by the

Lord when you stand before Him in glory. He not only enables you to live faithfully for Him here on Earth, but He will reward you in heaven for doing so. His Word clearly describes the path of life that brings blessing and reward: "You will show me the path of life; In Your presence is fullness of joy; At Your right hand are pleasures forevermore" (Ps. 16:11).[5]

To be anointed is to have meaning, direction, and purpose that God appoints, prepares, superintends, and revives along the way. It is the interpenetration of God's Spirit and yours. You are thus equipped so that you are not left to yourself. You possess the presence of the Most High with whom nothing is impossible. Anointing is God saying, "I have chosen you, and I am going to be with you!" Our inner peace, spiritual healing, and health derive from the harmony, joy, completeness, and anointed purpose in our alignment with God.[6]

Intimacy

Scripture promises that the most intimate desires of the human heart, aching for love, will be fulfilled by God Himself:

> For the devious are an abomination to the LORD; But He is intimate with the upright.
>
> —PROVERBS 3:32, NAS

The Hebrew word translated *intimate* means "to share secrets, deep, inward counsel, in audience with a person." The deepest longing of the human heart is to be known completely and accepted unconditionally. God Himself offers this love relationship to all who seek Him. That profound intimacy is available to all who pursue relationship with their Maker and Redeemer. Can you imagine sharing "secrets" with the Creator Himself? Receiving His counsel and guidance for living an anointed life? All of that and much more becomes a reality in the intimacy of relationship with God, through Jesus Christ and by His Spirit.

According to John Piper, to truly love God we must delight in a relationship with God that satisfies. Loving God is delighting in, cherishing, savoring, treasuring, revering, and admiring God beyond any gift—life and health notwithstanding.[7] When we truly love God with all of our heart, independent of our requests and expectations, and above our own needs, then we will find satisfaction, meaning, and purpose. We find, there, both eternal life and the inner healing for which we pine.[8]

We can draw very close to God on a personal basis, safely revealing our hearts and minds to Him. God call us to a life of intimacy. God cries out for us to know Him and beseeches us to live near to Him. He desires for us to understand Him and His inner workings, which have been and will be for eternity, and for us to know our place in those inner workings. Yet, we must open ourselves to Him. We have to ask Him to tear down the defensive, protective walls we build to prevent intimacy. Consider the psalmist's cry for intimacy: "Search me, O God, and know my heart; Try me and know my anxieties; And see if there is any wicked way in me, And lead me in the way everlasting" (Ps. 139:23–24).[9]

As our nation grows more obese, we are observing an entire culture seeking gratification orally through food. Some people are as addicted to eating as others are addicted to drugs, alcohol, sex, or other abnormal behaviors. If we seek our satisfaction in God, we will become "addicted" to His presence and find our deepest satisfaction in worshiping and adoring our Creator. All of our inadequacies, insufficiencies, and emotional vacancies in our lives, can be filled with Jesus.

Our radical gratitude for His grace, for His power to save us from our sin, for anointing our DNA and filling us with joy—all of this significance He gives to our lives can supplant the oral gratification people seek from overeating and other unhealthy, "out-of-control" behaviors. As we abandon our lives to God and begin to express radical gratitude to our Lord, we won't become victims of oral gratification to seek to calm our restlessness and mask our loneliness. We will celebrate our fulfillment in God alone.

Companionship

Enoch, the Old Testament saint who walked so closely with God that God took him to heaven, understood a depth of companionship with God that many have not yet discovered. Scripture simply says, "Enoch walked with God three hundred years, and had sons and daughters...And Enoch walked with God; and he was not, for God took him" (Gen. 5:22, 24). Someone commented that one day as Enoch walked with God, they ended the day closer to heaven than to Enoch's home. And God just said, "Come on, Enoch, and go home with Me."

Even without the understanding of the blood of Christ, or any molecular biological revelations of the marvelous creation of his DNA, Enoch pleased God—by walking with Him. I believe that radically intimate walk with God, becoming a loyal companion of God, results from a desire to appreciate Him for who He is and from a deep hunger for His presence.

This morning when I went to play golf and left my dog, Kippur, at home, it was hard to look into his eyes. I could see he wanted so much to go with me, but I just wanted to be with "the boys." In my relationship with Kippur, through spending time with him, I have won a place in his affections so that he adores me and wants only to be with me and to please me. Similarly, in my walk with God, as I spend time with Him in solitude, prayer, and reading His Word, I learn to adore Him and become radically grateful for who He is. As I enter more and more into His life, His Spirit mingles with mine. The anointing of the Holy Spirit is infused into me so that His walk becomes my walk in daily life. And I long more and more just to be with Him and to please Him.

My companionship with the Lord fills me with joy that springs from my adoration, appreciation, and gratitude to God.

It is a joy that resonates between me and the Lord through worship and prayer. It is the awe of appreciating His generosity, His glorious, meticulous, intricate, elaborate, integrated, design for all of creation. Yet, as in all true companionship, I feel at ease in His presence—the presence of the Divine. Perhaps the psalmist helps us articulate best this wonder of knowing our great God and being known by Him:

> O LORD, You have searched me and known me. You know my sitting down and my rising up; You understand my thought afar off. You comprehend my path and my lying down, And are acquainted with all my ways. For there is not a word on my tongue, But behold, O LORD, You know it altogether... Such knowledge is too wonderful for me; It is high, I cannot attain it... For You formed my inward parts; You covered me in my mother's womb. I will praise You, for I am fearfully and wonderfully made... How precious also are Your thoughts to me, O God! How great is the sum of them!
>
> —PSALM 139:1–4, 6, 13–14, 17

When we cultivate the kind of eternal perspective the psalmist had, we no longer see ourselves like we once did. We now live in anticipation of His eternal presence. We make all of our decisions based on that premise. We see that our life on Earth is short and soon passes away. But we are with the eternal God forever! When we focus on eternal imaginations, we can understand better how little the possessions and measures of worldly success matter. We can point ourselves toward eternity with Him, working enough to meet the needs of our daily lives without being consumed by the cares of the present day. Instead, we are consumed by our focus on our future with Him—a future that begins now as we are engulfed in His presence.[10]

True satisfaction comes through daily communion with God in an intimate relationship of love. Of course, Christ is the key to that intimacy, for we know God through Christ, and are known to Him through Christ. As we continually surrender our lives to Christ, we can become engulfed in His presence and enter into the fullness of God.

I know God as the One who saves the worst of sinners. Every day I strive to keep Him intimately involved in every aspect of my life. He totally intertwines the past, the present, and the future. He holds all the forces of the universe in the palm of His hand. It is important that we do not think of God according to some small, remote concept of One who created the world, sent Jesus to save it, and now observes us from a distance. God's people have the assurance that God is within us and around us. And He gives us a future to believe in. He wants us to be completely satisfied with Himself and the anointing He places on our lives.[11] May we learn to say with the psalmist, "As for me, I will see Your face in righteousness; I shall be satisfied when I awake in Your likeness" (Ps. 17:15).

Why not bow your heart before our awesome Creator, and ask Him to satisfy your deepest longings with His presence? Jesus declared, "Come to me…and I will give you rest" (Matt. 11:28). He will respond, for He summons you to choose to renounce your independent, self-reliant ways, and seek His love. As you renounce the erroneous idea of "haphazard chance" being the source of life, and embrace the loving heart of your Creator, you will begin to understand and appreciate the wonder that fills all of life.

The deepest fulfillment of our hearts and the greatest satisfaction for our unique DNA can only be found as we abandon ourselves in a frenzy of gratitude to the Creator of life! As we yield our lives to the providence of a loving God, He will anoint our DNA, reveal our purpose and divine destiny—and we will dance!

EPILOGUE

Exceeding gratitude for our Creator's plan is a profound perspective of life that fills our hearts and minds with promise, hope, joy, and happiness. It is based in a humble attitude of worship and adoration for God Himself, our Maker and Redeemer. Unfortunately, many people deny the existence of the Creator, whose handiwork is displayed in all of creation. Instead of turning to the light of God revealed in all of nature, they embrace dark, humanistic, secularist, or existentialist philosophies in their attempt to solve the mysteries of life. As a result, instead of finding fulfillment, satisfaction, and personal destiny in a God-centered perspective that leads to eternal life, they struggle to find meaning for their existence through their man-centered philosophies.

MAN-CENTERED PHILOSOPHIES

This denial of a Creator-God is the only explanation for the godless philosophies of origins as envisioned by Charles Darwin, for example, in his flawed theory of evolution. Of course, Darwin was not aware of the immense body of scientific discovery of the past two centuries. Yet, many scientists today still insist on preserving their man-centered philosophies, instead of recognizing our Creator-God in the awesome scientific realities they are observing on a daily basis.

The reality of "irreducible complexity" (which Darwin admitted would debunk his theory if discovered), and the overwhelming evidence of "intelligent design," as seen both under the microscope and through the telescope, give stark testimony against the theory of evolution. These and other scientific findings support sheer mathematical calculations of the immense improbability of complex life resulting from chance.

Even after considering our small planet Earth as a privileged planet among innumerable galaxies, with all the astrophysical conditions required to sustain the incredible level of life we enjoy; and after observing the microscopic single-cell zygote that produces human life in all its intricate, intelligent, interdependent systems; and after failing to produce even one living cell independently, many in the scientific community still deny the existence of an intelligent Designer. Blindness to the Creator, in light of the visible wonders of creation, is ultimately a result of choosing to live independently from God. It is a choice to adopt a man-centered existence rather than fulfill a God-centered destiny. The former is utterly lacking in gratitude for the gift of life; the latter is filled with exceeding gratitude for the Giver, as well as the gift, of life. The apostle Paul confirms this spiritual reality:

> For since the creation of the world His invisible attributes are clearly seen, being understood by the things that are made, even His eternal power and Godhead, so that they are without excuse, because although they knew God, they did not glorify Him as God, nor were thankful.
>
> —Romans 1:20–21

Especially considering the astounding scientific discoveries of the twentieth and twenty-first centuries, such as the human zygote, DNA, and the unfathomable expanse of the universe, it is amazing to think that much of the scientific community still fails the "gratitude test." Their proud independence fails to recognize God as the Creator of all. This sad reality can only be explained in the context of spiritual blindness, which is the norm for humanity apart from God's redemption. A man-centered mind-set results from the denial of God, the Creator-Redeemer. Where such existentialist philosophies govern minds, hopelessness, futility, and dark, idolatrous, worldviews are prevalent.

A Conversion Process

The good news is that God sent His Son, Jesus Christ, as a Redeemer, "that you should turn from these useless things to the living God, who made the heaven, the earth, the sea, and all things that are in them" (Acts 14:15). There is continual growth in our journey from spiritual blindness to experience an ultimately satisfying appreciation for our Creator-Redeemer. When we first turn our hearts to seek the living God, we realize the error of the godless philosophies of the world, with their sin, destructive standards, and values for life. We understand that the awesome world around us could not have been created by chance. And we become thankful for the Giver and the gift of life. We learn that the Giver of life came and died on the cross to obtain our pardon. When we trust Him alone to save us and not our works, He forgives our sin.

As we continue our pursuit of God, we experience deepening appreciation for the life Giver and all of life's wonderful gifts. This change of attitude will lead us out of spiritual darkness and confusion into a life filled with hope and promise. As we receive the eternal Word of life, our eyes are opened to spiritual realities by God's Word. Accepting Christ as the anointed One—the Messiah—our lives become anointed, divinely empowered, to live in satisfying relationship with Him. And we discover the ultimate enjoyment of purpose for life that reveals our personal destiny. Our divine relationship with our Creator-Redeemer deepens into adoration as we become eternally enthralled with God Himself. As our worldview is changed by divine truth, our attitudes are transformed by His grace and even our activities become God-centered. This divine anointing on our DNA brings great satisfaction to our lives—now and for eternity.

Unfortunately, because of a desire for independence from any superior power, it is a great difficulty for many men and women of science to accept the fact that there is a God. For the last one hundred fifty years scientists have tried to separate themselves from religion. They have become so wise in their own environment that they fail to acknowledge that they cannot explain the complexities they are discovering.

A scientist is looking through half a microscope when he or she fails to acknowledge that there must be a Creator, who has created the beautiful, intricate, scientific information—DNA—that is the substance of life. In the light of current scientific knowledge, it is simply not "scientific" to continue to embrace the theory of evolution. It cannot stand the scrutiny of scientific laws. The scientific knowledge we are discovering in the present century reveals too great a complexity of design to have occurred "by chance."

God-Centered Philosophy

It is time to humble ourselves and acknowledge the "Scientist-Creator" who created what we call "science." He understands how it was made and why. It is our knowledge of Him that will show us the secrets of life, scientifically and spiritually, and prepare us to live with Him for eternity. This temporal life is short in comparison to the unending life we will experience when it is over. Our greatest investment of time here should be to relate to the Creator of the universe, preparing our hearts for eternal destiny in His presence.

There is a direct connection between this present life and eternity. I suggest that the way we focus our minds now and the attitudes we cultivate in our journey of life will determine our eternity. For example, those who develop their musical capacity appreciate the varieties and intricacies of classical music. They have a deepened capacity and appreciation for music. In that same way, some have suggested that believers who have developed a deeper capacity for God on Earth will have a deeper joy and glory and wonder in heaven. What God bestows on us in heaven is related to the spiritual capacities we develop in this life. God will reward our mind-set and our personality for eternity to the degree we have become like Christ in this life.[1]

Scripture indicates that we will receive rewards in eternity according to the way we live our lives on Earth: "Do not be deceived, God is not mocked; for whatever a man sows, that he will also reap. For he who sows to his flesh will of the flesh reap corruption, but he who sows to the Spirit will of the Spirit reap everlasting life" (Gal. 6:7–8). Scripture is also clear that our attitude toward life should be one of rejoicing and thanksgiving: "Rejoice always, pray without ceasing, in everything give thanks; for this is the will of God in Christ Jesus for you" (1 Thess. 5:16–18). The apostle Paul prayed for the Colossian church and for all believers to be pleasing to God and to be thankful:

> That you may be filled with the knowledge of His will in all wisdom and spiritual understanding; that you may walk worthy of the Lord, fully pleasing Him, being fruitful in every good work and increasing in the knowledge of God; strengthened with all might, according to His glorious power, for all patience and long-suffering with joy; giving thanks to the Father who has qualified us to be partakers of the inheritance of the saints in the light.
>
> —Colossians 1:9–12

Paul clearly described the mind-set and attitude of a fruitful Christian who is preparing to receive a divine inheritance: patient, longsuffering with joy, and giving thanks. He characterized the Christian life as one in which we are "abounding in it [faith] with thanksgiving" (Col. 2:7). And he instructed Christians: "Whatever you do, do it heartily, as to the Lord and not to men, knowing that from the Lord you will receive the reward of the inheritance; for you serve the Lord Christ" (Col. 3:23–24).

To serve God *heartily*, carries the meaning of doing everything we do in such a way that we glorify God—with our whole mind, soul, heart, and strength. It is strongly reminiscent of what Jesus called the greatest commandment: "You shall love the LORD your God with all your heart, with all your soul, and with all your mind" (Matt. 22:37). This commandment embodies the idea of *exceeding gratitude* for our God. It describes relationship with Him that is built on thanksgiving, adoration, and worship. We begin to understand the church Fathers' expression in the Westminster Catechism: "Man's chief end is to glorify God and enjoy him forever."[2]

I have come to realize that my greatest sin of omission is this lack of exceeding gratitude for God Himself. When I seek to appreciate God fully, it makes me a better person, makes my life more productive, allows me to glorify God, and it lets me become what He ordained my DNA to express in the Earth. And all of this is accomplished without my struggling to be "good" through self-effort. As I humble myself to receive God's grace, deep adoration and gratitude fill my heart and mind, which results in godly living that abounds in thanksgiving.

To the end of receiving our eternal inheritance, it is vital that we learn to appreciate God and live a life abounding in thanksgiving to Him. Truly loving God—becoming enthralled with Him— is so much higher than serving Him out of a sense of duty without the joy of walking with Him in the path of obedience. Following a legalistic set of religious rules is not the response of a loving, grateful heart to the Creator-Redeemer. Our appreciation of God's grace that redeems us to enjoy eternal relationship with Him causes us to be humbly grateful for the gift of life. As we seek the grace of God in our lives, our mind-set and attitudes are transformed through gratitude to our Creator-Redeemer. This life perspective allows us to enjoy the anointed "dance of our DNA."

When the beloved disciple, John, received Christ as His Lord, he received revelation as well of the true origins of life:

> In the beginning was the Word, and the Word was with God, and the Word was God. He was in the beginning with God. All

things were made through Him, and without Him nothing was made that was made. In Him was life, and the life was the light of men...And the Word became flesh and dwelt among us, and we beheld His glory, the glory as of the only begotten of the Father, full of grace and truth.

—John 1:1–4, 14

If we fail to avail ourselves of this God-centered philosophy, we are in a sense rebuking the Holy Spirit, who gives us the wonderful gift of God's presence. We also fail to believe in Christ the Savior, denying His design of all of creation. As a result, we miss the profound perspective of life that offers so much promise, including eternity spent in the presence of God Himself.

Gifts of the Gospel

In the preface, I referenced John Piper's six stages of Christianity.[3] I would like to remind you again of their importance to your Christian walk. The heart of the *gospel*—good news—is God Himself. With that understanding, everything that leads us to God becomes a "gift" of the gospel. For example, if you let your mind go back to the beginning—before the beginning—you can imagine the *preplanning* of God when He determined all of creation and redemption as we know it. There are many mysteries to what theologians call the doctrine of *predestination*. What we understand clearly, however, is the call it gives us to worship our Heavenly Father, who is sovereign and reigns over all: "The Lord has established His throne in heaven, And His kingdom rules over all" (Ps. 103:19). God predestined or preplanned His Creator role and His relationship to His creation before time began.

While it has not been our intent to explore the broad interpretations of the doctrine of predestination, it is helpful to mention it in considering the concept of a Creator. It was God's desire to create—to design—an awesome universe, world, and human species.

Knowing the character of the Creator, as revealed in the beauty of creation, in the written Word, and through His Son, Jesus Christ, we cannot help but worship the loving heart of God. So preplanning the whole idea of life as we know it can be considered the first "gift" of the gospel.

The second gift of God to us is *creation*. The Bible clearly teaches that God created life by the power of His Word: "By faith we understand that the worlds were framed by the word of God, so that the things which are seen were not made of things which are visible" (Heb. 11:3). "You are worthy, O Lord, To receive glory and honor and power; For You created all things, And by Your will they exist and were created" (Rev. 4:11). To live independently from God means choosing to miss the wonder of exploring His purpose for all of creation and His purpose for your life.

Mankind spoiled the perfection of God's creation when the first couple chose to walk independently of God, disobeying His command in the garden. In order for God to enjoy the intimate love relationship He desired with mankind, made in His image, He enacted the plan of redemption that had also been a part of His preplanning. Our omniscient, all-knowing God effected His plan of creation, all the while knowing the unimaginable sacrifice it would require of Him to give His only Son to redeem the world from the ravages of sin.

The eternal Word of God would have to suffer the kenosis or emptying (see Phil. 2) and become the Son of God, "the Lamb slain from the foundation of the world" (Rev. 13:8). Through the *incarnation*, Jesus Christ became the perfect man and laid down His sinless life as a ransom to buy back a world full of sinful humanity. His incarnation can be considered a gift of the gospel, without which we would not have hope of being reunited with God, our Creator-Redeemer.

It is through the sacrifice of Christ at Calvary, laying down His life for the sins of the whole world, that believers have imputed to them the gift of *justification* in the eyes of God. Right standing before God—imputed righteousness—is for all who "believe in Him who raised up Jesus our Lord from the dead, who was delivered up because of our offenses, and was raised because of our justification" (Rom. 4:24–25).

This justification, or imputation of righteousness, is a wonderful, redemptive gift of the gospel. Yet, while justification is the heart of the gospel (there can be no "good news" without it), it is not the highest good of the gospel. The highest good of the gospel is the restored relationship with God, through Jesus Christ. John Piper explains:

> When I say that *God is the Gospel* I mean that the highest, best, final, decisive good of the gospel, without which no other gifts would be good, is the glory of God in the face of Christ [2 Cor. 4:6] revealed for our everlasting enjoyment. The saving love of God is God's commitment to do everything necessary to enthrall us with what is most deeply and durably satisfying, namely *himself*.[4]

To experience the glorious presence of God in our lives as we surrender our lives to Christ and continue to behold His splendor, is the highest good of the gospel. It has been God's loving desire from the beginning that His creation in His image—mankind—would walk with Him in intimate fellowship. This divine relationship would bring ultimate satisfaction and the infinite outpouring of God's love, which is His great joy. To that end, He has provided everything we need to be saved from our man-centered philosophies and mind-sets. John Piper explains the God-given ability of believers to behold the glorious light of the gospel:

> The best news of the Christian gospel is that the supremely glorious Creator of the universe has acted in Jesus Christ's death and resurrection to remove every obstacle between us and him-

self so that we may find everlasting joy in seeing and savoring his infinite beauty. The saving love of God is his doing whatever must be done, at great cost to himself, and for the least deserving, so that he might enthrall them with what will make them supremely happy forever, namely himself. Therefore, the gospel of God and the love of God are expressed finally and fully in God's gift of himself for our everlasting pleasure. "In your presence there is fullness of joy; at your right hand are pleasures forevermore" (Ps. 16:11).[5]

As we seek to live in the presence of God, doing all for the glory of God and fulfilling our eternal destiny, we will experience the *sanctification* of our minds and hearts. Holiness will motivate us to worship and adore our Creator-Redeemer in ever greater appreciation for Him. This sanctification, the cleansing of our desires, motivations, and actions, is a wonderful gift of the gospel. The process of beholding God and being changed is clearly explained in Scripture. The apostle Paul describes the cleansing power of Christ for believers' sanctification:

Husbands, love your wives, just as Christ also loved the church and gave Himself for her, that He might sanctify and cleanse her with the washing of water by the word, that He might present her to Himself a glorious church, not having spot or wrinkle or any such thing, but that she should be holy and without blemish.
—Ephesians 5:25–27

But we all, with unveiled face, beholding as in a mirror the glory of the Lord, are being transformed into the same image from glory to glory, just as by the Spirit of the Lord.
—2 Corinthians 3:18

It is clear from these Scriptures and others that we are cleansed and changed into the image of Christ by filling our hearts with the Word of God. As we do that, we receive the power of the Word to open our eyes to our eternal destiny. Of course, our ultimate destiny is to spend eternity in the presence of God.

The *consummation* or glorification of our lives is the ultimate gift of the gospel that brings us eternally to God Himself. This aspect of the gospel reveals to us life after death when we will experience the truth that: "For now we see in a mirror, dimly, but then face to face. Now I know in part, but then I shall know just as I also am known" (1 Cor. 13:12). It also speaks of the Second Coming of Christ when He will "transform our lowly body that it may be conformed to His glorious body, according to the working by which He is able even to subdue all things to Himself" (Phil. 3:21).

Yet, it is possible even in this temporal life to move from savoring the gifts of the gospel to ultimately enjoying God Himself. John Piper concludes:

> Eternal life is one of the most treasured gifts of the gospel...Jesus prays to his Father, "And this is eternal life, that they know you the only true God, and Jesus Christ whom you have sent" (John 17:3). In other words, the gift of the gospel called eternal life is not the mere extension of every earthly pleasure. It is the extension and perfection of the pleasures of knowing God and his Son Jesus Christ...All other gods must go. All other delights that are not delights in God must go—not because anything good must be taken away, but to make room for what is infinitely best, God himself.[6]

Through *exceeding gratitude for the Creator's plan*, we can *discover the life-changing dynamic of appreciation*. We can come to know in an intimate way "The God who commanded light to shine out of darkness, who has shone in our hearts to give the light of the knowledge of the glory of God in the face of Jesus Christ" (2 Cor. 4:6). As we gaze upon our Creator-Redeemer in the Word of God, His light will shine in our hearts, filling us with *exceeding appreciation* for Himself. Through humble worship and adoration, our eternal destiny will unfold and our DNA will dance with delight as we experience the ultimate satisfaction of fulfilling man's chief end—to glorify God and enjoy Him forever.

May the mystery, the romance, and the joy of totally abandoning yourself to the grace of God enthrall you with Him both now and forever.

More and more people are seeing this: they enter the mystery, abandoning themselves to God.

—Psalm 40:3

APPENDIX

D r. Richard Swenson asserts that we can learn to appreciate God's power and love by observing His creation. From the precise parameters of our planet to the faultless functioning of our human DNA, the grandeur of creation's scientific realities can evoke awe and appreciation in our hearts for God. In 2003 the Christian Medical and Dental Association honored Dr. Richard Swenson with the Educator of the Year award. He is an award-winning educator and best-selling author who has traveled to over fifty countries for purposes of speaking, practice, or study. Dr. Swenson has presented to such prestigious groups as the Mayo Clinic, members of the United Nations, the Pentagon, and members of Congress. He concludes: "The more we understand about God's power, the less we worry about our weakness."[1]

Commenting on the scientific marvels of the human body, as well as the unfathomable universe, Dr. Swenson exclaims, "Do we have any idea the level of power and precision we are witnessing here? What we need is a new vision of God—the real God—not some vague image...the kind of God Who stuns the physicists with symmetry; the mathematicians with precision; the engineers with design; the politicians with power; and the poets with beauty. Don't fear science; God invented it all. And a clear understanding of what He has done only enhances our view of Him."[2]

Continually probing the beauty of God's cosmos reality, scientists are astounded by the awesome facts they have discovered. For example, they know that our universe contains an estimated one hundred billion galaxies and that each galaxy contains an estimated one hundred billion stars. They have quantified at over one hundred parameters that had to be precisely related in order for life to exist on planet Earth. Today, there are almost six and a half billion people alive on our planet. Though our cultures vary dramatically, we share the same miracle—life. A clear, scientific understanding of what God has done only enhances our view of Him. His precision is impressive; His sovereignty is on display. How can such power fail to dominate our every thought and action, to rescue us from our everyday insecurities?[3]

Studying the handiwork of God, scientists have discovered that the mass of the universe is 10^{50} (ten followed by fifty zeros) tons. By multiplying that mass by the speed of light squared, we can convert that mass to pure energy; the result—a fantastically large number. There are 10^{79} elementary particles in the universe, counting neutrons, protons, and quarks. While scientists have been able to identify and calculate the mass and energy of this gigantic universe, *they have not been able to reproduce or create one ounce of mass or energy*. This fact resulted in the formulation of the first law of thermodynamics (represented by Albert Einstein's famous equation, $E = MC^2$), which states that energy or mass cannot be created—or destroyed.[4]

The level of precision of the universe is 10^{10} to the $27th$, a number that is humanly impossible to describe. The minute details of every movement of the stars, every element of the planets, every formative attribute of the Earth, are precisely what is needed to sustain life to the unfathomable degree that the most brilliant scientist could never begin to reproduce. The sheer magnitude of the universe that has been discovered to date is beyond our comprehension.[5]

Many of the estimated one hundred billion galaxies in the universe are irregular in shape or have none at all. Our Milky Way galaxy is a spiral shape with a center black hole. It is flat like a pancake and spins at the rate of a half million miles an hour. The planet Venus, which is the size of the Earth, has very long days because it takes eight months to rotate one time. And it is the only planet that is retrograde, meaning it rotates in the opposite direction from all the others in our galaxy. That rotation makes its atmospheric pressure ninety times greater than the Earth's. The upper clouds of Venus drip sulfuric acid. Constant surface hurricane winds, deafening thunder and lightning strikes, and a one thousand degree Fahrenheit surface temperature characterize the planet.[6]

The largest planet in our galaxy is Jupiter, which could hold one thousand Earths. Its rotation is so fast that one day is only eight hours long and its surface winds reach one thousand miles per hour. There is no known form of life on Jupiter, yet, it performs a very important role for our Earth. The precise placement of Jupiter protects the Earth from comets, which would strike the Earth one thousand times more frequently than they do, threatening our very existence. Saturn, which contains seven hundred fifty times the volume of the Earth, is the beauty queen of the Milky Way's planets. The beauty of its gigantic rings is exquisite. Two of its moons perform an extraordinary feat. Every four years they shift in their orbits, looking as though they are about to crash into each other. But then, at the last "moment" they do a kind of "dance"—and switch orbits.[7]

While we appreciate the beauty and fascinating aspects of the other planets, Earth is the only known inhabitable planet. For life to exist as it does, the precision of over one hundred parameters had to be exactly, mathematically defined to seemingly impossible limits: Not too much mass, not too little; not too close to the sun, not too far away; not too close to Jupiter, not too far away. The gravitational force had to be precise; the number of stars had to be precise; the moon had to be just the right size and in the right place, and the list goes on. Isaac Newton wrote in his book, *Principia*, (still touted as one of the most important works in physics), "Thus God arranged planets at distances from the sun."[8]

Robin Collins, Ph.D. is a highly influential professor of physics and philosophy who served as postdoctoral fellow at Northwestern University. Years of research have resulted in numerous books, including *The Well-Tempered Universe: God, Fine-Tuning, and the*

Laws of Nature. Collins explains: "When scientists talk about the fine-tuning of the universe they are generally referring to the extraordinary balancing of the fundamental laws and parameters of physics and the initial conditions of the universe. Our minds can't comprehend the precision of some of them. The result is a universe that has just the right conditions to sustain life. The coincidences are simply too amazing to have been the result of happenstance—as Paul Davies said, 'the impression of design is overwhelming.'"[9]

These great scientific minds attest to the power of God that set the universe in motion and watches over it with just as much care as when He created it. He is as involved in our personal "universe" of troubles and cares, plans and desires, hopes and dreams, as He is in the cosmos. As we seek to know Him and align ourselves with His sovereign plan for our lives, we can live in peace and freedom from all anxiety and fear.

Allan R. Sandage, renowned astronomer who was assistant to Edwin Hubble and then became his successor, has for half a century been a leader in our observational quest to understand the stars, galaxies, and the universe. Sandage has quantified the expansion of the universe in many important ways and was the first to recognize the existence of quasars without strong radio emission, leading the way to discovery of some of the most distant objects in the universe. He developed new observational techniques and opened new areas of inquiry in fields ranging from the pulsations of stars, to tests of cosmological models at great distances, to searches for quasars. When receiving the 2000 Cosmology Prize, it was stated that his lifetime contribution to extragalactic astronomy and cosmology, and his influence on his colleagues, is unmatched by any other astronomer.[10]

Dr. Sandage began his scientific journey as an atheist. He later confessed, "it was my science that drove me to the conclusion that the world is much more complicated than can be explained by science. We can't understand the universe in any clear way without the supernatural."[11] He recognized the sovereign power of the Creator that could not be matched, or even understood, by the finiteness of man's mind. Dr. Sandage found that in understanding the reality of the supernatural power of God revealed in the universe, and seeking to become acquainted with His divine essence—which is love (1 John 4:19), we can be delivered from all unbelief, fear, worry, and insecurity.

All of creation sings of the wonders of God's power and love. And the stars are seemingly the centerpiece of the heavens. The Old Testament prophet declared:

Lift your eyes and look to the heavens: Who created all these? He who brings out the starry host one by one, and calls them each by name. Because of his great power and mighty strength, not one of them is missing.

—ISAIAH 40:26, NIV

It is estimated that there are between 10^{20} and 10^{24} stars in the universe. All stars are hydrogen bombs, generating continual light and extreme heat. A *neutron star* is a small star by comparison, but very dense in mass. A spoonful of a neutron star would weigh one hundred million tons. *Pulsars* are neutron stars that can rotate one hundred times a second and emit radio waves. *Gamma ray bursts*, while they are not stars, deserve to be mentioned with these phenomenal extravaganzas of the night skies. They emit the most energetic form of electromagnetic radiation. Some gamma ray bursts are as bright as the rest of the universe combined. The surface of our sun converts four million tons of the mass of its surface into energy every second. That heat energy screams across the solar system, in the form of photons, and we receive one billionth of it to warm the Earth. So much heat energy is produced by our sun that if a pin head were heated to the core temperature of the sun and brought to Earth, it would kill everyone within one thousand miles around. Recently, the sun shot out a solar flare, which floated as a giant magnetic cloud, thirty million miles in diameter and moving at a million miles an hour.[12]

All the heavens demonstrate the reality of God in the cosmos. While these cosmic phenomena stagger our finite minds, we should be comforted to know that if God gives this much attention to the details of His creation, we can be assured that He is working in the details of our lives. We can bring to Him the cares that cause us worry. As we exchange the "pretend" realities seen through the eyes of worry for the true reality of our sovereign God who loves us, we will enter into peace and rest in His redemption. As the psalmist declared:

> How precious to me are your thoughts, O God! How vast is the sum of them! Were I to count them, they would outnumber the grains of sand. When I awake, I am still with you.
>
> —PSALM 139:17–18, NIV

Dr. Swenson explained the existence of the carbon atom as an example of seemingly impossible odds for life as we know it. Christian chemist George Bennett called the carbon atom "God's autograph."[13] Carbon is the fourth most common element in the universe and all of life that we have discovered is carbon based. It is the only element that has the properties needed for supporting the richness of life as we know it. Using hydrogen, oxygen, nitrogen, and other elements, it can form an infinite number of compounds. Scientists have measured over one million existing carbon compounds. Many thousands of these are vital to life processes. Carbon is unique among all of the elements; no other element can form the chemical bonds in carbon.

Yet, the formation of the carbon element is so unlikely that it should not be able to exist. Consider this simplified explanation of its formation. To form a carbon atom requires first that two hydrogen come together to form a *helium*. Then two helium come together and form a *beryllium*. This beryllium compound is very unstable—it lasts only for a billionth of a billionth of a second. In that tiny fraction of time, in order for a carbon atom to form, another helium needs to attach itself to the unstable beryllium. And it can't be just any helium in the area. The nuclear energy levels, or *resonance*, of the helium needed to attach to the beryllium must be precisely matched in order to form one carbon atom. Imagine all the carbon atoms required to form the basis of all of life as we know it meeting those exacting requirements for each of their formation.[14]

Fred Hoyle, brilliant British astrophysicist and a self-proclaimed atheist, predicted this "resonance number" for the "matching" helium and beryllium needed to form a carbon atom. Then he asked scientists at Cal Tech to scientifically calculate the number. They worked for a week with their computers to calculate the resonance number needed to form a carbon element. They discovered that the number Hoyle had predicted was the exact number that they calculated. This discovery shook Hoyle's atheistic worldview to the core. He said, "A common sense interpretation of the facts suggests that a super-intellect has monkeyed with the physics as well as the chemistry and the biology."[15]

Appreciating the "impossible," minute details of exquisite design required to form the basic building blocks of life should help us to rest in the omniscient, loving care of our Creator-Redeemer. As we choose to bow in humility before this unfathomable Creator-God, casting our care on Him, we realize how much He cares for us. Scripture clearly teaches: "Cast all your anxiety on him because he cares for you" (1 Pet. 5:7, NIV). Dr. Swenson sums up our confidence in God:

> The sovereignty, power, design, genius, majesty, precision, caring
> and intimacy of an almighty God takes away our fear, removes
> our frustration, and allows us to trust Him with the running of
> the universe. It allows us to...seek His will not our own, and

take our role instead of trying to have His role. To know Him is to trust Him and to trust Him is to rest in Him. As the psalmist declared: "The LORD is gracious and righteous, our God is full of compassion. The LORD protects the simplehearted; when I was in great need, he saved me. Be at rest once more, O my soul, for the LORD has been good to you. (Ps. 116:5–7).[16]

Albert Einstein helped to develop the laws of classic physics with his theory of relativity, presented in 1905 and his theory of general relativity developed in the years 1911–1915 that explain movement and gravitational pulls of the planets and their influence on all of life. These laws of physics rest on the certainty of measured values, like a clockwork machine. In fact, classical physics insists on measurable quantities and consistency.

However, for the study of the *subatomic* world of microscopic atoms and particles, like protons and neutrons, the reality of classic physics as we know it must be redefined. Between 1900 and 1930, Albert Einstein, Max Plank, Paul Dirac, Wolfgang Pauli, and others formulated the theory of *quantum mechanics*, which tries to provide accurate and precise descriptions for many phenomena that the "classical" theories of physics simply cannot explain.[17] However, the "laws" of quantum mechanics had to be defined by terms like *indeterminism, chance, unpredictability, randomness,* and *uncertainty*—words that were heresy to the ordered laws of classic physics.

At first, Albert Einstein hated the fact that, on the subatomic level, unpredictability, randomness, and uncertainty seemed the rule rather than the exception. While classic physics insists on precision, the universe proves to be indeterministic at its most basic level. When you try to measure the existence of microscopic particles that form the building blocks of life, you encounter uncertainty. It seems more like a cosmic game of dice than orderly precision. Einstein was appalled. He insisted, "God does not play dice with the universe." To the consternation of Einstein, an atom, under scrutiny, could simply disappear.[18]

Arthur Eddington, one of the most prominent and important astrophysicists of his time (1882–1944), was one of the first physicists who understood the early ideas of relativity along with Albert Einstein. He concluded that the physicist draws up an elaborate plan of the atom and then proceeds critically to erase each detail in turn. What is left is the atom of modern physics.[19]

Physicist Paul Davies, an internationally acclaimed physicist, writer, and broadcaster, is professor of natural philosophy in the Australian Centre for Astrobiology, Macquarie University, Sydney.[20] He describes atoms and subatomic particles as inhabiting a shadowy world of half-existence. An atom in subatomic space is like cotton candy that dissolves in our mouths—it disappears when we put it under scrutiny. You can't say anything about the future of these tiny particles that live a shadowy, ghostly, otherworldly existence. The unseen world on the molecular level simply does not follow prescribed rules or laws. Part of the problem is that the dimensions at the atomic level are occupied by seemingly empty space. The distance between atoms is a thousand times greater than the size of the atom. Even the atom itself is empty space. And 99.9 percent of the mass of a tiny atom is contained in its nucleus. Yet, the nucleus only occupies one hundred thousand billionth of the space of the entire atom. In this microscopic, sub-atomic world, matter possesses a degree of fuzziness, which cannot be precisely calculated or measured.[21]

And dimensions are not the only difference between the subatomic space and the world as we know it. The *behavior* of subatomic particles also differs greatly from the larger world. Every quantum bit has the potential to be here and there, now and then, a multiple capacity to act on the world, doing several different things at the same time. So startling were these discoveries, that Albert Einstein considered them heretical to the laws of physics. His friend, Neils

Bohr, wrote to him and told him to stop telling God what to do with His universe. Only after years of observing the mysteries of the microscopic world, which is much like going into a blind alley where no one has come out with satisfactory explanations, was Einstein finally able to accept its bizarre behavior.[22]

When this subatomic world was first explored in the early part of the twentieth century, it was also theologically threatening to some. Where was the precision of God as seen in the rest of the universe? Max Planck, one of the original scientists to formulate the theory of quantum mechanics in 1902, was not spiritually shaken about its implications. He said, "Both science and religion wage a tireless battle against skepticism and dogmatism, against unbelief and superstition, with the goal: toward God."[23]

Dr. Swenson asserts that quantum mechanics occupies the interface where physics and metaphysics meet. And he says he is glad that God doesn't reveal all of His secrets to us. We might ask how does it all work in such harmony on a macro level, yet when you examine it on a subatomic level it is so indefinable and mysterious? Obviously God wants us to see the beauty, power, and precision on a larger scale. But when we look at the subatomic reality, which is mysterious and indefinable, it points to God's sovereignty and His desire to reserve glory for Himself.[24]

According to Swenson, we worry when we try to anticipate God, not having an infinitesimal grasp of how great God's power is and how thorough, precise, and faithful He is. Science confirms the reality of God's brilliance. Yet, He can never be pinned down, as quantum physics shows us. He is life. He inhabits dimensions more profound than we can imagine. And He is love. His great love for us is measured by Calvary—the death of Christ, God's Son, to redeem mankind to eternal relationship with Himself. Considering scientific realities can be a catalyst to our recognizing our own frailty and finiteness when we consider the infinite power of God. As a result, we will be humbled and will listen more carefully when

He speaks. He said "Be still, and know that I am God" (Ps. 46:10). We can understand that He cares about us more than a billion galaxies. He works in our lives in a thousand ways at once. And the more we trust His sovereign rule, the less we worry about our future. There is no more comforting doctrine.[25]

Dr. Swenson concludes that the problem of perspective lies with us:

> The problem is the dimness on our side. God is undefeated and He is for us. In the end, sovereignty wins and His glory will be unrestrained. Finally, God will deliver us from our dimness, and we will rest under the shelter of the Most High.[26]

The apostle Paul encouraged the church at Ephesus "to grasp how wide and long and high and deep is the love of Christ, and to know this love that surpasses knowledge—that you may be filled to the measure of all the fullness of God" (Eph. 3:18–19, niv). He described God's power working in our lives in this striking way:

> Now to him who is able to do immeasurably more than all we ask or imagine, according to his power that is at work within us, to him be glory in the church and in Christ Jesus throughout all generations, for ever and ever! Amen.
>
> —Ephesians 3:20–21, niv

Understanding the reality of God in the unfathomable wonders of the cosmos can help your faith and challenge you to forsake your worry habits and anxious thoughts and to grasp the greatness of His love for you. In meditating on the grandeur of God's reality in the cosmos, you can learn to rest in His sovereign power and redemptive love for you. As you pursue relationship with Christ, you can lay aside anxious thoughts and fill your mind and heart with God's infinite love and power. Then you will find ultimate satisfaction in fulfilling His purpose for your life.

Foreword by Tom Woodward, Ph.D.

1. For more information see http://www.scienceandchristianbelief.org/articles/ McGrath%20article%20172.pdf#search=%22richard%20dawkins%20Christian%20 virus%20of%20the%20mind%22 (accessed October 6, 2006).

Preface

1. Information about David Hume available at http://www.allaboutphilosophy .org/agnosticism-faq.htm (accessed October 6, 2006).

2. *Wikipedia*, s.v. "Nihilism," http://en.wikipedia.org/wiki/Nihilism (accessed April 18, 2006).

3. Information about Soren Kierkegaard available at http://en.wikipedia.org/ wiki/Philosophy_of_S%C3%B8ren_Kierkegaard (accessed October 6, 2006).

4. *Wikipedia*, s.v. "Existentialism," http://en.wikipedia.org/wiki/Existentialism (accessed April 19, 2006).

3. John Piper, *God is the Gospel* (Wheaton, IL: Crossway Books, a publishing ministry of Good News Publishers, 2005).

Introduction

1. Guillermo Gonzalez and Jay Richards, *The Privileged Planet* (Regnery Publishing, Inc., 2004). Also a DVD produced by Illustra Media, www .illustramedia.com.

2. David Jeremiah, *Captured by Grace* (Nashville, TN: Integrity Publishers, 2006), 132.

3. Richard A. Swenson, M.D., "More Than Meets the Eye," DVD (Bristol, TN: Christian Medical & Dental Associations, 2005).

4. Ellen Vaughn, *Radical Gratitude* (Grand Rapids, MI: Zondervan, 2005), 70.

5. *Webster's New Collegiate Dictionary*, 9th ed., s.v. "Appreciation."

Day 1: The Transforming Power of Appreciation

1. "Charles Darwin's Natural Selection Theory," *Unlocking the Mystery of Life*, DVD, (La Habra, CA: Illustra Media, 2002).

2. James P. Gills, M.D. and Tom Woodward, Ph.D., *Darwinism under the Microscope* (Lake Mary, FL: Charisma House, 2002), 42.

3. Michael J. Behe, *Darwin's Black Box* (New York: Touchstone, 1996), 39.

4. John Piper quote available online at http://en.wikipedia.org/wiki/John_ Piper_(theologian) (accessed October 6, 2006).

5. *Webster's New Collegiate Dictionary*, 9th ed., s.v. "Appreciate."

6. Ibid., s.v. "Appreciation."

7. Ibid., s.v. "Grateful."

8. Vaughn, *Radical Gratitude*, 46.

9. Cicero quote available online at http://www.quotationspage.com/quote/2035 .html (accessed October 6, 2006).

9. Jeremiah, *Captured by Grace*, 1937.

10. James P. Gills, M.D., *Spiritual Blindness* (Lake Mary, FL: Strang Communications, 2004), 74.

11. Vaughn, *Radical Gratitude*, 71.

12. Charles Horace Mayo, *Aphorisms of Dr. Charles Horace Mayo, 1865–1939, and Dr. William James Mayo, 1861–1939* (Springfield, IL: Mayo Foundation for Medical Education and Research, 1988).

13. Richard A. Swenson, M.D., *More Than Meets the Eye* (Colorado Springs, CO: Navpress, 2000), 97.

Day 2: Discovering the Creator

1. Swenson, "More Than Meets the Eye," DVD (Bristol, TN: Christian Medical & Dental Associations, 2005).

2. Ibid.

3. Ibid.

4. *Unlocking the Mystery of Life*, DVD, (La Habra, CA: Illustra Media, 2002).

5. Ibid.

6. Mattin Durrani, "Physicist Scoops Religion Prize," *PhysicsWeb* (2002), http://physicsweb.org/articles/news/6/3/10 (accessed April 20, 2006).

7. John Polkinghorne, *One World, The Interaction of Science and Theology* (Princeton, NJ: Princeton University Press, 1987).

8. *Unlocking the Mystery of Life*, DVD, (La Habra, CA: Illustra Media, 2002).

9. Ibid.

10. Swenson, *More Than Meets the Eye*, 62.

11. Gills and Woodward, *Darwinism Under the Microscope*, 45.

12. *Unlocking the Mystery of Life*, DVD, (La Habra, CA: Illustra Media, 2002).

13. Ibid.

14. Ibid.

15. Swenson, *More Than Meets the Eye*, 73.

16. Francis Crick, *Life Itself: Its Nature and Origin* (New York: Simon and Schuster, 1981).

17. "Clay Pots," http://www.everystudent.com/wires/claypots.html (accessed October 5, 2006).

18. *Unlocking the Mystery of Life*, DVD, (La Habra, CA: Illustra Media, 2002).

19. Ibid., Stephen C. Meyer.

20. Jeremiah, *Captured by Grace*, 22.

21. Dr. Armand M. Nicholi, Jr., *The Question of God* (New York: Free Press, A Division of Simon & Schuster, Inc., 2002), 44–45.

22. Ibid.

23. Ibid.

24. Ibid., 46.

25. Ibid., 47.

26. Ibid.

27. Ibid.

28. Ibid.

29. Maltbie Davenport Babcock, "This Is My Father's World," 1901, public domain.

DAY 3: THE PHENOMENA OF NATURE

1. Swenson, *More Than Meets the Eye*, 113.

2. Ibid., 115.

3. *Nature Studies – Powell's Books*, http://www.powells.com/psection/NatureStudies.html (accessed 4/20/2005).

4. "All About Ants," Life Studies, http://www.infowest.com/life/aants.htm (accessed October 5, 2006).

5. Esther Quesada Tyrrell and Robert A. Tyrrell, *Hummingbirds: Their Life & Behavior* (New York: Crown Publishers, Inc., 1985).

6. Swenson, *More Than Meets the Eye*, 114.

7. Ibid., 115.

8. Guillermo Gonzalez and Jay Richards, *The Privileged Planet* (Regnery Publishing, Inc., 2004). Also a DVD produced by Illustra Media, www.illustramedia.com.

9. Ibid.

10. Ibid.

11. Stephen E. Jones, "Problems of Evolution," http://members.iinet.net.au/~sejones/PoE/pe06envr.html (accessed October 5, 2006).

12. Gonzalez and Richards, *The Privileged Planet*.

13. Ibid.

14. Ibid.

15. Ibid.

16. St. Francis of Assisi, "All Creatures of Our God and King," 1225, public domain.

DAY 4: THE DANCE OF DNA

1. Gills and Woodward, *Darwinism Under the Microscope*, 82, 120.

2. Ibid.

3. Dianne N. Irving, M.A., Ph.D., "Scientific and Philosophical Expertise," LifeIssues.net, http://www.lifeissues.net/writers/irv/irv_04person2.html (accessed July 19, 2005).

4. Ibid.

5. Ibid.

6. Swenson, *More Than Meets the Eye*, 63.

7. Ibid., 64.

8. Ibid., 65.

9. Ibid.

10. Ibid., 18.

11. Ibid., 66.

12. Gills and Woodward, *Darwinism Under the Microscope*, 184.

13. Ibid., 70–73.

14. Ibid.

15. Ibid.

16. Vaughn, *Radical Gratitude*, 202–203.

17. *Webster's New Collegiate Dictionary*, 9th ed., s.v. "Charisma."

Day 5: Anointed DNA

1. James P. Gills, M.D., *God's Prescription for Healing*, (Lake Mary, FL: Siloam, 2004), 12.

2. Vaughn, *Radical Gratitude*, 202–203.

3. *Webster's New Collegiate Dictionary*, 9th ed., s.v. "Adore."

4. Vaughn, *Radical Gratitude*, 204.

Day 6: God the Father

1. Swenson, *More Than Meets the Eye*, 69–70.

2. Ibid., 62–63.

3. Ibid., 64.

4. Ibid., 65.

5. Ibid., 67.

6. Lee Strobel, *The Case for a Creator* (Grand Rapids, MI: Zondervan, 2004), 37–39.

7. Sidney W. Fox and Klaus Dose, *Molecular Evolution and the Origin of Life* (New York: Marcel Dekker, revised edition, 1977), 43, 74–76.

8. Lee Strobel, *The Case for a Creator*, 37–39.

9. Ibid.

10. Ibid.

11. Ibid., 41.

12. Ibid., 42.

13. Ibid., 43.

14. Fuchsia T. Pickett, D.D., *God's Dream: His Eternal Plan for You* (Shippensburg, PA: Destiny Image Publishers, 1991), 3–5.

Day 7: Jesus Christ, the Son of God

1. Swenson, *More Than Meets the Eye*, 72.

2. Gerald L. Schroeder, *The Science of God: The Convergence of Scientific and Biblical Wisdom* (New York: Broadway Books, 1997), 102.

3. Swenson, *More Than Meets the Eye*, 70.

4. Ibid., 72.

5. Ibid.

6. Ibid., 19.

7. Ibid., 20.

8. Ibid., 18.

Day 8: God the Holy Spirit

1. Strobel, *The Case for a Creator*, 54–55.

2. Ibid.

3. Swenson, *More Than Meets the Eye*, 17.

4. Fuchsia T. Pickett, D.D., *Presenting the Holy Spirit, Vols. 1 & 2*, (Lake Mary, FL: Creation House, 1997), Vol. 1, p. 37.

Day 9: The Word of God

1. Gills and Woodward, *Darwinism Under the Microscope*, 184.
2. Ibid.
3. Ibid., 185.
4.Webster's New Collegiate Dictionary, 9th ed., s.v. "Appreciation."
5. Ibid., s.v. "Appreciate."
6. Web site: http://www.sacred-texts.com/chr/augconf.htm.

Day 10: The Commandments of God

1. Swenson, *More Than Meets the Eye*, 40–44.
2. Isaac Asimov, "In the Game of Energy & Thermodynamics You Can't Even Break Even," *Smithsonian Journal*, June 1970, 10.
3. Swenson, *More Than Meets the Eye*, 39.
4, Ibid., 40.
5. James P. Gills, M.D., *Imaginations*, (Lake Mary, FL: Charisma House, 2004), 4.
6. Don DeYoung and Richard Bliss, "Thinking about the Brain," *Impact*, February 1990, ii.

Day 11: Love

1. Swenson, *More Than Meets the Eye*, 23–24.
2. Blaise Pascal, ThinkExist.com, http://thinkexist.com/quotes/blaise_pascal/ (accessed July 24, 2006).
3. Vaughn, *Radical Gratitude*, 141.
4. C. S. Lewis, *The Four Loves* (Fort Washington, PA: Harvest Books, 1971), 117.
5. Ibid., 1–15.
6. Ibid. 1.
7. Ibid., 2–4.
8. Ibid., 3.
9. Quentin Hyden, M.D., *A Christian's Handbook of Psychiatry* (Grand Rapids, MI: Revell Books, 1971).
10. Ibid.
11. Lewis, *The Four Loves*, 11.
12. Ibid., 17.
13. Ibid.
14. Ibid., 6–7.
15. Ibid., 118.
16. Ibid., 31–32.
17. Ibid., 35.
18. Ibid., 36–37.
19. Ibid., 55.
20. Ibid., 58.
21. Ibid., 59.
22. Ibid., 61–62.
23. Ibid., 94–95.

24. Ibid., 17.

25. Ibid., 98.

26. Ibid., 137–139.

27. Ibid., 140.

28. Jonathan Edwards, *A Treatise Concerning Religious Affections,* Introduction, http://www.ccel.org/e/edwards/affections/religious_affections.html (accessed 10/18/06).

29. Henry Scougal, *The Life of God in the Soul of Man* (Ross-shire, Scotland: Christian Focus Publications, 2002).

30. Ibid.

31. Gills, *God's Prescription for Healing,* 134.

32. George Matheson, "O Love That Wilt Not Let Me Go," 1882, public domain.

Day 12: Salvation of Mankind

1. Swenson, *More Than Meets the Eye,* 144–45.

2. Ibid.

3. Sharon Begley, "Science Finds God," *Newsweek,* July 20, 1998, 49.

4. Swenson, *More Than Meets the Eye,* 185.

5. Ibid., 184.

6. John Piper, "All Things for Good, Part One," Desiring God, June 9, 2002, (accessed October 5, 2006).

Day 13: Forgiveness

1. Charles Darwin at "Christian Apologetics and Research Ministry," www.carm.org/evo_questions/darwineye.htm (accessed December 10, 2003).

2. Gills, *God's Prescription for Healing,* 13.

3. Vaughn, *Radical Gratitude,* 204–205.

4. Gills, *God's Prescription for Healing,* 13.

5. R. T. Kendall, *Total Forgiveness,* (Lake Mary, FL: Charisma House, 2002), 52.

6. Ibid., back cover.

7. Ibid., 170–174.

Day 14: Imputation

1. Swenson, *More Than Meets the Eye,* 25–27.

2. *Webster's New Collegiate Dictionary,* 9th ed., s.v. "Impute."

3. Swenson, *More Than Meets the Eye,* 25–27.

4. Ibid.

5. Martin Luther quote available online at http://www.foundationsforfreedom.net/Topics/Faith/Faith012.html (accessed October 5, 2006).

6. Martin Luther, "Concerning Christian Liberty," http://www.iclnet.org/pub/resources/text/wittenberg/luther/web/cclib-2.html (accessed February 10, 2006).

7. Martin Luther, quote found in *Women of Destiny Bible,* NKJV, (Nashville, TN: Thomas Nelson Publishers, 2000), 1375.

8. *The New Unger's Bible Dictionary,* s.v. "Imputation."

9. Gills, *Imaginations*, 211.

10. Henry Barraclough, "Ivory Palaces," 1915, public domain.

DAY 15: GRACE

1. Swenson, *More Than Meets the Eye*, 28–30.

2. Strobel, *The Case for a Creator*, 62.

3. Ibid., 63.

4. Ibid., 65–66.

5. Vaughn, *Radical Gratitude*, 140.

6. Jeremiah, *Captured by Grace*, 171.

7. Ibid., 86–87.

8. Vaughn, *Radical Gratitude*, 120–121.

9. Gills, *God's Prescription for Healing*, 23.

10. Ibid., 24.

11. Ibid., 29.

12. Jeremiah, *Captured by Grace*, 132.

13. Samuel Stennett, "Majestic Sweetness Sits Enthroned," 1787, public domain.

DAY 16: FAITH

1. Strobel, *The Case for a Creator*, 106.

2. Ibid., 110–120.

3. Ibid., 120.

4. Ibid., 126.

5. Robert M. Augros and George N. Stanciu, *The New Story of Science* (New York: Bantam, 1986), 70.

6. *Fausset's Bible Dictionary*, s.v. "Faith."

7. Ibid.

8. Oswald Chambers, *My Utmost Devotional Bible* (NKJV) (Nashville, TN: Thomas Nelson Publishers, 1992).

9. Ray Palmer, "My Faith Looks Up to Thee," 1875, public domain.

DAY 17: THE CROSS

1. Swenson, *More Than Meets the Eye*, 37–38.

2. *Webster's New Collegiate Dictionary*, 9th ed., s.v. "Surrender."

3. Gills, *God's Prescription for Healing*, 29–30.

4. James P. Gills, M.D., *Believe and Rejoice*, (Lake Mary, Fl.: Creation House, 2004), 33.

5. *Webster's New Collegiate Dictionary*, 9th ed., s.v. "Joy."

6. Gills, *Imaginations*, 168–69.

7. Ibid.

8. Judson W. Van De Venter, "I Surrender All," 1896, public domain.

DAY 18: PEACE

1. Gills and Woodward, *Darwinism Under the Microscope*, 74.

2. Ibid., 75.

3. *Brown-Driver-Briggs Hebrew Lexicon* (Peabody, MA: Hendrickson Publishers, Inc., 1996).

Day 19: Prayer

1. Gills, *God's Prescription for Healing*, 101.

2. Randolph C. Byrd, "Positive Therapeutic Effects of Intercessory Prayer in a Coronary Care Unit Population," *Southern Medical Journal* 81, 1998, 826–828, www.godandscience.org/apologetics/smj.html (accessed March 10, 2003).

3. Ibid.

4. Gills, *Believe and Rejoice*, 57.

5. Ibid., 58.

6. John Piper, *Desiring God: Meditations of a Christian Hedonist* (Portland, OR: Multnomah Press, 1991).

7. Gills, *The Dynamics of Worship*, 37.

8. Gills, *Rx for Worry: A Thankful Heart*, 44–45.

9. Gills, *Believe and Rejoice*, 59.

10. Pickett, *Presenting the Holy Spirit, Vol. 1*, 177.

11. Gills, *Imaginations*, 66.

12. *Webster's New Collegiate Dictionary*, 9th ed., s.v. "Intercede."

13. Gills, *Imaginations*, 191.

14. Ibid., 192.

15. William Walford, "Sweet Hour of Prayer," 1845, public domain.

Day 20: Divine Testings

1. Swenson, *More Than Meets the Eye*, 30–33.

2. Ibid., 35–36.

3. Ibid., 93.

4. Andrew Murray, *Humility*, (New Kensington, PA: Whitaker House, 1982), 38–39.

Day 21: Purpose: Divine Destiny

1. Gills and Woodward, *Darwinism Under the Microscope*, 72.

2. Ibid., 197–99.

3. Strobel, *The Case for a Creator*, 147.

4. Gills and Woodward, *Darwinism Under the Microscope*, 197–99.

5. Ibid.

6. *The Westminster Shorter Catechism*, found at http://www.shortercatechism .com/resources/wsc/wsc001.html (accessed December 6, 2005).

7. Thomas O. Chisholm, "O to Be Like Thee," 1897, public domain.

Day 22: Divine Rest

1. Gills, *God's Prescription for Healing*, 80.

2. Ibid., 83.

3. Strobel, *The Case for a Creator*, 126.

4. Ibid., 150–51.

5. *Matthew Henry's Commentary on the Whole Bible*, New Modern Edition, Electronic Database, s.v. Genesis 2:2–3.

6. Biblesoft's New Exhaustive Strong's Numbers and Concordance with Expanded Greek-Hebrew Dictionary, s.v "Rest."

7. Gills, *God's Prescription for Healing*, 83.

8. Ibid., 5.

9. John Piper, *God's Passion for His Glory* (Wheaton, IL: Crossway Books, 1998).

DAY 23: DIVINE COMFORT

1. Swenson, *More Than Meets the Eye*, 79–81.

2. Ibid.

3. *Webster's New Collegiate Dictionary*, 9th ed., s.v. "Comfort."

4. Ibid., s.v. "Solace."

5. W. Phillip Keller, *A Shepherd Looks at Psalm 23* (Grand Rapids, MI: Zondervan Publishing House, 1970), 35.

6. Gills, *God's Prescription for Healing*, 16–17.

7. Vaughn, *Radical Gratitude*, 74.

DAY 24: MARGIN

1. Swenson, *More Than Meets the Eye*, 94–95.

2. Richard A. Swenson, M.D., *Margin: Restoring Emotional, Physical, Financial, and Time Reserves to Overloaded Lives*, (Colorado Springs, CO, Navpress, 1992).

3. Russell D. Robinson, *An Introduction to Helping Adults Learn and Change* (Milwaukee: Omnibook, 1979), 38. Idea credited to Howard McClusky.

4. Swenson, *Margin*, 103.

5. Ibid., 108.

6. Ibid., 116.

7. Ibid., 120.

8. Ibid., 121.

9. Ibid., 122–124.

10. Martin Shaffer, *Life After Stress* (New York: Plenum Press, 1982), 91.

11. Swenson, *Margin*, 135–140.

12. "How long is the Average Work Week in the U.S.?" found online at http://www.libraryspot.com/know/workweek.htm (accessed July 14, 2005).

13. Dolores Curran, *Stress and the Healthy Family* (San Francisco: Harper and Row, 1985), 157.

14. Dr. James Dobson, *Dr. Dobson Answers Your Questions* (Wheaton, IL: Tyndale, 1982), 27, 28.

15. Swenson, *Margin*, (Colorado Springs, CO: Navpress, 1992), 153–159.

16. Ibid., 173.

17. Ibid., 174–175.

18. James P. Gills, M.D. and Ronald H. Nash, Ph.D., *A Biblical Economics Manifesto*, (Lake Mary, FL: Creation House, 2002).

19. Swenson, *Margin*, 218–220.

20. William D. Longstaff, "Take Time to be Holy," 1882, public domain.

Day 25: Healing

1. Gills, *God's Prescription for Healing*, xviii.
2. Ibid., 18, 81.
3. Jeremiah, *Captured by Grace*, 188.
4. Gills, *God's Prescription for Healing*.
5. Ibid., 48–54.
6. Ibid.
7. R. C. Byrd, "Positive Therapeutic Effects of Intercessory Prayer in a Coronary Care Unit Population," *Southern Medical Journal* 81, 1988, 826–829.
8. Gills, *God's Prescription for Healing*, 169–170.

Day 26: The Human Struggle

1. Gills, and Woodward, *Darwinism Under the Microscope*, 163–165. Chapter authored by Thomas E. Woodward, Ph.D.
2. Ibid.
3. R. T. Kendall, *The Thorn in the Flesh* (Lake Mary, FL: Charisma House, 2004), 2–3.
4. Ibid., 8.
5. Ibid., 9.
6. James P. Gills, M.D., *The Prayerful Spirit* (Lake Mary, FL, Creation House, 2003), 88–89.

Day 27: Waiting on the Lord

1. Gills, *God's Prescription for Healing*, xviii.
2. Swenson, *More Than Meets the Eye*, 37.
3. Ibid.
4. Gills, *God's Prescription for Healing*, 97–98.
5. Ibid., 99.
6. Gills, *The Prayerful Spirit*, 45.
7. Ibid., 46.
8. Ibid., 117–118.
9. Gills, *God's Prescription for Healing*, 188.
10. Ibid., 190.

Day 28: Relationships

1. Gills, *God's Prescription for Healing*, 24–25.
2. Ibid., 108.
3. Ibid.
4. Swenson, *More Than Meets the Eye*, 100.
5. Gills, *Imaginations*, 186.
6. Swenson, *More than Meets the Eye*, 51.
7. Gills, *Believe and Rejoice*, 41.
8. Gills, *Dynamics of Worship*, 150.
9. Gills, *Imaginations*, 211.
10. Gills, *Prayerful Spirit*, 121.
11. Ibid.

Day 29: Joy

1. Strobel, *The Case for a Creator*, 182.

2. Gills, *Believe and Rejoice*, 5.

3. C. S. Lewis, *Surprised by Joy* (Orlando, FL: Harcourt Brace, 1956).

4. Gills, *Believe and Rejoice*, 6.

5. Ibid., 11.

6. Gills, *God's Prescription for Healing*, 85.

7. Gills, *Imaginations*, 168–69.

8. Gills, *Believe and Rejoice*, 22–23.

9. Gills, *Believe and Rejoice*, 23–24.

10. Ibid., 70.

11. Norman Cousins, *Anatomy of an Illness*, (New York: W.W. Norton Co., Inc., 1979).

12. *The Westminster Shorter Catechism*, found at http://www .shortercatechism.com/resources/wsc/wsc001.html (accessed December 6, 2005).

Day 30: Presence of God

1. Gills, *God's Prescription for Healing*, 49–50.

2. W. Wayt Gibbs, "Cybernetic Cells," *Scientific American* 55, August 2001.

3. Gills and Woodward, *Darwinism Under the Microscope*, 56–57.

4. Gary Thomas, *Sacred Pathways* (Grand Rapids, MI: Zondervan, 2000).

5. Gills, *Imaginations*, 437.

Day 31: Satisfaction

1. Gills and Woodward, *Darwinism Under the Microscope*, 85–86. Chapter authored by Dr. Philip Johnson, J.D.

2. Gills, *Believe and Rejoice*, 45.

3. Gills, *Dynamics of Worship*, 175–76.

4. Gills, *God's Prescription for Healing*, 136.

5. Ibid., 137–38.

6. Ibid., 139.

7. John Piper, *All Things for Good, Part One*, June 9, 2002, www.desiringgod .org/library/sermons/02/060902.html (accessed September 20, 2003).

8. Gills, *God's Prescription for Healing*, 135.

9. Gills, *Imaginations*, 82.

10. Ibid., 45.

11. Ibid. 66.

Epilogue

1. Gills, *Imaginations*, 28.

2. Benjamin B. Warfield, "The First Question of the Westminster Shorter Catechism," in *The Westminster Assembly and Its Work*, in *The Works of Benjamin B. Warfield*, vol. 6 (reprint, Grand Rapids, MI: Baker, 2003), 379–400.

3. The concepts of the "gifts" of the gospel were drawn from John Piper's book, *God is the Gospel* (Wheaton, IL: Crossway Books, a publishing ministry of Good News Publishers, 2005).

4. Ibid., 13–14.

5. Ibid. 147.

6. Ibid., 123.

Appendix

1. Richard Swenson, *More than Meets the Eye*, DVD presentation (Bristol, TN: Christian Medical & Dental Associations, 2005), www.cmda.org.

2. Ibid.

3. Ibid.

4. Ibid.

5. Ibid.

6. Ibid.

7. Ibid.

8. Ibid.

9. Lee Strobel, *The Case for a Creator*, (Grand Rapids, MI: Zondervan, 2004), 129–130.

10. Allan R. Sandage, Staff Astronomer Emeritus, The Observatories (Pasadena, CA) Carnegie Institution of Washington, 2000 Cosmology Prize Recipient, as found at http://www.petergruberfoundation.org/sandage.htm (accessed June 24, 2006).

11. Ibid.

12. Richard Swenson, *More than Meets the Eye*, DVD presentation, (Bristol, TN: Christian Medical & Dental Associations, 2005), www.cmda.org.

13. George Bennett quote available online at http://home.insightbb.com/~gbennett47/autograph.html (accessed October 12, 2006).

14. Ibid.

15. Ibid.

16. Ibid.

17. Ibid.

18. Ibid.

19. Sir Arthur Eddington, biographical article found at http://www.usd.edu/phys/courses/phys300/gallery/clark/edd.html (accessed June 29, 2006).

20. Paul Davies, "The Third Culture," found at http://www.edge.org/3rd_culture/bios/davies.html (accessed June 29, 2006).

21. Richard Swenson, *More than Meets the Eye*, DVD presentation (Bristol, TN: Christian Medical & Dental Associations, 2005), www.cmda.org.

22. Ibid.

23. Ibid.

24. Ibid.

25. Ibid.

26. Ibid.

ABOUT THE AUTHOR

James P. Gills, M.D., is founder and director of St. Luke's Cataract and Laser Institute in Tarpon Springs, Florida. Internationally respected as a cataract surgeon, Dr. Gills has performed more cataract extractions with lens implantations than anyone else in the world. He has pioneered many advancements in the field of ophthalmology to make cataract surgery safer and easier.

As a world-renowned ophthalmologist, Dr. Gills has received innumerable medical and educational awards, highlighted by 1994–2004 listings in *The Best Doctors in America*. Dr. Gills is a clinical professor of ophthalmology at University of South Florida, and was named one of the best ophthalmologists in America in 1996 by ophthalmic academic leaders nationwide. He has served on the board of directors of the American College of Eye Surgeons, the board of visitors at Duke University Medical Center, and the advisory board of Wilmer Ophthalmological Institute at Johns Hopkins University. Listed in Marquis' *Who's Who in America*, Dr. Gills was Entrepreneur of the Year 1990 for the State of Florida, received the Tampa Bay Business Hall of Fame Award in 1993, and was given the Tampa Bay Ethics Award from University of Tampa in 1995. In 1996 he was awarded the prestigious Innovators Award by his colleagues in the American Society of Cataract and Refractive Surgeons. In 2000 he was presented with the Florida Enterprise Medal by the Merchants Association of Florida, was named Humanitarian of the Year by the Golda Meir/Kent Jewish Center in Clearwater, and was honored as Free Enterpriser of the Year by the Florida Council on Economic Education. In 2001 The Salvation Army presented Dr. Gills their prestigious "Others" Award in recognition of his lifelong commitment to service and caring.

Virginia Polytechnic Institute, Dr. Gills' alma mater, presented their University Distinguished Achievement Award to him in 2003.

In that same year, Dr. Gills was appointed by Governor Jeb Bush to the board of directors of the Florida Sports Foundation. In 2004 Dr. Gills was invited to join the prestigious Florida Council of 100, an advisory committee reporting directly to the governor on various aspects of Florida public policy affecting the quality of life and economic well-being of all Floridians.

While Dr. Gills has many accomplishments and varied interests, his primary focus is to restore physical vision to patients and bring spiritual enlightenment through his life. Guided by his strong and enduring faith in Jesus Christ, he seeks to encourage and comfort the patients who come to St. Luke's and to share his faith whenever possible. It was through sharing his insights with patients that he initially began writing on Christian topics. An avid student of the Bible for many years, he now has authored eighteen books on Christian living, with over six million copies in print. With the exception of the Bible, Dr. Gills' books are the most widely requested books in the U.S. prison system. They have been supplied to over two thousand prisons and jails, including every death row facility in the nation. In addition, Dr. Gills has published more than 185 medical articles and authored or coauthored nine medical reference textbooks. Five of those books were bestsellers at the American Academy of Ophthalmology annual meetings.

As an ultra-distance athlete, Dr. Gills participated in forty-six marathons, including eighteen Boston Marathons and fourteen 100-mile mountain runs. In addition, he completed five Ironman Triathlons in Hawaii and holds the record for completing six Double Ironman Triathalons, each within the thirty-six-hour maximum time frame. Dr. Gills has served on the national board of directors of the Fellowship of Christian Athletes and in 1991 was the first recipient of their Tom Landry Award.

Married in 1962, Dr. Gills and his wife, Heather, have raised two children, Shea and Pit. Shea Gills Grundy, a former attorney, now full-time mom, is a graduate of Vanderbilt University and

Emory University Law School. She and husband, Shane Grundy, M.D., presented the Gills with their first grandchildren—twins, Maggie and Braddock. They have since been joined by Jimmy Gills and Lily Grace. The Gills' son, J. Pit Gills, M.D., ophthalmologist, received his medical degree from Duke University Medical Center and in 2001 joined the St. Luke's staff. Dr. Pit and his wife, Joy, are the proud parents of Pitzer and Parker.

Believe and Rejoice: Changed By Faith, Filled With Joy
  Observe how faith in God can let us see His heart of joy.
  ISBN-10: 1-59979-169-2   ISBN-13: 978-1-59979-169-2

A Biblical Economics Manifesto (with Ronald H. Nash, Ph.D.)
  The best understanding of economics aligns with what the
  Bible teaches on the subject.
  ISBN-10: 0-88419-871-5   ISBN-13: 978-0-88419-871-0

Come Unto Me: God's Call to Intimacy
  Inspired by Dr. Gills' trip to Mt. Sinai, this book explores
  God's eternal desire for mankind to know Him intimately.
  ISBN-10: 1-59185-214-5   ISBN-13: 978-1-59185-214-8

*Darwinism Under The Microscope: How Recent Scientific Evidence
Points to Divine Design* (with Tom Woodward, Ph.D.)
  Behold the wonder of it all! The facts glorify our intelligent
  Creator!
  ISBN-10: 0-88419-925-8   ISBN-13: 978-0-88419-925-0

The Dynamics of Worship
  Designed to rekindle a passionate love for God, this book
  gives the who, what, when, where, why, and how of worship.
  ISBN-10: 1-59185-657-4   ISBN-13: 978-1-59185-657-3

God's Prescription For Healing: Five Divine Gifts of Healing
  Explore the wonders of healing by design, now and forever-
  more.
  ISBN-10: 1-59185-286-2   ISBN-13: 978-1-59185-286-5
  HARDCOVER
  ISBN-10: 0-88419-947-9   ISBN-13: 978-0-88419-947-2

Imaginations: More Than You Think
Focusing our thoughts will help us grow closer to God.
ISBN-10: 1-59185-609-4   ISBN-13: 978-1-59185-609-2

Love: Fulfilling the Ultimate Quest
Enjoy a quick refresher course on the meaning and method of God's great gift.
ISBN-10: 0-88419-933-9   ISBN-13: 978-0-88419-933-5

Overcoming Spiritual Blindness
Jesus + anything = nothing. Jesus + nothing = everything. Here is a book that will help you recognize the many facets of spiritual blindness as you seek to fulfill the Lord's plan for your life.
ISBN-10: 1-59185-607-8   ISBN-13: 978-1-59185-607-8

Rx for Worry: A Thankful Heart
Trust your future to the God who is in eternal control.
ISBN-10: 1-59979-090-4   ISBN-13: 978-1-59979-090-9

The Prayerful Spirit: Passion for God, Compassion for People
Dr. Gills tells how prayer has changed his life as well as the lives of patients and other doctors. It will change your life also!
ISBN-10: 1-59185-215-3   ISBN-13: 978-1-59185-215-5

The Unseen Essential: A Story for Our Troubled Times...Part One
This compelling, contemporary novel portrays one man's transformation through the power of God's love.
ISBN-10: 1-59185-810-0   ISBN-13: 978-1-59185-810-2

Tender Journey: A Story for Our Troubled Times...Part Two
Be enriched by the popular sequel to *The Unseen Essential*.
ISBN-10: 1-59185-809-7   ISBN-13: 978-1-59185-809-6

The Worry Disease

This colorful pamphlet teaches how to banish worry by trusting in God and thanking Him always!

<small>Pamphlet</small>

Transform Your Marriage...Into a Sweet, Tender Journey

In an elegant twenty-four-page booklet, Dr. Gills encourages couples to develop a new closeness with each other and the Lord.

ISBN-10: 1-879938-11-1 I   SBN-13: 978-1-879938-11-3